ARISE

SIR SEAN CONNERY

BY JOHN PARKER

JOHN BLAKE

Published by John Blake Publishing Ltd,
3, Bramber Court, 2 Bramber Road,
London W14 9PB, England

www.blake.co.uk

First published in hardback in 2005

ISBN 1 84454 084 7

British Library Cataloguing-in-Publication Data:

A catalogue record for this book is available from the British Library.

Design by www.envydesign.co.uk

Printed in Great Britain by Creative Print & Design (Wales)

1 3 5 7 9 10 8 6 4 2

Papers used by John Blake Publishing are natural, recyclable products made
from wood grown in sustainable forests. The manufacturing processes
conform to the environmental regulations of the country of origin.

Photographs © Rex Features

CONTENTS

PREFACE

The year 2005 marked the 50th anniversary of Sean Connery securing his first credited role in a movie called *No Road Back*. In the intervening years, he had put together a remarkable body of work which had been, quite deliberately, a diverse mix of topics and genres, alternating through massive blockbusters aligned to the pop culture of the day to difficult, low budget movies of literary or subjective merit which he knew from the outset would barely register in the box-office charts. Over the years, he has been bestowed with just about every honour and award that his peers could bestow, including an Oscar, a BAFTA, two Golden Globes, three Golden Laurels and various international and national honours. The French anointed him with title of *Chevalier de la Legion d'Honneur* (one of their highest decorations), Edinburgh – his birthplace – gave him the seldom bestowed Freedom of the City, Germany and Japan both provided national awards of merit and President Bill Clinton presented Connery with the JF Kennedy Center award for lifetime achievement and contribution to the performing arts, the most important award in American cultural life.

The United Kingdom came late to this scenario. As will be seen as we progress through this account of his life, he has been continually ignored by those who choose to grant national honours and awards in Britain despite the fact that he had been internationally recognised as one of the most significant actors of the 20th century, not least as the on-screen creator of the most famous image in British movie history, James Bond, which was of course just a small slice of his outstanding repertoire. The Bond films he helped launch were produced in Britain and officially became part of Hollywood legend in 2004 when recognised as the biggest grossing series in international movie history. Yet, not only was Connery ignored for British honours, he was the subject of a downright veto by the bitchiness of modern British politics, coupled with a smear campaign, which precluded him from receiving a knighthood or any other national distinction in spite of the fact that, apart from all the above, he had been one of the largest individual benefactors of Scottish charities in modern times. What follows, however, is not a promotional exercise on behalf of Sean Connery. He has never been the easiest of men to deal with but, as many will testify in the forthcoming chapters, he is a man of honour who expects no less of those he does business with.

Sean Connery is, in many respects, a man alone in the international movie scene. He clearly has many, many friends and contacts at all levels of his business, but he does not join the social scenes of Hollywood or New York or London. He has also been the sole arbiter of the way his career has developed, and certainly in the latter stages he tried to involve himself at every level of whatever film he was making, more recently as producer as well as star. His relationship with the media soured during the Bond era and he 'went private' after years in the public eye during which he often experienced a level of intrusion usually reserved for The Beatles. Nothing in Connery's life seemed off limits: one day while standing at a urinal in Tokyo he looked up to discover a Nikon lens pointing down at him. The whole business had such a deep and lasting effect upon him that after his divorce from Diane Cilento in 1973 he stood outside the court and made the following announcement: 'As from this day I will have no comment to make on my private life. Nothing of my private life will ever be divulged to the press with whom I do not have an especially good relationship, because I have no press agent. To simplify matters I intend now to keep private matters private.'

It is a statement of intent that Sean Connery has pretty well adhered to in the intervening years. A former British prime minister once said public figures carry the burden of what he described as the cruelty of modern publicity, and it is easy to have sympathy with Connery's view: after all it is also his right. He generally only gives interviews in connection with his work, his charities and his affiliation to Scottish Nationalism, and studiously avoids any discussion of personal matters and private thoughts. 'Why should I reveal my soul to a complete stranger?' he once said to a writer who had called for a chat. Thus I did not seek co-operation from Sean Connery himself in the preparation of this book, and while treading the precarious path of trying to avoid intrusion into his privacy I was pleasantly surprised at the number of his friends and colleagues (out of the 148 with whom I made contact) who were willing, even eager, to give their views, impart their stories and recount anecdotes for the first edition of this biography. Many others have assisted in bringing this account up to date.

While respecting the wishes of those who requested off-the-record conversations, I would like to make a special note of appreciation for all who gave of their time by granting me interviews, answering my telephone calls, replying to my correspondence or helping in any other way. These people include: Joss Ackland, Candice Bergen, Honor Blackman, Klaus Maria Brandauer, Jill Craigie (Mrs Michael Foot), Cheryl Crane, Edward Fox, James Fox, Ronald Fraser, Lt Col Peter Gibbs (for the Princess

Royal), Lewis Gilbert, Sir John Gielgud, Kenneth Haigh, Robert Hardy, Ken Hankins, Charlton Heston, Michael Hayes, Ian Holm, Alex Kitson, Gerry Lewis (for Steven Spielberg), Robert Lewis, Herbert Lorn, Karl Malden, Anna Massey, Michael Palin, Donald Pleasence, Alvin Rakoff, Maurice Segal (for Albert 'Cubby' Broccoli), Maureen Stapleton, Eric Sykes, Trevor Wallace, Robert Watts, Alan Whicker and Fred Zinnemann.

For help with other research I am indebted to: Sheldon Leonard, Directors Guild of America; Professor Ronald L Davis, head of the Oral History Collection, the DeGolyer Institute of American Studies, Southern Methodist University of Dallas, Texas; the staff of the Doheny Library and Special Collections Department at the University of Southern California, Los Angeles; the staff at the Library and special collections archive of the Academy of Motion Pictures Arts and Sciences, Los Angeles; the American Film Institute Library and Archive, Los Angeles; the Performing Arts Library, Lincoln Center New York; the British Film Institute for video and film facilities, and the Tasiemka Archive, London.

1

STAIRWAY

The chances of Sean Connery ever making it even to the bottom rung of the ladder to film stardom were slight, and if he surmounted that hurdle any bookie his paternal grandfather used to run for would still have given astounding odds on him becoming what Steven Spielberg described as one of the top five actors in the world. From a background of deprivation and poverty and with the merest of education, one could talk in terms of a million-to-one shot. 'No wonder,' said actor colleague James Fox, who was thoroughly taken by Connery's disciplined and creative presence after working with him in 1990, 'he rather despises the privilege system of our country, but battled on to show his contemporaries who is the *real* star.'

'Privilege' was not a word the Connerys were familiar with. Home was a tenement, 176 Fountainbridge, on Edinburgh's south-western slopes where the more depressing of the city's factories and steam-powered manufacturing plants had been built during the Industrial Revolution. Father Joe was a Scotsman through and through, though his own father was Irish, a part tinker from the County Wexford area who had arrived in Scotland in the 1890s looking for work, stayed and married a local girl. Mother Effie (neé McLean) was 20 when she married and ambitious for a family of her own. Joe had no skills and even labouring work was scarce at the end of 1929 when their first child was on the way.

That child was born on 25 August 1930 at 6.30pm and given the name Thomas. He slept in the bottom drawer of the wardrobe in his parents' bedroom, moving to a convertible settee in the kitchen-cum-sitting room when he was five. The family lived in just these two rented rooms. The lavatory was on the landing, shared with other families on that floor. The stairway was unlit and reached via a dark hallway. During the day conflicting odours reached 176 Fountainbridge: the acrid smell from the North British Rubber Company (where Joe worked for a while) overlaid by an additional bitterness from the brewery opposite and moderated by the aroma from Mackay's sweet factory down the road. 'They weren't the worst slums in Edinburgh,' said Alex Kitson, later a national labour leader who was born in the next street, 'but they were bad enough. They were small and damp, not very healthy for a young family. But despite the deprivations we were all relatively happy; normal working families struggling to make ends meet. That's life, and it was no different to millions across the country. You worked and slept, and on Friday nights you got drunk. That was it.'

But keeping a job was a problem. Unemployment continued to rise as the Depression bit. Men went to the factory every day hoping for work but sometimes did not get it, and Joe Connery, like dozens of other young husbands, considered emigrating south or even abroad. Effie, however, liked the clannishness of 'the stair' and appreciated having supportive neighbours. She was careful with the family finances and they got by.

Those who gave accounts of Tommy Connery's early life, when the seekers of minutiae went in search of 'background and colour' after he became famous, confirmed that as a boy he was mad about

2

sport, especially soccer, and when he wasn't kicking the toes out of his black boots he would be sitting in a corner reading a comic. His former schoolfriend, John Brady, remembered that even in his pre-teens he was an avid reader but otherwise was no great scholar. He attended Tollcross Primary School and there learned, parrot-fashion, his times tables along with the 40 or so other children in his class. Their training ground was the street, where the toughest fared best. Apart from football, occasionally fishing for nothing in the Grand Union Canal or strolling down to the Meadows, a park ten minutes walk away, there were few diversions.

The birth of brother Neil in 1938 did not help the already difficult financial situation. Joe Connery had changed jobs, been out of work and was tenuously employed again. Tommy realised it was within his ability to help and got a job at St Cuthbert's Dairy Stables around the corner in Grove Street. He was paid a few shillings a week to help on the carts, getting up at dawn and delivering milk around a mile of side streets and tenements before going to school. Tommy chose the milk round, according to his mother, because 'he was daft on horses ... always taking my dusters to rub down the milk horses. And he loved driving the cart.'

Tommy was intent on paying his share of the rent. He further supplemented his – and the family's – income by doing a paper round and working for a local butcher. Before he was ten he already sought to control his own destiny, something which became a hallmark of all he did in his future professional life.

He appears to have been a boy who thought much about his position and his surroundings, and his own reminiscences seem tinged with an undercurrent of loneliness, or at least a loneliness in thought. He has spoken variously of his awareness that as far as his family was concerned it was a case of 'make your own bed and lie on it'; he said he neither sought advice nor received any. He was undoubtedly blessed with a loving mother and an occasionally absentee father whose threats of breaking his bottom in the event of misbehaviour seemed to be more verbal than actual. Yet, in their humble world, young Tommy Connery's tough life instilled within him a strong determination which blossomed in a variety of ways, such as his later rejection of the most coveted screen role available to any of the handsome young movie stars of his age and, later still, having the courage to do battle with the most influential of Hollywood studio executives who he felt had been cheating him.

He recognised this trait in his nature and also recognised its source. He professed to have no regrets about his harsh upbringing and in the mid-1960s he commented,

'I had to make it on my own or not at all and I would not have preferred it otherwise. Absolutely not. This sort of motivation is the great thing that's lacking in present-day society. Everything is so smooth running, so attainable, that one is deprived of initiative, lured into a false sense of security. In the days before the war, with high unemployment, many people simply put in an appearance every morning at the factory although they knew there was no chance of work. Sheeplike, they felt they just had to go. Today everything's handed to them on a platter ... society medicine has taken the worry out of being ill. If there is malnutrition of any kind in this country – and I think there is – then it's self-inflicted. The only competition you'll find today is the conflict between those few who try to correct a wrong, and the majority who hope it will just cure itself in the end.'

Connery would soon reject questions which attempted to prise from him views on modern living because his experiences tended to produce a controversial response not easily understood in the cold light of a chat show, where the host might throw it back in his face. It happened several times, including the above occasion when the interviewer implied that the only form of competition his upbringing had taught him was adeptness in verbal and physical abuse. Connery replied that was not really true; he was not a violent man. Those who found him rude and aggressive usually provoked that kind of response. He liked getting on with people, but did not bend over backwards to be nice just to show that initial impressions were wrong. 'As a young man,' said Alex Kitson, 'he was tough, but not rough, if you see what I mean. You had to know how to handle yourself around our way, but he did not go out looking for trouble.'

During the war years, Joe Connery went to work at Rolls Royce in Glasgow, which meant he only got home at weekends. Tommy Connery had moved to Darroch Secondary School. He was a strong, lean boy, used to being up and about by 5am, but home circumstances meant that he was unwilling to follow anything other than a basic education, from which he would extract himself at the earliest opportunity. Craigie Veitch was in Connery's class at Darroch, an old Georgian building, gaunt and grey, that somehow remained in use until the late-1980s. He recalled that those who went to the school were destined for technical and craft jobs, or for no particular career at all:

'Darroch was staffed by no-nonsense teachers with strong right arms, the better to belt you with; the plus-12 girls in print dresses and rough-and-ready boys whose school uniform was a pullover and short trousers topped off in winter with a balaclava helmet. Our English teacher always insisted that the well-rounded man must be accurate in his spelling and he kept to hand a largish Chambers dictionary which he would bounce on the head of any boy thick enough to think that "seize" was "sieze". We were versed in poetry, too, but I cannot recall Connery ever being called to the front of the class to recite lines. There was nothing of the long-haired poet about schoolboy Connery. He was big and he was as hard as nails in an easy-going way and anyone at school who messed him about got a thick ear and a black eye. One torrid encounter, Connery v Anderson, went the best part of 12 bloody rounds in the playground before the janitor and two teachers managed to break it up.'

Other contemporaries remember that football and work took preference over all else for Tommy Connery, school running a weak third. Occasional escape from the dark zones of Edinburgh became possible on Saturday afternoons or Sundays when they could afford the bus fare and leave the city grime for the countryside near Dunfermline where Effie's parents, Neil and Helen McLean, had set up home for their retirement. They had rented a cottage and there were chickens for fresh eggs. Water came crystal clear from the spring, and milk direct from the cows on a farm not far away. There were ponds to play in, frog spawn to collect, and a huge carthorse to ride. These were luxuries for a boy from the city, and now his brother Neil, six in 1944, was old enough to join him. Grandfather Neil was a plasterer who rose to Public Works Foreman before retiring to the country. For the Connerys it was a culture shock being able to get close to farm animals and play football on real grass in wide open spaces. Grandfather McLean taught the two brothers how to take nourishment from raw fresh eggs by piercing a hole in each end and sucking the contents out – the poor man's equivalent of oysters, he would say. The memory was one which especially stuck with brother Neil: 'We regarded this as a big delicacy and such things are not easily forgotten or dropped. Sean liked to swallow raw eggs long into adulthood … more than that, these other-world experiences formed a bond between us that was never broken.'

It was an idyllic period for the brothers that they remembered and talked about in later life; Connery himself often referred in interviews to this grandfather who drank a bottle of whisky a day to wash down plenty of food, usually cold. The old man managed to put the record straight before he died at the age of 93, telling a newspaper reporter who came to call that his secret for a long and healthy life had actually been plenty of exercise.

Films meant no more to Connery then, in the 1940s, than they did to any other boy or girl in the locality. Tommy occasionally caught up with the golden age of Hollywood in the Blue Halls, a colourful and misleading name for the local cinema at Fountainbridge. Tuppence would buy a seat for the Saturday morning *Flash Gordon* or one of the endless B-movie Westerns pumped out by Hollywood like animated comics. The screens were full of talented kids – Mickey Rooney, Jackie Cooper, Jane Withers, Shirley Temple, Freddie Bartholomew, Deanna Durbin – who provided fresh-faced, middle-class images which never went down too well in the poorer areas. Their specially written stories, like Mickey Rooney's Andy Hardy series, were billed as representing a major swing from the Hollywood sophistication of the late-1930s to represent the everyday problems faced by an everyday family.

The kids of Fountainbridge would have loved to face such 'problems', and thus they were alienated from the pictures. More appealing were the Dead End Kids with Huntz Hall, Leo Gorcey and company, who had sprung to the screens in a series of stories involving mild hooliganism and adolescent humour, which in truth bore little resemblance to the reality of the slum children they were supposedly portraying. Tommy Connery did not, by all accounts, have many screen idols of that era. He was most taken with Westerns, or any film that featured horses which, after football, became an early passion.

He left Darroch Secondary School before his 14th birthday. There was fresh pressure on the family. His father Joe had been off work, having sustained injuries to his arm and face in a work accident in Glasgow, and his mother was struggling to keep the family on the 30 shillings a week she earned from cleaning. They became even more reliant on the earnings of elder son Tommy, who was giving her £2.10s every payday from his earnings on the milk round and newspaper deliveries, topped up by other part-time work wherever he could find it.

At 14 Tommy was working from dawn to dusk in three jobs, with the milk round providing the major part of his income while also indulging his hobby for horses. He had been given charge of his own animal, Tich, the smallest in the dairy's stables, and he lavished the horse with affection and care, returning most evenings to feed and groom him. Tich was his pride and joy, especially when he won a highly commended prize for the best turned out dray horse. Future union organiser Alex Kitson recalls that it was a job for life in the dairy if you got past 16. 'They looked after you so long as you were a hard worker, and many milkmen stayed for long service,' he said. 'But there was always a general clearing out when lads got to 16 because they had to be paid more money.'

In spite of the poverty surrounding the family, Tommy had been surprised to discover that his mother had been putting away some of his rent into a Post Office savings account, to which he was thriftily adding as much as he could. Within a couple of years he had accumulated £75, a princely sum in immediate post-war Scotland and almost enough to put a deposit on a house for his family except that his father had only just found a new job – with a removal company – after being off work for almost two years with the injury. Their own removal to better conditions was out of the question.

In anybody's language Tommy was a wealthy young man among his friends on the stair. One night, soon after his 16th birthday, he announced that he had decided to spend the money on a Triumph or BSA motorbike. He was rapidly disabused of this idea by a stern father and dashed out of the flat, angry that he could not spend his hard-earned money in the way that he wanted, in spite of the assurances he gave that it was not his intention to join one of the gangs.

Soon after two men trundled up the stairs with a piano. Tommy had paid £56.10s for the second-hand instrument. No one in the flat played and the thing aggravated the cramped conditions in which the Connery family survived, but it was a fine status symbol. Joe wanted it out straight away, and Tommy promised he would take lessons. It was an altogether odd gesture, never really explained, though it perhaps displayed a need to buy something that would be a monument to his hard work, or was an act of defiance to show that he could do exactly as he pleased with his own money – apart from buying a motorbike.

There were other stirrings. Tommy Connery had been running around with newspapers and milk since he was nine – more than seven years. His life since he left school had become something of a drudge: up at dawn, delivering milk until three in the afternoon, home for a snack and out again for the paper round. In the evenings and at weekends he played soccer for Grove Vale Juvenile and later graduated to a more senior side, Oxgangs Rovers.

There were occasional treats such as the cinema, trips to see his grandparents and some sporting outings, but otherwise his outlook improved not a jot from one day to the next. It bothered him when he came back from the cinema, having glimpsed the colourful images of those other worlds. If he wanted to get on he needed money, and he would never grow rich on a milkman's pay.

As Tommy approached his 17th birthday he was assessing his future. There were all kinds of pressures building up. Adolescence itself was enough, but it went deeper. His social life extended to soccer, cinema and local dances. His home life was not unhappy, but two grown men and a third, young Neil, coming up on the rails was like locking three stags in a small barn. Joe's authority was being challenged merely by Tommy's presence; Tommy himself must have felt hemmed in and did not always enjoy his father's humour. One day when two girls came to call, Joe went to the door and said he was sorry but 'Tam' could not come out as his mother was bathing him.

Tommy resolved he would not remain there much longer.

If he wanted to see the world beyond Edinburgh, which he had only ever left for brief excursions, then he would also have to think of leaving home and Fountainbridge. He sought no help or guidance, he just discarded ideas and replaced them with others as quickly as they came to him. He had already rejected being 'put to a trade'. Many of his schoolfriends had signed up for three- or four-year apprenticeships on little money to learn plastering, painting and decorating or one of the many other crafts. Tommy did not want that.

He had heard talk of boys who had joined the Merchant Navy, which was regrouping and recruiting after the war, and Tommy finally decided to run away to sea with the Royal Navy. The actuality wasn't quite as romantic as that. One day when his mother wasn't looking he boarded a tram to deliver him across the Firth to the naval shore base of HMS *Lochinvar* at South Queensferry and there signed on for seven years active service with a second term of five years in the Volunteer Reserve to follow. He returned home taken by curious feelings of guilt, jubilation and apprehension.

Brother Neil recalled the mayhem caused in the Connery household that evening by Tommy's announcement. To say that Effie was upset was an understatement. Joe protested that he might have had the courtesy to tell them before taking such a step, but inwardly he was not at all displeased with his son's decision; he was even proud. It would give him the discipline of service life and keep him off the city streets, and there was the added advantage of reducing the demands on space in the flat made by a growing young man.

In the days before his departure he boasted to his friends that he was off to see the world. Exotic ports with a girl in every one beckoned, and mates listened wide-eyed and open-mouthed to the adventures this lad who had seldom ventured out of Fountainbridge could expect to encounter in his new life.

Once more, the reality was rather more mundane. Connery proceeded with enthusiasm through the rigorous training programme, first at the naval gunnery school then into an anti-aircraft unit and finally he was given a posting to HMS *Formidable*, based at Portsmouth. By then the impetus of his new life was already beginning to flag. True, the uniform was smart and in the dance halls of austere post-war Britain servicemen were still heroes. He was also treated with some respect by his former friends when he returned to Fountainbridge on leave and showed off his latest acquisitions – twin tattoos engraved on his right forearm, in fine naval tradition, one night when drink had been taken with colleagues. They read 'Scotland Forever' and 'Mum and Dad', which might have been clues to homesickness, even though he had travelled no further than Portsmouth Harbour.

Connery was already doubting that the Navy was the solution to his problems; he apparently replaced one set of restrictions with another and he could not easily attune to naval discipline after relying largely on his own self-control for years. For a young man of such independent spirit, used to making his own way in the world and suffering the consequences, he now found that he was not even allowed to think for himself. The money was poor, too, especially if he had not done well at poker, and there was no sign of his travelling abroad. Worse, he doubted his ability to settle to Navy life and was especially unsure that, because of his minimal education, he could meet the challenge of rising through the ranks to a reasonable position, like Petty Officer.

All in all, it began to worry him and get on his nerves. Within a year he was suffering stomach pains and was removed to the sick bay where doctors diagnosed a duodenal ulcer, then a serious complaint that could prove fatal. At 19 years old Able Seaman Connery was on the verge of a breakdown and the medical officer placed him in the care of the naval hospital for eight weeks. Throughout he kept silent, bottling up the feelings, hoping that eventually it would all come right. It did. He was summoned before a naval medical board and told that he was to be discharged on medical grounds. He would be granted a disability pension of 6s 8d a week and he returned, tail between his legs, to Fountainbridge and the Fountain Bar.

In spite of the bravado, Connery was troubled by his failure to achieve his aim of travel and excitement. He was unhappy about moving back with his parents, which would be seen almost as an admission of defeat, but he had no alternative. The gloomy thoughts that had enveloped him before he joined the Navy descended again with even greater anguish – the surroundings, the lack of privacy for a man of almost 20, the whole situation.

The only temporary solution – and he intended that it should be only temporary – was to get a job in the locality. His qualifications were limited to muscle and brawn, just like his father's, for there were few opportunities in Edinburgh for a man trained in anti-aircraft gunnery.

An unsettled period followed, roaming from one job to the next, taking them as they came for the pay and nothing much else; steelworker, corporation road worker, delivering coal, odd-job man, labourer, cement-mixer attendant and so on. He appeared not to bother about the quality of work, so long as there was overtime and the decent reward of £10 or so every Friday – still good money in 1950 – to finance a social life beyond the Fountain Bar and get among the girls. His parents were worried about him for he was moving from one job to another sometimes after only a few weeks, or even days. Again and again, they advised him to settle to a trade, but he never would.

Connery realised that it was a thoroughly unsatisfactory existence, and it seemed that he would become trapped in the same level of life that his father and his friends had accepted virtually without question. He even applied his mind to learning a skill, which he had previously vowed never to do, by joining a scheme run by the British Legion (he had been automatically registered with the organisation as a disabled ex-serviceman).

The Legion's work in this area was renowned and its charitable facilities enabled him to take up a scholarship to a training course. A variety of options were on offer – building trades, haircutting and carpentry among them. He opted to study French polishing and eventually landed a job with a family firm of cabinet makers, Jack Vinestock and Co., in the summer of 1950.

Tommy Connery was no more than a bench assistant, learning a craft and working with experienced hands on everything from tables to coffins. Jack Vinestock, son of the company's founder, remembered him most for his liveliness and not for his abilities or even potential as a French polisher. He might have made the grade, but his old boss doubted that he had either the talent or the patience for the craft.

From Connery's point of view, however, there was a particular advantage to be gleaned from his time with Vinestock's – his first introduction to the theatre. One of his fellow workers, John Hogg, worked evenings and weekends at the King's Theatre which was in Leven Street, not far from Connery's home. It was one of the more refined centres of theatrical endeavour and staged operas during the Edinburgh Festival.

Hogg worked there partly out of interest and partly for the extra few pounds it brought in. Like most backstage hands, he assisted with everything from dressing the players to helping with scenery. Connery, that Christmas of 1951, was tall, strong and very fit from doing body-building at a local club. He was taken with the idea, though he had never set foot in a theatre in his life and the only reason for doing so now was the additional money. Hogg took his young workmate along to the King's and introduced him to the stage manager. Connery began working as a general hand backstage and was soon mixing with a curious band of people with whom he discovered a certain affinity.

It was a seasonal task and did not lead to an immediate rapport with the theatre. He was still bogged down in a no-man's land, striving to free himself from the shackles of Fountainbridge but every two steps forward were matched by one and a half back. The job at Vinestock's ended early in 1952. There was talk of becoming a professional footballer. His skills on the soccer pitch had attracted the interest of several minor league scouts and he became a part-time professional with Bonnyrigg Rose, later being offered professional terms with East Fife which would have provided him with a signing-on fee of £25. Connery decided it was an offer he could refuse and continued to talk and dream about getting out, of travelling the world, but the opening for him to dart through had yet to appear. Instead he used his physique and secured a job as a lifeguard at Edinburgh's large outdoor Portobello pool. He did not know it, but he was heading towards his historic moment of destiny, the one that movie stars talk of as the most important decision of their lives.

The summer of 1952 was long and hot. There were girls aplenty and Tommy Connery – now more popularly known as Big Tam –

could virtually take his pick, and usually did. He was a catch for any young woman in Edinburgh; he was good looking and mysterious. Few, however, made it up the stair to meet Effie because he was not ready for any serious relationships.

He was a familiar figure among the young set through soccer, his lifeguard job and his Saturday night mooching at the Palais, which boasted one of the largest dance floors in Scotland (over 1,500 people could be expected when the swing bands of the era attracted the jivers and the boppers). The Palais even employed Big Tam as a bouncer for a time and few dared tackle him.

Then came another brief flirtation with the theatre. Anna Neagle was on tour with a show entitled *The Glorious Years* which was booked into the Empire for five weeks. Her production manager advertised in the *Edinburgh Evening News* for extras for crowd scenes; Connery applied and, being six-foot two and attractive, was appointed a guardsman, a non-speaking role which merely entailed his hovering at the back of the stage. It was supposed to be casual work but something was stirring deep down, though quite what it was Connery did not know. 'He had no hankering for the theatre,' his pal Alex Kitson recalled. 'It was just another job to him.'

He had no anchor. He was off on any jaunt that provided money without great effort, and he was mobile having finally bought a motorbike out of a £90 lump-sum payment received from the Navy to wind up his disablement pension.

He became an artist's model at Edinburgh College of Art for seven shillings an hour, posing with nothing more than a G-string to cover his incidentals; he would travel to Manchester on his motorbike for other modelling assignments for Vince Studios; he was photographed for a body-building magazine which paid decent hourly rates; he topped up his weekly earnings by doing casual shifts for an undertaker, French polishing the coffins. Later he took what appeared to be a more permanent job in the press room at *Edinburgh Evening News* which at last offered something he might settle to. Yet Connery had no such ambitions and was soon telling his mates it was temporary. This was Big Tam Connery, ducking and diving, weaving in and out of this and that, making money and spending it, looking good and feeling it … except that still he was going nowhere.

Until …

Charles Atlas had started something. The world-renowned body-builder's image stared out from newspaper and magazine advertisements, helping six-stone weaklings improve their physique after having sand kicked in their face. The image appealed to 1950s youth and the male meat market became a thriving business. A former Mr Scotland, Archie Brennan, saw Connery at the Dunedin Weightlifting Club and said he should take it up professionally; he reckoned that with weight training he could have the kind of physique to win prizes. Ray Ellington, the singer-bandleader who played at the Palais and did workout sessions with Connery, also gave him words of encouragement. Jimmy Laurie, another of the club members who was older and more advanced in the art, thought about it too, and did not see the point of waiting. He had been pawing over an announcement for the Mr Universe competition and began to get ideas that others would think above his station. Why did not he and Connery enter?

2

LUCKY BREAK

One bit part as a crowd-scene extra in an Anna Neagle show had not inspired thoughts of a stage career in the mind of Tommy Connery. It was merely a way of earning extra cash. And nor was there the slightest thought, when he and his pal Jimmy Laurie set off from the Dunedin Weightlifting Club for London to enter their Mr Universe contest, that it might lead to anything other than temporary small-time fame in the world of the male body-beautiful.

Unlike his eventual contemporaries he did not move into acting through the motivation of burning desire, a precocious talent as a child or, like Richard Burton, progression derived from opportunities which presented themselves in his youth. Today Sean Connery does not care to be compared with anyone and there are those who would say there is no point in comparing Connery with Burton anyway, but the similarities between the two men accentuate their differing paths to stardom.

Robert Hardy, a close friend of Burton's from Oxford days, detected striking similarities between the two actors almost from their first meeting. By then Connery had been in the business for several years and had taught himself some of the rudiments of acting that Burton learned at school. Hardy, charmingly resourceful in memories, recalled, 'I remember having a drink with Sean once somewhere near Lancaster Gate; we were rehearsing a play at Shepherd's Bush and sitting on a bar stool. I looked at him and thought to myself then how much like Burton he was – not in looks; I think it was that sort of nationalism that they both had, and the retained accent, which crystallised my view. Connery said he had an admiration for Richard Burton and he knew we were great friends and we started talking about him. There was something about Sean that reminded me of Rich in that though they were both from different national backgrounds they were startlingly similar in their speech and movement. I told him then that he would go a long way.'

There was another comparison. As Melvyn Bragg observed in his biography *Rich*, Richard Burton made his own luck, literally forcing himself out of the industrialised environment of Wales as Connery did out of Fountainbridge. When they both made it, it produced within them an awesome self-confidence that was easily taken as arrogance, which perhaps it was.

In other ways they were as different as chalk and cheese. Though Burton's background was humble (he was the 12th child of an alcoholic miner) he had paid attention at school, read a lot, appeared in school plays and altogether showed the academic promise that Connery had shunned in favour of earning money. Connery, early on in his career, lacked the advantage of education and learning. Another disadvantage was the very limited contact Connery had with people outside his circle whereas, as Hardy's recollections of Burton's youth graphically illustrate, the Welshman went to Oxford and formed an immediate rapport with the university hellraisers. He was flung into a social and literary whirl that Connery neither experienced nor had any means of entering through normal channels.

Their relative positions in 1953 could not have been more

different. As Jimmy Laurie and Big Tam headed south on Connery's motorbike from 'Auld Reekie' to 'the smoke' (as London was commonly described then by all from the provinces who professed connections in the big city) Burton's acclaim was already such that his Hamlet opened a breathtaking 39-week season at the Old Vic, as Connery's Mr Universe contest was being staged at the old Scala Theatre in West London.

The theatre itself had seen better days – and certainly a lot more entertaining nights – as a collection of men gathered from various parts of the globe. Their preoccupation was the size of their pectorals and biceps, and against them the two hopefuls from the lower west side of Edinburgh looked decidedly provincial and ordinary. They surveyed the competition despondently; the truth was that the Dunedin lads were almost comically small.

Connery was in better shape than his friend and won bronze in the lighter division. Laurie was dismayed at his own lack of success and both men blamed the Americans: they were much bigger and had not been labouring under the British disadvantage of food rationing. Connery and Laurie had discussed becoming professional body-builders, but now they were seriously disillusioned. It was especially disconcerting for Connery to discover that in order to be successful in this field it was clearly necessary to sustain an almost freakish physique based upon bulk. Connery was equally surprised to learn this physique could only be achieved by avoiding any overexertion other than specialist exercise.

He had all but decided that this kind of life offered nothing for him when, by chance, a fellow competitor, Stan Howlett, told them how he was using his own body-beautiful in the back row of the chorus in *South Pacific*, a task which required no special abilities since the main requirement was muscular good looks. Furthermore, a touring company of the show was being put together and auditions were being held that very week.

The idea of a provincial lad on the town in London getting cast in a musical of international repute with famous stars of stage and screen would have seemed as preposterous as the plot for any show – except that it happened. Connery had already appeared on stage, albeit in a crowd scene, and in a verbal CV such a minuscule event could quite easily be transformed into a claim of reputable stage experience when set alongside such stars as Anna Neagle. He was a quarter of the way there already. On Howlett's advice, he and Laurie pooled their resources, moved into a rented bedsit, did their homework on the show and then gate-crashed the auditions for the touring version of *South Pacific*.

Connery exaggerated his abilities during the interview. Of course he could dance, but the producer little knew that the Fountainbridge Palais had been the sole arena of his performances to date. Singing? Yes, of course … though his only stage had been in his mother's kitchen or with his friends at the Fountainbridge Bar. He also made much of his Navy experience.

He was given some lines of dialogue to read out and dropped the pages halfway through. As he began picking them up, he heard the director curse him for being clumsy, decided that there was no point in continuing and started walking to the wings. The director called out and told him to read the words again. He got a second chance and soon found himself in a collective audition in which he more or less mouthed one of the songs from the show and did a few fancy steps that he later admitted were a hangover from his ballroom dancing.

Fortunately, as Howlett had pointed out, the producers were not looking for singers, dancers or actors, but handsome, agile guys who would look and sound like a bunch of butch sailors. The chosen few would not even be chorus boys, just muscle men whose party piece would be the lively routine for one of the show's most famous numbers, 'There Is Nothing Like A Dame'.

Perhaps the only time Connery's inexperience showed was at the end as potential hirelings were being considered. Traditionally no one ever mentioned money. It was simply not done to enquire about one's recompense; actors were glad enough to get the work and trusted in God that the producers would not be too mean.

Connery, neither aware of such etiquette nor concerned with it, walked to the front of the stage and yelled down to the stalls where the show's producers and management were considering their options.

'What's the wage?' he demanded of anyone who might hear. When Billy Connolly tells this story, the quote becomes 'What's the pay, Jimmy?'

It wasn't Jimmy, it was Jerome ... Jerome White, the producer, who was naturally taken aback by such an inquiry and replied tetchily, 'It really doesn't concern me.'

'Well, it concerns me,' came the reply.

Connery was assured that matters of finance were only discussed if and when the part was offered. It seemed even then an unlikely possibility, but White was apparently taken by Connery's movement on stage and assigned him a role in the back row.

Connery received the news a couple of days later at the lodging house where they were staying. The wage was £12 a week and he would have turned a double somersault had he been capable. His luck was not shared by Jimmy Laurie, who eventually accepted that there was no alternative but to return to Edinburgh and pick up where he had left off, back to the grindstone and the mundane after his brief flirtation with the glamour of London.

Connery resigned from his job and the almost unbelievable news spread like wildfire around the tenements of Fountainbridge that Big Tam Connery – or Shane, as he had lately become known in the wake of the Alan Ladd film of the same name – had gone and joined the theatrical profession, akin to saying he had run away to join the circus.

It did not come as a great surprise to his few close friends, however. Nothing would surprise them about Tommy Connery. He could have been successful in any proper job – like a French polisher, an undertaker, a milkman or a steelworker. He could even have been a footballer, but threw away the chance of security in a trade to become a singer/dancer in a fancy London show instead. No matter. At least he had escaped, and with a bit of good fortune and a fair wind Edinburgh would not see him again.

The feelings of his family and friends ranged from pride and admiration for his sheer guts to the predictable comment going around the press room at the *Edinburgh Evening News*: 'He'll be back, tail between his legs.' If the truth was known, he himself doubted this remarkable break would lead to anything of substance; he had been lucky and he should enjoy it while he could because tomorrow it might be over and he would be back cleaning the rollers of the presses.

It was his mother, reflecting later as only mothers can with their remarkable insight, who decided that the moment had finally arrived and Tommy Connery would not be seen on the stair again except for visits. For Connery the realisation that he might be at the beginning of an exciting career was slow to conquer the more usual and natural mercenary thoughts about 'How much?' which generally superseded the one of 'How long?' The words 'career' or 'calling' did not even come into the reckoning at this stage, and on his own admission he was more interested in the job because of the travel prospects – visiting almost every part of the British Isles.

It also appears to have struck Connery in between auditioning for the part and actually taking it up that once learned and rehearsed there would be little to do in the daytimes while on tour. It was the old attitude of income over effort on which he had so far survived.

The work entailed six evening and two matinee performances each week, amounting to less than 20 hours in all. It was, according to his reckoning and even accounting for rehearsals, dressing, make-up and the rest, very good money for a relatively undemanding task. Set against the 18-hour days he had been used to in his youth it was nothing.

He would have most of his days free to do as he wished, play football, or perhaps do part-time work. It still had not sunk into his brain – nor would it for some time – that to proceed further, to become an actor, to go on in this new life he had accidentally stumbled into, he would have to undergo a complete sea change in attitude, demeanour and intent, not to mention a desire to learn. At that point it was all a bit of a laugh and a thrill and, once mastered, the chanting of songs in the back line of the chorus was going to be a doddle.

Connery quickly established himself as a popular member of the cast, especially among those of his own age group and who, like him, were not experienced, although several of them later recalled he was a loner, a man of independent mind and spirit with no intention of going along with the crowd simply because it was expected of him.

He played poker on Friday nights when they got paid; he played soccer wherever he could and generally became involved with the social life of the cast which built up as the tour went on. This particular tour was one of the most successful ever staged by any company, either before or since, and was among the last of the touring companies to record such a success in the provinces, making its way around the country two or three times. Such large-scale endeavours would soon become impossible through cost, and dwindling theatres and support.

But then, in 1953, *South Pacific* was booked into towns and cities across the British Isles and in some it stayed for a run of eight to ten weeks. By the time they reached Edinburgh on the first circuit around Britain, Connery was well into the part and was understudying for more important roles. His salary had been increased, but for the time being he remained one of the chanting, hand-springing boys at the back.

It was sufficient, however, to instil considerable pride among his family who all turned up at the King's Theatre, where he had once worked backstage, and they and his friends gave his appearance on stage a special cheer. His brother Neil, still living in Edinburgh today and having carried on the trade of decorator, remembered that first visit of the show to Edinburgh and found Tommy Connery happier than he had ever known him; he was sure then that he would stick at it. Tommy, he said, spoke enthusiastically about the future and was eager to prove himself; he wanted to do well even to the point of over-enthusiasm about his abilities. He did not seem to have a thought that he might be trying to run before he could walk and this was once again interpreted by some of his colleagues as arrogance. The very idea that this young man from nowhere could be a 'star' jarred with some of the more experienced, and slightly cynical, professionals in the cast.

During the first stop in Manchester, booked at the Opera House for nine weeks, two developments occurred which were to affect the shape of Connery's career. Robert Henderson, who was playing Captain Brackett in the show, and Connery were staying at the same boarding house. They had become good friends. Henderson, then 47 and with a long list of theatrical credits both as an actor and a director, was able to pass on tales of his experiences both in his home country of America and in Britain. Connery was intrigued and fascinated by his new friends in the showbusiness world and Henderson became a father figure to Connery, undoubtedly a major influence in his early interest in the theatre.

Henderson was always quick to deny that he discovered Connery, claiming the talent and ability were already there, within him. What Henderson did was to help unlock it and inspire an interest in further study, which until then had been dormant.

Connery was suddenly keen, even anxious, to learn. Henderson said he happened to come along just at the point the young Scot seemed to have decided on self-improvement. As they walked to their digs one night after the performance, Henderson suggested that Connery spend some of his free time reading. He mentioned Ibsen, and had to explain who the influential modern dramatist was. Connery wanted to know more and Henderson suggested a reading list of plays, giving him the titles of *Hedda Gabler*, *The Wild Duck* and *When We Dead Awake*, not expecting to hear another word about them. He was surprised to discover that Connery had quickly devoured all the titles and now wanted to spend time discussing them and their meanings. It progressed from there.

Henderson gave him a list of books that he felt had influenced modern theatre, including Proust's *A la Recherche du Temps Perdu*, Stendhal's *Charterhouse of Parma*, Tolstoy's *War and Peace*, Stanislavski's *My Life in Art* and Thomas Wolfe's *Look Homeward, Angel*. Again, Connery checked them out from the library and spent hours of heavy reading.

He persisted with what Henderson described as admirable dedication. The older man also suggested that Connery try to curb his accent. It was undoubtedly strong and his natural pronunciations were a problem, especially for English producers and directors. While he did calm the accent down and rid his speech of some of the more dialectic Robs Roys, he seems even then to have made a deliberate decision to keep his own identity and not become just another acting voice.

In the middle of this first wave of self-improvement an opportunity presented itself to provide Connery with an immediate escape route into the more familiar – though equally glamorous – world of soccer. A regular member of a South Pacific XI which turned out against local football teams while on tour, he played against a Manchester United junior team watched by Matt Busby, the Manchester United manager. Busby remained for the entire match and was seen to be enjoying a tightly fought tussle won by the showbiz team.

Connery played his usual tough and spectacular game as an attacking forward and was changing after the match when Busby arrived, asked him to step outside for a moment and offered him a job at Old Trafford. The offer was an enticing £25 a week, almost double what he was getting in *South Pacific*, and he was sorely tempted to say yes without hesitation. However, he said he would consider it overnight and let Busby know his decision the following day.

He sought out Robert Henderson and asked his advice. Henderson said he believed that with luck and hard work

Connery could become a good actor, and for that reason he believed he should reject Busby's offer. The thought of joining a major soccer club played on his imagination all night. He weighed up what Henderson had said, worked out his own list of pros and cons and finally concluded that he would decline. Connery admitted later it was one of the toughest decisions he had made in his life: 'I really wanted to accept because I'd always loved the game. But I stopped to assess it and asked myself what's the length of a footballer's career? A top-class footballer could be over the hill by the time he was 30, and I was already 23 – but more than that I wanted something that would last and so I decided there and then to become an actor, because it was fun. It turned out to be one of my more intelligent moves.'

Producer Jerry White was in Manchester that week and when he heard that Henderson had advised Connery to turn down Matt Busby's offer he flew into a rage. 'Are you mad?' White shouted. 'This boy will never make it as an actor. He could have earned himself some fame and a decent living for a few years … he'll never do that in this business.'

Henderson remained confident that he had given his protégé the correct advice, and was vindicated over the coming weeks as Connery increased his reading, sitting in libraries wherever they might be, reading and re-reading the works that Henderson had suggested. He progressed so well that Henderson led a deputation from the cast to have Connery promoted from the chorus when the part of Lieutenant Buzz Adams – created in the original show by Mary Martin's son Larry Hagman – became vacant.

This unusual occurrence impressed Jerry White. Connery became Adams and faced his first night as an actor. It was not a large part but it was important. He had to inform Captain Brackett (Henderson) that the Japanese had landed in the Pacific islands. It was a small speech which, the cast agreed, he delivered with impressive intensity and apparently without a nerve in his body. And when the show next came round to Edinburgh, he was reported in the local newspaper as a 'star' of South Pacific. His name had also changed to Sean, a variation on Shane, and he was on his way.

There were other relationships on that long, hard road around the countryside of the British Isles. There had to be; the show ran for almost two and a half years and the players were living in each other's pockets. Meanwhile, Connery had purchased a small tape recorder and would recite Shakespeare and speeches from Ibsen and Shaw. He gradually curbed the worst deep tonal valleys of his accent but the speech therapy largely consisted of grammatical and interpretative exercises. One of the cast, Carol Sopel, was very close to him for some time and there was talk of them marrying, but perhaps that was wishful thinking among a sentimental cast anxious for a celebration involving two of their most popular members. For whatever reason Carol and Sean's romance ended, and that was just as well because another guide in the education of Sean Connery was just over the horizon, and was to remain in his life for some considerable time.

Julie Hamilton was then 21 and a freelance photographer working for various national newspapers and magazines. At the time she lived in the London home of her mother, the writer Jill Craigie, and stepfather Michael Foot, a future Labour Party leader. One night in April 1956 she had arranged to meet her actor friend, Ronnie Fraser, who was appearing in a play at the Lyric Theatre in Hammersmith. After the show they went to a local pub where Fraser introduced her to a young fellow Scot, Sean Connery, to whom she took an instant dislike. Her first impression was that he was 'a bit of a yob', in untidy attire, tattoos on his arms and several unattractive gold teeth. She thought he had a 'silly shy smile' and was a touch boring.

They met again casually several times after that, and Julie's attitude towards Connery did not improve until the day they both attended Fraser's wedding to his girlfriend Lizzie. Julie was a bridesmaid, and Connery joined Fraser in turning out in full Scottish regalia. After the reception Julie took Sean to her parents' house – they were away that weekend – and their love affair began.

By then Connery's run in *South Pacific* was at an end and he was facing a rough patch. He had been sharing digs with three other actors, and according to his brother Neil was 'reduced to travelling about London looking for work on a rusty old boneshaker of a bicycle which he bought for five shillings'. He never once let his family know of his precarious plight. Lodgings were always a problem and there was a succession of cheap digs until Julie found a more pleasant alternative.

In fact, it was a room in the apartment of journalist Lew Gardner and his wife Merry Archard, who shared a first-floor flat in Brondesbury Villas, Kilburn. Merry had met Julie while working on a women's magazine.

Lew Gardner, later to become well known for his work on Thames Television's *World In Action*, had never been what one would call well off since he moved to London, and letting a room at a mere 12s 6d a week supplemented the family budget. At the time he worked for the Communist Party newspaper, the *Daily Worker*, having been succeeded in his former role as Corby district reporter for the *Northampton Chronicle and Echo* by the present author. He was fired for painting Communist slogans on the road, something of a recommendation to the *Daily Worker* whose employees were encouraged to donate a percentage of their salary to the cause. Gardner, now sadly dead, eventually quit Communism over Soviet excesses in eastern Europe, but in the meantime Sean Connery's rent came in very handy.

Julie became an influential figure in Connery's early days in London. Michael Foot and Jill Craigie were well known for their left-wing views and were prominent in the emerging Campaign for Nuclear Disarmament (CND). Julie went for showbusiness rather than political subjects. She was well educated, had studied theatrical history and was often found in theatreland seeking photographic possibilities.

Julie was confident, a necessary trait for any woman to survive in Fleet Street in the 1950s when it was totally controlled by men. Female photographers in particular were a rarity. She especially appealed to Connery because she had a bright, sharp sense of humour, was a fast talker, like himself, and in his current quest for theatrical and literary knowledge proved to be a sympathetic source of data and discussion.

These were lean times for Connery. Peter Noble, film columnist for many years on *Screen International*, recalls him turning up in response to an advertisement for a babysitter; he would do it to earn ten shillings. This did not surprise his landlords, the Gardners – after all, they were letting out a room for the same reason and for not much more money.

Connery continued his reading and went to elocution lessons when he could afford them. Lew Gardner lent him some books, including a 13-volume set of the complete works of Stalin which Lew had no further use for. He discovered, however, that Connery did not wish to read them either – they were used to prop up a three-legged double bed he had bought cheaply.

The Gardners were impressed by Connery's Scottish canniness. When short of cash, he would bargain for the cheapest piece of meat and turn it into a large stew which he would keep on the stove for days. Finding work was a problem, which is why he was grateful for Julie Hamilton's contacts; she also knew her way around London and theatreland, which was important. Even so, the period immediately after *South Pacific* was fairly unproductive. Connery was realistic enough to know that he could not yet be classed as an actor, but did not let that stop him, hoping that experience in small stage and screen parts would eventually catch up with his ambitions. And that meant simply tackling anything.

When Robert Henderson was asked to direct a production of Agatha Christie's *Witness For The Prosecution* at the Kew Theatre he offered Connery a walk-on part as a court usher for £6 a week, which was gladly accepted. When the run ended he was out of work for months and had to face the usual list of excuses. At 20th Century Fox he was rejected for a small role in *Boy On A Dolphin* because he was too tall. Rank auditioned him for a part in *High*

Tide At Noon, but then said he was too dark. Michael Bentall let him down at the Old Vic by telling him, 'You don't fit into the composition here. Take elocution lessons. Study your diction.'

This seems to have been the source of a degree of bitterness and resentment. When Connery had become a star *without* ditching his accent and was being questioned about the quality of Bond movies, he angrily defended his roles by saying, 'And quality isn't to be found only in the Old Vic. Old Vic or Old Smith, the hell with it! What does it matter? Above all, I certainly don't have the snobbishness or the bad taste to spit on something that gives me success and money, and anyway in my job there's room for every kind of acting.' Obviously certain things, certain people, certain memories stuck in his craw.

But there was some hard graft before anyone would want to interview Sean Connery. Some nights in the impoverished Gardner household they sat around reading poetry, particularly Burns. Sean's version of Scots Wha Hae was especially remembered; he recited it in a dramatic whisper as though confiding to a group of friends.

The friendship with Julie continued, and while Connery and Michael Foot got along well Jill Craigie was less sure about her daughter's involvement with a penniless young actor, although she certainly never pressurised Julie to examine the relationship more closely.

Julie and others advised a scattergun approach to job hunting and Connery applied for everything, from work as a film extra to roles in repertory, in the hope that a number of parts would present themselves from which he could make his selection. It did not happen quite like that and a string of bit parts followed, providing little more than an observation post for his learning. He watched, listened and absorbed everything. His first role before the film cameras was in 1954 when he was an extra in the Herbert Wilcox film *Lilacs In The Spring*, starring Wilcox's wife Anna Neagle making her second appearance in Connery's life – or was it he in hers?

Theatre work was spasmodic, often part time and unrewarding, but it was work. At Kew there were appearances in two further plays, *Point Of Departure* and *A Witch In Time*, and Connery secured repertory roles at Oxford, as Pentheus in *The Bacchae* and later appearing with Jill Bennett in the Eugene O'Neill play *Anna Christie*. He was walking on in television drama and graduating slowly to speaking parts, playing three roles in a BBC production of *The Condemned* and also a small-time crook in an episode of *Dixon Of Dock Green*, which a year later became the early training ground for Connery's future best friend, Michael Caine, a regular bit-part player in the series.

But there was nothing regular about Connery's employment. He was still chasing, pushing and sometimes begging. He combed the columns of the trade press and telephoned producers and casting directors personally. Towards the autumn of 1955 there were more promising developments, though minor. He had already secured his first speaking part in a B-movie called *No Road Back*, starring the Canadian actor and former singer Paul Carpenter, Margaret Rawlings and, for added attraction, an imported American name, Skip Homeier. It was the pattern for British movies to have a second-string American 'star' to lead an otherwise British cast. Connery was once again chosen for his likeness to a director's perception of what a crook might look like; tall and agile, potentially dangerous but fairly brainless. He was playing second fiddle to Alfie Bass, one of that merry band of British actors who appeared in just about every such movie made in British studios in the 1950s. The film was typical of those churned out for second-feature slots in a declining cinema market by Gibraltar Pictures.

Connery, all muscle and eyebrows and with a mop of unruly hair, was for the most part silent, and when he did have something to say he had to act out a speech impediment which, coupled with his accent, did not augur too well for immediate recognition as a star performer. He played a character called Spike, which was a change from Jock – the normal name given to characters who spoke with a Scots accent in British films – and this scene with Paul Carpenter was just about his longest speaking part in the movie.

Carpenter: *Now Spike, when you get inside the Lake Street building I want you to go right up to the top … get out on to the roof and climb across to Constines.*

Connery: *I-i-is there a sk-sk-sk-skylight?*

Carpenter: *Yes, you'll have to prise that open, let yourself inside the building and work your way down three flights till you get to ground level.*

Connery: *W-w-what about the C-c-constines wa-watch-wa-watchman?*

Carpenter: *You and I will have to take care of him when I get inside …*

Though a small part, the dialogue caused Connery some problems and the stuttering did nothing for his image. Carpenter, a man with a cruel humour especially as his 'star' aura faded into the bottom of a whisky glass, was egged on by the joker Alfie Bass to suggest that Connery might apply to the director, Montgomery Tully, to straighten out the dialogue to make it less banal and dump that awful stutter. Carpenter, in dispensing this, left out two rather important details: that Tully himself wrote the script, and was personally affected by a speech impediment when aroused.

In all innocence, Connery duly approached the director to suggest an alteration to the script. Tully, so the story goes, dismissed his request angrily: 'Hu-hu-who the f-f-fuck do you think y-y-you are? L-l-larry Olivier?'

The movie was shot in six weeks at Pinewood and in spite of an alluring publicity campaign extolling the alleged excitement of an 'Underworld Queen entangled in a web of crime, murder and romance' it disappeared without trace. It provided little for anyone to be proud of, but for Connery it was a start. Years later, when he was a star as James Bond, *No Road Back* returned to haunt him. A continental film distributor dug out a print of the movie, repackaged it with subtitles and billed it as Sean Connery starring in *The 007 Gangster Club*. During one showing of the film in Rome the crowd turned nasty when they discovered the deception.

Enterprising billers of old movies are never averse to cashing in on the name of a major star in later years. Actor Herbert Lom recalled for me, 'I first met Connery on a British picture called *Hell Drivers*. He played a small part. We had what was then called a star-studded cast – Stanley Baker, Pat McGoohan, Peggy Cummins, Dickie Attenborough, myself and a few others and, of course, Sean Connery's name was never mentioned anywhere. I saw the picture advertised recently for a re-run on television and it said, "*Hell Drivers* ... Starring Sean Connery". Full stop. I suppose that is a compliment and fame indeed and those of us who have worked with him are proud of that ...'

Lom, later to cap his international fame appearing with Peter Sellers in the *Pink Panther* movies, was right about the star-studded cast. It was Connery's first experience of working alongside some of the bigger names of the British film business. Stanley Baker, who was to become a close friend, Patrick McGoohan, a rival when James Bond was being cast, David McCallum, who was to emulate Connery's later success with his own spy series, William Hartnell, the first Doctor Who, fellow Scot Gordon Jackson, another later friend and himself 'Jock' in so many British post-war movies: they were all there in that movie which was filmed towards the end of 1956 and screened in the summer of 1957. Few who saw the film first time round will forget the impact of the daredevil truck driving of Stanley Baker and Patrick McGoohan, though Connery's part was unfortunately beyond recall. *Hell Drivers* was reissued in the 1960s, when most of the stars had become internationally famous for other works.

Two other films Connery appeared in that same autumn were less auspicious, and providing a mere listing for his CV. First was a tiny role in a dull melodrama called *Time Lock*, about a boy trapped in a bank vault, written by Arthur Hailey and based on a Canadian television play. The production team of Gerald Thomas and Peter Rogers went on to greater renown producing the *Carry On* films.

Next came a film which promised more than it delivered. *Action Of The Tiger* was a poorly constructed tale of a French girl attempting to rescue her brother from political imprisonment in Albania. Director Terence Young held a press conference to announce that his movie, with Van Johnson, Martine Carol and Herbert Lom, would illustrate how the industry could ward off the rising threat from television. It would have superb outdoor filming in exotic locations and lavish and thrilling adventure action with which the small screen could never compete. It was to be shot all over Europe in Cinemascope and, with MGM behind it, success seemed guaranteed.

Unfortunately such a promise was difficult to uphold. Van Johnson was particularly lacklustre and his leading lady, Martine Carol, observed that the bit-part player Sean Connery, whose only important scene was an attempted sexual assault on her, should have played the lead. Terence Young also admired Connery's rough-edged presence which he said reminded him of an early Kirk Douglas. Connery was sure the film was going to be a winner, as were the producers who laid on a celebrity night world premiere at the Empire, Leicester Square, in August 1957.

By then Terence Young knew very well that he had not been able to rescue his project from the depths of dullness to which it had descended and he felt rather sorry for the newcomer Connery who approached him and asked respectfully, 'Sir, am I going to be a success in this?'

'No,' said Young bluntly, well aware that it was no fault of Connery's. 'But just keep on swimming. Keep at it, and one day I'll make it up to you.'

He kept his promise.

3

MOVIE STAR

Kenneth Tynan noticed the 'out of w-w-work a-a-actor' who came down to a club behind the Haymarket Theatre on Friday nights in the 1950s, cautiously buying a couple of long-lasting halves of bitter and was there, it appeared to Tynan, to stand next to, rub shoulders with, or eavesdrop on some of the well-known people who gathered at the small bar. In observing this activity, Tynan at least paid Sean Connery a back-handed compliment – that he recognised him as an actor; out of work a lot of the time, true, but an actor nonetheless and there was something to be said for that early recognition. The club, the Buckstone in Suffolk Street, had become the watering hole of the young theatre world. It was run by an actor named Gerald Campion, later famous as a television Bunter, who was as bouncy and bossy as he was in that role and used to serve good, cheap food and drinks well beyond the licensing hours.

Peter Finch was a regular, as were Stanley Baker, Maxine Audley and Emlyn Williams. Wendy Hiller used to drop in for a boiled egg after appearing in *The Heiress* at the Haymarket, while

Tynan himself held court like a peacock prince in his purple suit, and yellow shirts with pink feathers in the buttonhole. Was Connery a disciple hoping to sit at the feet of some of the established prophets of the British theatre, a man seeking enlightenment from the words of wisdom he might overhear, or just an underemployed actor doing his own intelligence work in the hope of picking up the hint of a job? I suspect primarily the latter was the motive because he didn't care for snobbery in any form, but at the same time he was able to observe and absorb. No doubt he formed an early impression of Kenneth Tynan, a rather more detailed one than Tynan had formed of him.

The Connery memory is a long one. Fifteen years later he was sitting in a restaurant lunching with Tom Hutchinson, who was going to write a piece about him in the *Guardian*, when Tynan walked by. The doyen of critics had probably long forgotten his early encounters with Connery in the Buckstone Club. Not so Connery. 'K-k-kenneth f-f-fucking T-t-tynan,' Connery mimicked. 'He spends his life criticising plays from a position of lofty principle and then dives into a show like *Oh! Calcutta* which isn't half so well presented as Raymond's Revuebar where I was only the other night. Even though the Revuebar champagne is bloody pricey.'

Sean Connery has never been overfond of critics, against whom he has occasionally directed more venom than he has against the most hated of the species, the gossip reporter, but it was critical acclaim that brought him to public attention and started off the clamour for his signature on the bottom of a contract. He might counter that he earned such acclaim, and it only became possible firstly because of the opportunity he was provided with for giving the performance, and secondly by the performance itself.

If, perchance, the critics helped the process, fine and thank you very much, but by and large he would quietly have wished to take the credit for himself and be ever thankful to the man who gave him the opportunity, a Canadian director named Alvin Rakoff. The moment came out of the blue, like one of those barely believable plots for a Hollywood movie when the star can't go on and some unknown stand-in gets his big break and becomes an overnight success. Well, it was almost like that for Connery.

The breakthrough came at a time when the BBC was pioneering a new line in live television drama, inspired by the competition from the recently arrived independent television. Innovative writers and directors were being sought, against the advice of a strong lobby in the television medium that they should not risk experimentation with the unknown. Those pressing for wider boundaries of dramatic presentation could point to American television where, buried between the commercials and the jingles and the game shows, there was already a strong theatrical movement which had produced many exciting new writers and actors and had actually shown the movie industry the way with a string of live drama productions.

Charlton Heston was among those who transferred from television to the big screen, and his route could have been a model for Sean Connery. He explained for me the way it happened: 'The big studios just would not let their actors anywhere near television. It was war and they could not see how television could become part of the film industry; it was not seen as a remotest possibility. The theatre people wouldn't do it either; they thought it was rather tacky, so that left a whole new medium open to a bunch of 25-year-olds whose prime qualification was that they were unemployed. A whole lot of us including Maureen Stapleton, Jack Lemmon, Jimmy Dean, Walter Matthau, all got started in the early days of television doing the drama shows, and what a training ground that was.

'Here we were racketing around inventing a medium because the network television people didn't know what to do either. They came to me and asked if we could do *Macbeth* in 90 minutes, with 10 days' rehearsal. I said we could and in the space of 18 months for Studio One I did *Julius Caesar, The Taming Of The Shrew, Jane Eyre* and half a dozen other classics. The actor doesn't draw breath who isn't going to get good with those parts. What it did do was provide a group of unknown actors, writers, directors, with an opportunity that could never be repeated either in film or on television.'

Gradually, as live drama established itself on American television, it was copied and monitored in Britain, and there was an unexpected bonus in this for Sean Connery. The most successful new production on American television in recent months was Rod Serling's play *Requiem For A Heavyweight* which had starred Hollywood actor Jack Palance, fresh from his lead in Clifford Odets' *The Big Knife* in 1955. He was considered a *big* star and one of the few Hollywood non-conformists who had lowered himself by appearing on television.

Requiem For A Heavyweight was the tale of Mountain McClintock, a boxer with a heart of gold, forced to retire through an eye injury and suffering the gradual humiliation and degradation of show wrestling and, finally, appearing as a clown. It was a slightly clichéd tale, but otherwise a reasonably compelling story, especially for British television where such lavish productions with an imported Hollywood star were virtually unknown.

The BBC bought the play for British audiences and Alvin Rakoff, who had won awards with his last national television production *Waiting For Gillian* in 1955, was hired to direct the drama, which was scheduled to go out live on 31 March 1957 from the new Wood Green Television Centre. Rakoff had already earned a reputation in Canada and Britain and was among the early pioneers of trying new, often experimental theatre for British television. He was a good choice to team up with the actor Palance, a man known for both his professionalism and his fiery, volatile manner.

As it transpired, Rakoff would not have to work with Jack Palance who cried off because of an overrun in his Hollywood commitment the very week the show went into rehearsal. Rakoff found himself without a star. Lists of names and possible replacements were drawn up and among those under consideration was Sean Connery. Rakoff had directed Connery in television as an extra for *The Condemned* and was so enthusiastic that he gave him three parts.

Rakoff told me, 'What struck me about him more than anything was his effort to please and his determination to get things right. I liked him very much because of this enthusiasm and freshness. I had already booked him for a small part in *Requiem* but hadn't really thought of him for the lead.'

Rakoff's then girlfriend and later his wife, Jacqueline Hill, who was the co-star in *Requiem*, mentioned Connery's name as the day of hectic consideration progressed without success.

'Why don't you see him?' she said to Alvin. 'You've got nothing to lose.'

Rakoff was worried about Connery's accent. Jacqueline remained sure he could overcome that problem but, more importantly, he would appeal to women and that almost off-the-cuff remark made Rakoff take notice. When he saw Connery again he became convinced that the actor possessed visual qualities which would be especially appealing, 'but quite frankly, his acting wasn't brilliant.' His reading was suspect but, at the same time, dubiously impressive; the Scottish burr provided an oddly authentic touch to the punch-drunk, mid-Atlantic voice that the part demanded. Rakoff believed there was more to it than that, more to it than just an actor fitting well to a role and reading it impressively. Connery's innocence as an actor brought almost naive interpretations which would have been impossible to achieve from an experienced professional, and this innocence provided the quality required for a man knocked half senseless during a career in the ring. It was quite different from the stumbling, shuffling character portrayed by Palance.

The only real doubt was in Connery's build and physical appearance. He was not exactly the knocked-about-heavyweight sort in an era when boxing top-weights were in the mould of Freddie Mills, then flirting with showbusiness and also considered for the role. Connery's sharp and handsome features, with not a hint of a broken nose or cauliflower ear, did not give him the look of a battered ex-champ. Rakoff convinced himself he could live with that, called Connery and offered him the job. 'What I especially remember about the phone call was that Connery was tremendously grateful. I think he instinctively knew that this was a major role, the first one of his life, and he could make something of it. I did, too.'

The fee, the standard one-performance-only fee for a non-ranking actor was £35, but that did not matter. Connery would have done it for nothing. He was apparently nervously ecstatic. Even so, Rakoff was well aware that he had a hair-raising week of rehearsals ahead for what was a difficult production even without the last-minute change of leading man. It involved a multitude of sets, and being such a major television production all eyes were on him – not merely the critics and the pundits outside, but also the BBC mandarins from within.

All week long Connery was edgy but confident. At his room in Brondesbury Villas he worked hard. Julie Hamilton spent hours helping him rehearse his lines and his landlords, the Gardners, kept up a supply of tea and sympathy. All in that close circle were inspired by Connery's determination to succeed. 'I don't think for a moment,' Julie Hamilton said, 'that he ever considered failure. I don't think he dared think of anything other than making it work.'

Meanwhile, during the daytime, rehearsals proceeded at the television centre and Rakoff still found it necessary to try to get Connery to lighten his accent. He was convinced, though, that Connery had the ability to become a competent actor. He has since made no extravagant, retrospective claims that he discovered Connery, although he did recall that he fought against others in the BBC drama hierarchy who watched the last day's rehearsals before live transmission and were not convinced about Connery's talent. Some – preparing to get themselves prematurely off the hook if anything should go wrong – doubted he was the right choice for the part. One man said Rakoff had put his own career on the line by choosing him.

And so the big night came.

Friends in London were glued to their sets, and Connery's relatives in Edinburgh were more nervous than himself. Families from the stair crowded into the Connery living room to watch a son of Fountainbridge who had become a star. 'By heaven, that was smashing,' said Joe Connery when it was over. His wife Effie was close to tears.

At the television centre that Sunday night congratulations were offered from cast and technicians alike, who knew that Connery had successfully grappled with the most demanding task of his career. The bit part he had been booked for, incidentally, in the last scene where the manager walks away with a new young fighter, was taken by an uncredited young actor named Michael Caine.

After the customary drink in the BBC pub Connery caught his bus home, exhausted but pleased, to await the reviews. Much rested upon what the critics said, more so in those days than now; they would also give the signal to the movie industry, whose leading producers were keeping a cautious eye on the upstarts of television drama to spot new ideas and the arrival of talent.

Connery was quiet but apparently confident that he had done enough to spark some kind of reaction that would kick-start his career, and he had. Reviews were good. *The Times* said that he displayed a 'shambling and inarticulate charm' and the following day the telephone began to ring at the office of his recently acquired agent, Richard Hatton. Perhaps with more of an element of luck than skill, Connery had hit the spot and became an immediate target for producers waving long-term contracts.

This was not unusual. Although the old studios system was dying the death, the Rank Organisation was still running a fairly comprehensive list of stars and major Hollywood distributors like 20th Century Fox were attracted by the tax incentives on offer to movie-makers in Britain. Fox had publicly announced it would pursue an ambitious programme of films made within the British Isles. The studios, along with other independent film-makers, were always on the lookout for talent and so Rank and 20th

Century Fox came running with offers. The latter, said Hatton, was especially appealing because of its international arena while Rank, though well connected in Hollywood, was by and large a British-based company.

Connery did not display any great rush to join either. He must have been elated by this interest, but he instructed Hatton to play a holding game and took off to Edinburgh with Julie Hamilton for a short holiday. Such a technique, though capable of giving any agent heart flutters lest the offers might be withdrawn, remained his modus operandi in later years.

The trip to Edinburgh became another crossroads, in more ways than one. During the past months Connery and Julie Hamilton had become close enough for marriage to be discussed. He was 27 years old, and men of his age in Fountainbridge were talking of marriage by then. So, apparently, was Julie Hamilton since she made a point of revealing that her mother Jill Craigie was not in favour. 'Marrying an actor, and not a very successful one, was not the done thing,' she recalled. This did not affect Connery's relationship with Michael Foot, from whom he would seek advice and occasionally indulge in long conversations about politics. Craigie, a screenwriter, often tipped him off about jobs and helped in other ways. He showed his gratitude by buying her a puppy which they called Vanessa, and it eventually became famous as it was photographed time and again with the Foots on their Aldermaston marches and elsewhere.

Now it was Julie's turn to meet Connery's parents. They drove to Scotland in her sports car, since he did not drive, and he had no qualms whatsoever about taking his friends back to his roots and those two rooms on the stair. For whatever reasons, the relationship between himself and Julie became strained. His brother Neil said it first showed one evening when, while they were all sitting around the fireside, Connery made a signal to Neil which indicated the two of them should go out for a drink. This they did, leaving Julie to chat to Effie. Later she appeared at the Fountain Bar, complained about being left alone and they had a row. Neil reckoned the relationship was all but done for. Jill Craigie was not especially upset that they were drifting apart and had not altered her view when I spoke to her in 1992.

'Julie was quite convinced he would get on in life,' she said. 'She was sure he would become a big star. But personally I had my doubts and frankly I did not fancy him as a son-in-law. She was certainly very much in love with him and they lived together for a while when he got his own place in Wavel Mews. I provided him with a certain amount of furniture which I never got back, incidentally. The thing that struck me during their friendship was that he had very, very rough manners and great tattoos up his arms. My daughter had terrible trouble with her spine around that time and she had been in hospital for a serious operation, and I remember he used to let her carry heavy suitcases. You may judge that I wasn't altogether taken with him. I thought he would be very hard and a tough sort of person and I did not think he would make my daughter happy, and that was my chief concern. She, on the other hand, was quite convinced he was going to be a big star. She had a very good instinct about that and predicted a good future for several others, including Leslie Bricas. I thought he'd got something to him, certainly a creative streak. Julie worked hard with him, and I think she had a lot to do with bringing him out. She had the contacts in the theatrical world; she certainly encouraged him and would spend hours reading over parts with him. I was also working in films myself at the time, writing a script for Gregory Peck's *Million Pound Note*, but Julie had a better view of his abilities than I think I had at the time. The breakthrough came when there was a move towards regional accents and Sean came very much into that category. Anyway, that was our impression as opposed to my daughter's. And I still think she would have been very unhappy if anything had come of her relationship with him.'

Back in London after their Scottish trip, Connery decided to accept the 20th Century Fox offer of a long-term contract as the one most likely to benefit his career to the full – an assessment which eventually proved to be wrong. Fox paid him quite well, around £120 a week, but did not rush him into any immediate employment. It was television that continued to explore his abilities, most notably as Mat Burke in Eugene O'Neill's Pulitzer Prize-winning play *Anna Christie* – in which Connery had taken a role at Oxford – now adapted as a one-hour television drama and screened in the ATV Playhouse series in August 1957.

It was, by any standards, an enticing part as the lover of a prostitute seeking to redeem her self-respect. In the starring role was Australian-born actress Diane Cilento. She was 24 years old, described in the gossip columns as a 'top-drawer sex kitten', and married to the Italian writer Andre Volpe. She and Connery met for the first time at a reading, and Cilento reckoned she did not take to him immediately; she thought he had a rather large chip on his shoulder. She was also to criticise his brusque manner and the tendency towards unfettered criticism of others – by which she presumably meant he told it straight. The match had all the makings of an interesting screen partnership, a fact which was assured by the very task they were about to perform.

The demanding play required intense research and rehearsal, for O'Neill had ensured that the actors portraying the two leading characters needed to establish a rapport. Connery, already familiar with the play, suggested to Cilento that they rehearse privately, away from the pressures of the television studio. Cilento agreed and invited Connery to the apartment she shared with her husband. There is an old adage about opposites attracting, and Connery and Cilento were certainly opposites in background and upbringing, although they were similar in their single-minded determination. He described her as a very independent person, very much like himself and like no one he had met. He was enthralled and there was sufficient chemistry between them to make *Anna Christie* a highly polished production.

Diane Cilento was to become the next most influential and important figure in Connery's life, although the full implications of this almost fatalistic encounter would remain, for the time being, within their private thoughts. It also finally spelled the end of his relationship with Julie Hamilton. She has told of that realisation when he awoke one morning, and said, 'What incredible eyes Diane has got.' Julie said she knew at once what was happening, and challenged him. The upshot was that Julie collected her things and walked out: 'I went home to my parents' house and cried for days.' She did not see Sean again for three years, by which time she had married and had a baby son, while still pursuing a highly successful career in photo-journalism.

Work was also curiously disconcerting at this time. He had signed a seven-year contract with Fox just as the old time film-makers in Hollywood were in their death throes. The most famous of all the big studios, MGM, which Louis B Mayer once boasted had more stars than in Heaven, was letting many of its famous names go. Judy Garland had been ejected, penniless. Clark Gable, Gene Kelly and Lana Turner were all released. Some were jubilant at escaping from the studio system that had cocooned them and cared for their every need and whim; others were bitter that they were being discarded after years of exploitation.

For Sean Connery, a man who became a model of independence and self-management in future years, a seven-year deal with Fox – a studio which itself was but a couple of years away from the edge of bankruptcy – could so easily have meant a ticket to nowhere. There was a ridiculous and very real prospect on the horizon: having made it big on television, having been wooed by the movies, having secured a long contract and a fat cheque, he might then languish in the studio back lot waiting for some casting director to remember his name.

But Connery was not prepared to compromise. Even before he had been accepted for his debut major Hollywood role, which would guarantee him worldwide exposure for the first time in his life, he was quite definitely set on *not* taking the first offer that came along and had no intention of giving up his independence.

In spite of his precarious financial state and a most earnest desire to become a star, he clearly started as he meant to go on, and he would bow to no one. This comes through loud and clear in a press release written in London for Paramount, but subsequently halted by the head of department. It is a remarkable document which reads like a statement of intent for the rest of Connery's working life, and was written in what the studio bosses might have considered a dangerously subversive tone. It could not have been bettered by Connery himself. I discovered the apparently suppressed hand-out among files in the Library of the Academy of Motion Pictures Arts and Sciences in Los Angeles. Dated November 1957, it reads:

> *Sean Connery, the handsome, virile young Scotsman has been in motion pictures for only a little over a year but has already proven that he has a mind of his own and nothing, not poverty or success, is going to change it. When Sean Connery doesn't like something, he doesn't do it ... two Hollywood companies waved financially juicy contracts under his nose but Sean did not like the idea of being tethered by a contract and refused, even though the rent was falling into arrears and he couldn't always buy a tank full of petrol for his motor scooter. Finally, 20th Century Fox secured his signature by promising him greater leeway in the selection of roles. But Sean has not sullied his Scots independence. Twice Fox offered Sean films in Hollywood; twice Sean refused, even though some of his opportunistic friends advised him that independent thought was one thing but the chance to make a film in Hollywood was quite another. The parts, Sean maintained, were not right and he held out even though the landlord was pounding heavily on the door. Connery says, 'If you compromise your independence for any reason, there's not much use living. If you compromise it for something as fleeting as money you are already dead ...' He is not hiding the fact that he likes his current job very much. The part is right, he says.*

The part should have been right. Connery was to star opposite Lana Turner, the original MGM Sweater Girl who had made them millions and had enjoyed her hey-day with several husbands and even more high-profile affairs, which typically made more headlines than her work. She had recently been released from her bondage to MGM, although she had remained there long enough for a young Jack Nicholson, then a messenger in the *Tom And Jerry* office, to catch sight of her as he lay on the grass during his lunch break. Now, in the autumn of 1957, she was bringing her entourage and a little bit of Hollywood to London, searching for a young and vibrant male lead to join her in an important new project.

Coincidentally, one of her last films with MGM was on a loan-out to Fox with another British actor, Richard Burton, who co-starred in a remake of their 1939 hit *The Rains of Ranchipur*. It ultimately faded at the box office in spite of a controversial advertising campaign by the studio featuring Burton sneering at her, 'I wonder what the word for you is in Hindi … in English it's got one syllable.' Then she went straight into filming *Peyton Place*, which was to revitalise her flagging career. After 18 turbulent years in which her films had earned MGM over $50 million she was out on her own. 'I've been sprung,' she announced happily. 'I'm a free agent again. I can work for anyone I like, do anything I like. For 18 years I was a fixture in the Thalberg Building. If they'd got a rotten picture and couldn't get anyone to play in it, they'd say "Give it to Lana". Well, not any more they don't.'

After completing *Peyton Place*, she followed the route of many other Hollywood stars of the mid-1950s to Europe with a script, a director, a production team and financial backing from Paramount to make her first picture for her own newly formed company, Lanturn Films. The movie was Joseph Kaufman's *Another Time, Another Place* and in advance of her arrival she announced that she would be looking for a British co-star. She had script approval, meaning she had final say over the finished words, and cast approval, meaning that she could select the male 'love interest' for the film, a story set during the London Blitz in 1944. Fox put Connery's name forward for a loan-out to Lanturn and Paramount, only to discover there were 300 other aspirants for the part of dashing BBC correspondent Mark Trevor, a married man who has an affair with the American journalist played by Lana Turner. Connery got the part, personally selected by Turner.

Determined as ever to make it work, he began meticulous research for the film. Commandeering a tape player, he persuaded the production people to get hold of 133 recordings of the most famous wartime broadcasts made by correspondents in London, both well-known BBC reporters and the American commentators who became famous for their reports from the Blitz, such as Edward R Murrow and Quentin Reynolds. Then Connery spent two weeks listening to the tapes in preparation for his role. Director Lewis Allen was so impressed that he had several recordings played to the entire cast before shooting a scene, and was convinced this heightened the emotions.

Allen made the point to everyone present, however, that they should not get too impressed by the history of the era. It was a love story, not a war film – and so it was. Connery was a fictional lover, but even so he found himself plunged into a sensational piece of Hollywood history that ended in violent death and a threat on his own life. True enough, he seemed to get along very well with Miss Turner who was ten years his senior, although that didn't matter because she claimed to look ten years younger, which was probably true. There was an excellent working relationship between them that was so obvious it became a draw for the British media. It was a good story: an unknown British actor playing opposite a Hollywood screen goddess who was apparently enjoying the experience very much indeed.

The press pack danced fairly constant attendance from the time initial filming began in Cornwall in late September 1957. The place was filled with the excitement of a Hollywood set, and villagers became extras or fascinated spectators. Location work was completed by early October and the production was moved into

Borehamwood Studios. In the close proximity to London journalists, there was a certain hype – assisted by the studio press office – about the off-screen relationship between Connery and Turner. Lana's daughter Cheryl Crane said there was nothing to it; they were making a picture together, became friends and occasionally dined out. Like many others, Connery found Turner more vulnerable than her tough image indicated, and 'a lovely lady' to work with. It was sufficient to arouse the curiosity of Lana's current boyfriend, a nasty hooligan – hoodlum would be overstating his importance – named Johnny Stompanato who arrived suddenly in London from Los Angeles intent on warning off his imagined British competition.

The romance between Stompanato and Turner had become a curiosity, especially since separating from her current husband, former Tarzan Lex Barker, in February 1957. She was now approaching 40 and, after a history of associations with the world's most attractive men, her latest love affair was both inexplicable and, in the eyes of her closest friends, dangerously shameful.

She had in the past found excitement, as did many stars, running occasionally with the hoodlum crowd that achieved semi-respectability in Hollywood after the war, especially following the arrival of Bugsy Seigel whom she met on a number of occasions. Turner also knew the infamous gambling racketeer Mickey Cohen and through him met Stompanato, a sharply dressed small-time crook with a physique that matched many a Hollywood star. In fact, in the half light of a nightclub he could easily have been mistaken for Sean Connery.

Cheryl Crane described Stompanato as her mother's 'backstairs lover' and he was the last person the film's backers wanted hanging around in London, where promiscuity was much more frowned upon than in America. In her 1982 autobiography, *Lana*, Turner admitted she tried to keep Stompanato out of London because he 'might damage the picture'. But Stompanato wanted to be with Lana and came to London with the idea of becoming an executive producer of this and other films she might make.

Friends said that their quarrels began when Turner refused to risk either her name or her money to help him and eventually the rows began to affect her work.

Stompanato assumed that her young co-star was stealing her away. It was then, Turner later told the police, that the gangster flew into a rage and threatened her over and over again: 'You'll never get away from me. You'll never get rid of me.' She said she was terrified of him and that he threatened her with death or disfigurement and had held a razor to her face and a gun to her temple. Once he almost strangled her with such force that her vocal cords were bruised and she was unable to work for almost three weeks.

Finally there came a confrontation between Stompanato and Connery. Turner makes no mention of it in her autobiography and merely says she had become so worried about what her boyfriend might do that one of her studio people arranged with Scotland Yard to get him put on a plane back to America. Cheryl Crane's description was rather more dramatic:

'Gossip inevitably put my mother in bed with any man she smiled at, but people working on *Another Time, Another Place* were persuaded that Mother and Sean really were having a secret fling. They had a certain familiar air with each other. Stompanato was forbidden to visit the set. Instead, he was forced to spend his time at their rented house in Hampstead. Then one day ... seized with anger and jealousy, John forced Mother's chauffeur to drive him to the studios, where he stormed inside and waved a gun at Connery and told him to stay away from Mother. Unperturbed, [Connery] flattened John with a right to the nose. After he lost the confrontation with Connery, his frustration towards Mother boiled over ... just before Christmas. He knocked her around, nearly smothering her with a pillow before she tore away and was saved by a maid who heard screams. Mother's larynx was bruised in the struggle and the next day on the set she could barely speak. A publicist called it laryngitis, explaining that her facial swelling had been caused by a piece of canvas flapping loose in the wind.

By chance [one of Lana's aides] introduced her over lunch a few days earlier to one of the top men at Scotland Yard. A phone call now set the wheels in motion ...'

The whole business was kept quiet. Not a word leaked out to the press of the disruption caused by Stompanato's arrival, nor of Connery flattening the irate gun-toting lover. Stompanato was quietly expelled from the country. At Christmas there was added interest in the Turner–Connery situation with the release of her film *Peyton Place*, which had opened to excellent reviews and, more importantly, re-established Lana Turner as a big box-office attraction. To be associated with what on the face of it was a successful venture with one of the most famous actresses of the decade augured well for Connery. The boy from Fountainbridge had travelled far, and the story of the poor-kid-made-good line which was being pumped out by the press office was a decent match for his co-star, allegedly discovered working at a Hollywood soda fountain.

That apart, Connery knew by then that it was not a happy film. From his point of view it was a blessing that he was killed in Italy after 25 minutes of dialogue. The film thereafter descended into a rather banal and watery plot featuring Turner and Connery's screen wife, Glynis Johns. Turner blamed everyone else for its lack of sparkle.

'I had never liked England,' she said. 'The damp, bitter climate depressed me and I could never seem to shake the malaise. In Cornwall, where we shot on location, the food and lodgings were grim. Then there were problems with the script and I quickly realised that the picture was a poor vehicle for me. The actors were inexperienced, as I remember. It was one of Sean Connery's first films and he often missed his marks and forgot his key lines, to the annoyance of the director. Because I was co-producer I had to work to smooth things out to ensure that the schedule went ahead as planned.'

All in all, Connery was probably glad to see the back of that one; but he had certainly not heard the last of Johnny Stompanato.

Lana Turner went back to America early in the New Year and 20th Century Fox looked around for something for Connery. Weeks went by and for the first time in his life he was drawing money for doing nothing. Then, out of the blue, Hollywood called – and this time he was wanted there, in the film capital itself, working for one of the most prestigious companies. The chance arrived when Walt Disney began casting his next major film, *Darby O'Gill And The Little People*, a project he had personally nurtured for years. The charming Irish fantasia, about a caretaker who falls down a well and is captured by leprechauns who allow him three wishes, had been around for a long time. Disney originally had the screenplay written in 1947 and later visited Ireland himself to pursue a location for filming, but in the end settled for massive sets to be built inside the Disney Studios in Burbank, California, while external scenes were shot on a ranch in southern California.

Once the decision had been made, Disney sent his team to Britain to find an Irish cast and bring it back to the US for filming, due to start in May. Fox, who still had nothing of their own suitable for Connery, agreed to loan him out and after viewing his 25 minutes in *Another Time, Another Place* the Disney people offered him the part. Irish, Scottish, what the hell? Who could tell the difference?

Connery was slightly dubious about taking the job but Henderson, his mentor from *South Pacific* days, told him not to give it a second thought because very few people who had worked for Disney suffered as a result.

Preparing to leave for Hollywood, he had rented out his recently acquired mews house in north London to actor Ian Bannen, and the immediate future looked cloudless. Then the second instalment of the Lana Turner sensation burst into the headlines worldwide, dragging him with it. Turner and Stompanato's romance had been forced into the public glare with their return from a holiday in Mexico in March 1958 to attend the Academy Awards. Headlines recorded LANA FLIES IN WITH MOB FIGURE. She looked apprehensive and nervous at the award ceremonies for which *Peyton Place* had received seven Oscar nominations, including Best Actress, although won none.

It was generally recognised as her best work since *The Bad And The Beautiful* with Kirk Douglas, and the continued publicity ought to have given a boost to her movie with Connery. Then, on the night of 4 April 1958, Turner's daughter Cheryl, then just 14, plunged a carving knife into the stomach of the unsuspecting Stompanato after listening to another terrible row in which he threatened various kinds of violence. Stompanato died in a pool of blood at their feet. So began the massive publicity of the biggest scandal to hit Hollywood since the good old days.

That Connery arrived in Hollywood at the height of it was an unfortunate coincidence. In the weeks of headlines that followed as Cheryl faced a possible murder charge, certain letters written by Lana Turner to Stompanato while she was filming *Another Time, Another Place* in England found their way into the newspapers. They had been in the hands of Stompanato's relatives and were given to the newspapers by Mickey Cohen, angry that his former associate had been disposed of in such a manner. The letters ranged between innocence and intimacy, and made excellent breakfast-time reading for the millions following the case around the world. Some gave details of how Connery had taken Turner and Cheryl to shows around London and thus Stompanato's friends and family assumed, as the gangster had done, that there was a romantic involvement.

Connery was staying at the Hollywood Roosevelt Hotel ready for the filming. One evening he received a telephone call from a representative of Mr Mickey Cohen, who was apparently prepared to put a contract out on Connery's life. First he offered some 'friendly' advice which amounted to 'Get your ass out of town'.

Connery was not prepared to do as suggested, in spite of the implication that he might not live to see another picture if he did not; he was, after all, there to do a job of work. He did, however, take advice on the matter from senior executives at the Disney Studios who warned him to be careful. Death threats had been received by Lana Turner and Cheryl Crane's lawyer, Jerry Giesler, and it was not beyond the capabilities of Mob personalities to have him permanently propping up a section of the new Santa Monica Freeway. He packed his bags, moved out of the Roosevelt and into a rooming house in the San Fernando Valley called the Bel Air Palms Motel.

The publicity raged. During the inquest and subsequent court hearing on the case against Cheryl, an enterprising picture editor at *Life* magazine sorted out stills of some of Lana's screen appearances in court – as the killer of her husband in *The Postman Always Rings Twice*, as the witness in *Cass Timberlaine* and again on the witness stand in *Peyton Place*.

Meanwhile, Paramount executives decided a bandwagon was rolling which they ought quickly to climb aboard. Never ones to miss such an opportunity, they pulled out all the stops to get an early print of *Another Time, Another Place* rushed into the cinemas and premiered by the end of April – four months ahead of schedule. With *Peyton Place* still drawing huge box office receipts and promising to be one of the biggest earners of the year, there were similar hopes for Lana's new film. Unfortunately, it was not to be. By now a backlash was building and, of course, *Another Time, Another Place* was not in the same class. Connery came out of it reasonably unscathed from a mass of mauling reviews. Set against the real-life scenes that were being played out in all quarters, there was simply no comparison.

Nor was there any comparison with Connery's current job at Disney, where he was keeping his head down and his face out of the Lana Turner saga. He made a point of not contacting her or answering any press enquiries about the case – a wise decision, in which he was advised by the Walt Disney organisation which had been monitoring the situation very carefully. Such a high-profile case could easily smear their whiter-than-white operation. The fantasy tale provided a ready-made escape for Connery from the harsh realities of life in Beverly Hills. *Darby O'Gill And The Little People* was a film he enjoyed making. He was surrounded by a fine cast, an amusing group intent on enjoying the experience as much as he was; it included Janet Munro, Kieron Moore, Albert Sharpe and Estelle Winwood.

Walt Disney, for whom the project had a special significance since it was virtually his brainchild, called in at the Burbank Studios almost daily. With the headlines raging outside, he took a benign, fatherly interest in Connery and would often stop for a conversation. Work was hard and disciplined; they went to bed early and rose early and Connery was happy to conform. He played the character of Michael McBride, a young man sent to replace the ageing caretaker Darby. The old man attempts to arrange a love match between McBride and his own daughter Katie, played by Janet Munro, and during the course of this romance Connery sings 'Pretty Irish Girl', subsequently released as a single.

It was in many ways his most professional performance yet, better than *Requiem For A Heavyweight*, although some New York critics were less than flattering about his acting which, one said, amounted to little more than the ability to look good dancing. The usual stunning effects of any Disney production of this sort ensured that the film contained some electrifying, and terrifying, moments. Disney chose to stage the world premiere in Dublin's massive Theatre Royal in June 1959, making *Darby O'Gill And The Little People* an assured success. The stars of the film all turned out, with Walt Disney himself, and were introduced on stage prior to the screening by compère Pete Murray. It opened in London in July and then throughout the country and in America to excellent houses. So high had Connery's star risen that when Disney's blockbuster *Sleeping Beauty* was premiered at London's Astoria the following month, he arrived in an open carriage with Janet Munro, Kieron Moore and Diane Cilento. It had become Connery's first global success, and for the first time he was beginning to look like a star.

4

BRIDGE TO
THE MOON

Sean Connery's sexuality figured in his credentials as an actor from an early stage and became an essential ingredient in his rise to stardom. It must have been pleasing – to start with – to have girls falling at his feet, but when he had achieved fame it became tiresome to face the endless questions that were fired at him about his women. In the end it turned full circle and was pleasantly amusing and ego-boosting to be voted the sexiest man in the world at the age of 60.

Alvin Rakoff chose him for *Requiem For A Heavyweight* partly because of his sex appeal; it was a key factor in his selection as Lana Turner's screen lover – for he was no great actor then – and other directors for whom he worked early on in his career mentioned his rough-edged quality and animal magnetism. It was a built-in mechanism that barely needed exaggeration, an almost instinctive attribute which was more important to him than he realised. It is obvious now, and it has been confirmed by many close to him, that he had great difficulty coming to terms with the demands of public sexuality – and probably never has.

The first difficulty to be encountered was that the media expected him to act out the role for them in real life, but he did not join the extrovert band of Hollywood stars who conducted their love affairs in public, as if they were unable to differentiate between truth and fiction. He certainly had a talent for attracting affection, but unlike some of his colleagues he rigorously defended his view that relationships were a totally private area of his life. He not only refused to talk about them from the outset, he eventually became angry at the way writers tended to blur the lines between himself, his private life and his screen roles.

Early in this media pursuit of his private love life he said to a close friend that it could be likened to 'screwing in public' and he was not going to lower himself. The same friend redrew the analogy for me years later: whatever Connery did on stage or in front of a camera was in the public domain, because he had placed it there; everything else was private.

The audience is never allowed backstage at a theatre because it would destroy the illusion created by the actors out front, and similarly no one – not the audience, the cameras or the media – was allowed behind the scenes of his life once he was off stage. Eric Sykes was impressed by his ability to shrug off his acting role instantly. 'Many cannot do that,' Eric told me. 'If Peter Sellers, for example, was playing a vicar he would be the vicar, the nice guy on screen and off for the duration. If he was playing a villain, he would be villainous to us with a fearsome intensity. Sean could just walk away from it, as if he was switching off the lights.'

Connery's social attitudes on a broad front were almost puritanical, verging on the naive. This probably harked back to life on the stair, when sex was not only seldom talked about in the family but was, by necessity, performed quietly in snatched moments simply because of the restrictions imposed by families living in crowded rooms.

During his adolescence he had been successful in the art of wooing. Connery has admitted losing his virginity at an age so young he could not even remember it, yet he remained in control and apparently ignored the temptations of the new permissiveness as being a distraction from his single-minded aim of becoming a successful actor. Contact with this new and exciting world, expanding as he moved into his late-20s to even wider horizons, presented him with some interesting challenges that went completely against the 'people like us' syndrome of the working classes.

People like them did not go abroad for their holidays, fly in aeroplanes other than in wartime, stay in hotels, drink French wine (or any wine other than British sherry or Sandeman's Port at Christmas). People like them did not own cars, or even have a driving licence unless to drive a lorry. People like them had never dived into a swimming pool that was not filled with a hundred screaming children, nor travelled by taxi unless in an extreme emergency. People like them … He was one once, but now he wasn't. His contract salary from 20th Century Fox gave him the wherewithal to expand his lifestyle and broaden his outlook while past repressions could be identified and discarded.

As they went, and he began to take the stepping stones into the domain of the middle class – even occasionally the upper class – temptations were inevitably ever present, especially in the company of those groups of actors, artists and extroverts known and envied through history for their cavalier attitude to sexual morality. Connery's sexuality, which some would point to as the key to his sway over an audience, did not develop into a notoriously overt catalogue of real-life and high-profile bedroom scenes like Beatty or Nicholson, even though his masters would have wished it in the interests of publicity.

He sidestepped the scandals, and the innuendo – with the exception of the Lana Turner affair which was not of his making – that surrounded some of his contemporaries was minimal. When his screen appearances became eventually filled with blatant, sometimes sadistic, sex, it seemed to have had the effect of forcing out his own determination to avoid personal linkage.

This was apparent from quite early on and was recognised by

those who worked with him. Honor Blackman, for example, who starred with him in *Goldfinger* and whose romp in the hay became an iconic Bond scene, was almost embarrassed to talk about Connery's sexuality.

In a British Academy of Film and Television Arts' tribute to him in 1990 she was called upon to make a small speech and, referring to her judo scene in that film, she had to say with all the double entendre she could muster, 'And we finished up in the hay, and I mean that literally … It's a wonder the hay didn't catch fire.' When I read that quote back to her a couple of years later, she said, 'Oh gosh, don't remind me. It was something I had to recall for an anecdote. And it really wasn't like that at all. The whole scene was just so professionally managed by Sean that sex really did not get a look in. It never did, but it did not affect the way he appeared on screen which was the archetype of virility and sex appeal.'

Looking back over almost three decades since she made the film, she remained moderately astonished that Connery steadfastly avoided headlines of a sexual or scandalous nature. By the law of averages very few in his position have been able to achieve such apparent squeaky-clean normality, forcing debate as to whether he was either lucky in keeping dalliances quiet or that he simply never indulged in anything that could lead to trouble in the first place. The former proved to be the case and, in attempting to explain not merely his sexuality but his ability to draw an iron curtain down over his private life, it might be said that it had never been different. Singularity seems to have been difficult and he appears to have needed the presence in his life of a strong woman. But his needs in those career-forming years were not those of many men, who may have been spoiled by caring mothers and who expected to have their every whim attended to by a young bride. Men with his background were the bread-winners and the dinner had to be on the table when they came home from work, their shirts clean and ironed and the socks darned. That would have been his life in the tribal normalness of Edinburgh that went with a job in the print room of the *Edinburgh Evening News*.

His needs were different. He apparently sought from his serious female companions a willingness, even a desire, to contribute to his own preoccupation at that time, which was to pursue his goal for self-improvement and betterment as an actor. Nothing else mattered, or so it seemed, to a number of his friends of successive eras whose comments I was able to compare.

Yet neither was there any talk of the fashionable word 'insecurity'. His life went through phases of insecurity enforced by struggling to make ends meet, but those who know him well say it was not a word that could be applied to him personally. Emotion and feelings were shown only as part of his performances on stage or in front of the camera. If he possessed private fears they were kept backstage, and those around him were shown a confident and determined face. Perhaps because it was comparatively late in life that he finally set his course, he refused to be deflected by pleasure seeking or irresponsible frippery.

A woman was important and there was an important woman waiting. Connery's return from America after completing his film for Disney was followed by a jaunt to Africa for an insignificant loan-out role in *Tarzan's Greatest Adventure*, starring Gordon Scott in the title role, which added nothing but experience and exotic locations to Connery's career. It was a fairly barren period workwise, although his relationship with Diane Cilento – which had begun quietly 'in the background' while she was in the final stage of her faltering marriage to Andre Volpe – was beginning to gather pace. Connery, meantime, moved onwards and upwards. Friends who considered Julie Hamilton to have contributed to laying the foundations of Connery's future would soon realise that she paled to insignificance alongside the altogether more forceful character of the new woman now firmly in his life.

Don Prince, a 20th Century Fox executive who watched Connery grow from an unknown into a major star, gave an uncompromising, if slightly cynical, view of this developing situation in the following terms: 'Her name was Diane Cilento – and you spell it Pygmalion. She coached Sean and tutored him; she put thoughts into his head and showed him how to play for better effect ... She was the making of Sean Connery.' Having spoken to a number of acquaintances of both, this exaggeration was not hugely wide of the mark; he, after all, would do nothing he did not want to do.

Cilento was like no one he had yet met in the business. According to first-hand accounts, the impression was quite mutual and it arose, at least on her part, when they were performing the ATV production of *Anna Christie*. Cilento, an experienced, RADA-trained actress, found herself relying heavily on Connery, who had prior knowledge of the play, and accepted his advice and suggestions as if he was some trusted old tutor. Conversely, she was able to comment constructively on his performance. He had found someone who actually respected his work and who was interested in it from an unselfish point of view. It became a sort of professional mutual admiration club which soon developed beyond.

Like Julie Hamilton, Cilento was not initially attracted to Connery, put off by what could be called his commonness and lack of manners verging on boorishness. There was also a certain Celtic aloofness which Diane classified as an almighty chip, but it was more likely to have been a mask for his inherent shyness. Once she had brushed away the chip, however, she found him sexually appealing and, more importantly, she discovered a man's man with no airs or graces. A rough-cut diamond, as Terence Young once said; a man who hated falsehoods and phoneys, who walked around in a turtleneck sweater, sloppy jeans and sandals not for effect but because he liked doing so and who paid not the slightest attention to what the establishment expected. He was, in short, his own man.

On her part, Cilento had much to offer Connery. She was upper class, well educated, had travelled the world, was an experienced actress and a passionate reader and writer although her formal education, like his own, had virtually ended when she was 14. She was filled with knowledge and was as ambitious as Connery. Her family itself provided an intriguing background.

Her father was Sir Raphael Cilento, whose own father fled to Australia due to his involvement with the Italian patriotic movement originated by Garibaldi. Raphael Cilento became renowned for his research into tropical diseases and was knighted by the British for his services to medicine. Her mother, Phyllis, was an eminent gynaecologist and of their five children three went into the medical profession, while Diane chose the performing arts and another sister became an artist.

Diane was a rebel in her youth, always in trouble at boarding school. She moved through her education with energy to spare, seemingly selecting a route which most appealed to her and avoiding both convention and the gymslip uniformity normally imposed upon the young gels of her age. I came across an interesting and lucid description of her, which probably cannot be bettered, while searching through the archives of gossip columnist Hedda Hopper, who spent some time with Cilento soon after she had settled in with Connery.

The Hopper papers, in the special collections repository of the Library of the Academy of Motion Pictures Arts and Sciences in Los Angeles, included the following notes, apparently never published in full, which, love or hate Miss Hopper, are pertinent and topical for inclusion here:

> Few young stars come into motion pictures with training and experience like Diane Cilento's. A small, vivid girl with straight cornsilk blonde hair, green eyes and a wide flexible mouth, she is a mixture of French, Scottish and Danish on her mother's side and her father ... is Italian. Diane's life has been spent in Australia, England and the US and each place has contributed to her colour and technique. Since she has won honours in both legitimate theatre and television, I was curious to know where she got her training.

63

Hopper went on to record how Diane had provided her with 'a dizzying account' of her life, beginning at the age of six with ballet lessons in Queensland, continuing through her boarding school days in Australia and then on to Washington Irving High School in New York when her father was working for the World Health Organisation. She joined the Fokine Ballet School at Carnegie Hall when she was 15 and followed that with two years at the American Academy of Dramatic Arts and then work experience at the acclaimed Barter Theater in Virginia, first as an electrician's assistant and then taking small parts. She went on to England before her 18th birthday, gained a scholarship to the Royal Academy of Dramatic Arts then went into repertory with the Manchester Library Theatre.

Hedda Hopper's notes record this explanation by Cilento for her movement through such a diverse training ground of opportunity: 'I was aggressively independent in those days. During my five terms with RADA I earned money serving in a wine shop where I also got my meals, so it wasn't unprofitable. For a time I also sold programmes in a circus and, in all, I sought opportunities to study life from different angles.'

She was still a teenager when she appeared in a Manchester production of *Romeo And Juliet* and her notices were such that she quickly moved to London's West End to appear in *Arms And The Man*. She was the last person Sir Alexander Korda placed under contract and he cast her in *The Passage Home* with Peter Finch and Anthony Steel, the only girl in a cast of 30 men for which she was voted Britain's most promising actress in 1955. From this, she moved straight into Robert L Joseph's London production of *Tiger At The Gates*, in which she was cast as Helen of Troy opposite Michael Redgrave. When the play moved to Broadway she won the New York Critics Award for Best Actress of the Year.

Like Connery, she had shunned blank-cheque overtures from Hollywood, having 'hated the thought of being tied down at that point'. In the meantime, she had met and married the Italian Andre Volpe, variously described as a writer, a student, a journalist and a trainee film director. They were married, following a whirlwind three-week romance, at Kensington Register Office in February 1955 after he had proposed to her in Rome on the Via Gloria.

The marriage had a shaky start. She was working in *Tiger at the Gates*, and then went on to other things. He was travelling back and forth to Rome where he was due for call-up in the Italian military. In March 1957, when she was appearing in *Zulieka* during its pre-London run in the provinces, the newspapers descended upon her when there was a scene at an Oxford hotel. Cilento, who had a tendency to wildness, smoked cigars and rode a scooter around London, was good gossip column copy. The play had been difficult and she had refused to let Volpe visit her. She was depressed and soon afterwards checked into a nursing home before going off to Italy, chased by reporters to whom she made a statement about problems with the play when script changes were made only five minutes before curtain-up.

She had barely recovered, and also discovered she was pregnant, when she returned to London to appear with Connery in *Anna Christie* in August. The following month she flew home to Australia for the birth of her daughter Giovanna Margaret, leaving Connery in charge of her motor scooter.

Though Cilento's training and experience was far broader than Connery's, she had been under such heavy pressure that her confidence was drained. She needed a reliant shoulder and, as she told Hedda Hopper, Sean Connery eventually brought a stability to her life that she had failed to achieve in those fast and furious years since she cast off parental shackles and began making her own way. And yet, Connery was exciting and unpredictable, just as she was – although she hated the description, saying it was like one of those dreamed up by a studio publicist. At the time it seemed to fit both of them.

There was, perhaps, a reciprocal need in Connery, too. 'We did not fall in love for a year or more after our first meeting,' Diane once said. 'He was not nearly as attractive in those early days.'

By then she had returned to her apartment in Bayswater with her daughter. Her marriage to Volpe was all but over and her relationship with Connery crystallised in 1959, which was not a good year for either of them with him bereft of decent work and Diane falling ill. However, the affair was marked by its discretion. Few even knew of their friendship outside what appeared to be a professional association. She wanted to avoid publicity in her personal life at all costs.

At some point the couple enrolled in a school of movement run by the Swede Yat Malmgeren, a former member of the Kurt Jooss Ballet Company who had devised a sort of therapy for actors and dancers which was mysteriously described as 'cohesive terminology'. It was not merely physical in nature, but designed to improve expression of thought and communication with others. Connery, who used to attend group sessions with Malmgeren three times a week, described it as 'a remarkable period for me, proving that with proper exercises you can reshape your physical structure by attacking yourself from within'.

The exercises were a forerunner of many similar forms of self-hypnosis and alternative therapy which later exploded into popular cults like transcendental meditation. Yat's techniques have been credited with assisting Connery to develop movement, a key feature of his performances as James Bond and which, incidentally, he recommended to his son Jason when he began acting 20 years later.

In that regard Connery and Cilento were ahead of the fashion, and apparently never averse to experimenting with mental and physical alternatives designed to tune the mind and body to achieve the peaks of ability. Robert Hardy described to me an occasion a few years later when he was staying with the Connerys while rehearsing a West End play, co-starring Hardy and Cilento, which Sean was directing. 'They had this extraordinary box upstairs which I believe was zinc lined and he persuaded me to get inside it, as they did, each morning. It was like a coffin on its end. Apparently it was supposed to concentrate one's energies.

Both Sean and Diane used it. I don't recall that it had any particular effect on me, but who knows? They swore by it and used it all the time, which I thought bizarre.'

Connery's movement classes ran parallel to his reading and study. Among his books was one on the life and work of Constantin Stanislavski, the guru of Method actors such as Marlon Brando, James Dean and Rod Steiger. Connery had left it rather late in life to conform to the edict of the American writer John Burroughs: that a youth gathers his implements to build a bridge to the moon. Even so, Connery was certainly acquiring a box of tricks, and he added to it like a squirrel stores away food for the future. The absorption factor continued, not least in connection with the latest trends which towards the end of the 1950s developed into something of a revolution, but unlike most of his male contemporaries he was self-taught. He was like one of those old-style jazz pianists who could out-perform the product of meticulous tuition because, although he might be rough around the edges, he had no pre-set boundaries. In fact, Connery has been known to talk with some derision about the snobby products of acting academies who believed that they had been 'taught' how to act as if they were learning maths.

It was all experimentation and improvisation, which in a way was what Stanislavski was writing about. Not only that: for an actor who could not go to one of the tutorial establishments like the Royal Academy of Dramatic Arts or had not had the kind of schooling which provided the opportunity to study and perform the classics, there was no other way than self-tuition and work experience. The nearest the British studios ever had to the American star-making system was the rather limp Rank Charm School. But Hollywood studio schools, where the likes of Rock Hudson – a truck driver from the midwest – were taught every conceivable aspect of the art had all but ceased. They were old hat although, as Charlton Heston said in their defence, they gave a young actor a chance to bat.

But new wave American screen actors had started talking about 'organic' motivations 'from within', and these concepts had made their way across the Atlantic in a number of major films. With the competition of television to films in full flow, the time had arrived for a complete overhaul of anything that was happening on screen, otherwise the industry faced total collapse. As Joss Ackland, among the large group of promising young actors scouring the world's stage for the breakthrough, recalled for me,

'The movies of the 1950s had become a wasteland. America produced large-scale epics with grey plots in glorious garish Technicolor and slow, coy, romantic comedies that had no connection with reality. Only a few moments of magic broke through: *High Noon, On The Waterfront, Twelve Angry Men* and the occasional musical, *Seven Brides For Seven Brothers, Singing In The Rain* and *A Star Is Born.* Marlon Brando had magnetism and the new age of frustrated teenagers identified with James Dean. In England there were tepid films about alligators, mermaids and doctors, where James Robertson Justice parodied a fading class. Bodies relaxed and became free as we discovered rock'n'roll … and it was not the 20-year-olds who set the rules and created fashion, it was the teenagers.'

Young actors ignored the developments at their peril. Stanislavski and the Method had a few supporters in Britain, including Kenneth Haigh who had created the role of Jimmy Porter in John Osborne's *Look Back In Anger*, a play which Connery recognised as something of a milestone, even a watershed, in theatre and television generally. It was one which would affect him directly because it was the beginning of a trend leading to the so-called 'new wave' in Britain, around which a body of writers established themselves but whose work, Haigh despairingly recalled, became somewhat trivialised in the popular press by talk of kitchen-sink dramas and northern accents.

The truth was that new writers were dealing with new, often social issues, and it was a total contrast to the kind of films being produced in Britain until that time. 'Who cared about the British film industry then?' said Haigh. 'They were turning out stuff like

Doctor Up Your Snatchbox, or something. Who gave a fuck about that? When writers began to deal with serious issues, the popular newspapers had to find an angle, and it all became chronicled in a rather glib way.'

The teachings of Stanislavski came to the fore when actor and director Bobby Lewis and actress Cheryl Crawford founded the Actors Studio in New York in 1947. Lee Strasberg and Elia Kazan later imposed their own theories and Lewis subsequently left, but the whole movement was so controversial that it became a focus for all modern actors. Though Brando and Dean were well-known exponents, there were many others who became famous, giving credence to the Method as a necessary experience for future stars. Montgomery Clift, Carroll Baker, Eli Wallach, Karl Malden, Maureen Stapleton, Marilyn Monroe, George C Scott, Paul Newman and Grace Kelly were among those who had had early exposure to the system.

It had become such a talking point between 1955 and 1960 that Laurence Olivier decided to drop into the Actors Studio in New York and see what it was all about, a timely adventure when he discovered that Monroe, his co-star in *The Prince And The Showgirl*, had attended sessions there before working with him.

It was a popular theory of student actors that the exercises and discussion points developed by Stanislavski and improvised by the Actors Studio would lead to better and more innate performances away from the normal perceptions of acting out a role, and, more importantly, to the understanding of acting and characterisation. Stanislavski believed that the actor's inspiration should come from deep within himself, almost from a spiritual base, and not just from applying himself to the memorising of lines.

The best example of the clash between acting's old school and the Method was described to me by Julie Harris, who starred with James Dean in *East Of Eden*. Dean's screen father was the veteran actor Raymond Massey, who found immense difficulty in dealing with the way Dean operated. When a scene was not working Dean would stand there motionless, swearing violently and using the foulest words he could think of to vent his frustration. Massey walked off the set immediately. 'I have never heard anything like it in my life,' he complained to director Elia Kazan. 'I cannot work with this man a moment longer. You never know what he is going to do or say. Can't you make him say the lines the way they are written?'

Maureen Stapleton, one of Bobby Lewis' star pupils, in a long discussion about her work and early tuition at the Actors Studio, told me that she believed that any young actor of the period, in Britain or the US, would have benefited from studying Stanislavski; there was always some element that could be applied to any given situation in theatre or on film, and she pointed to a long list of students who had followed herself, Brando and Clift to the Actors Studio who eventually became stars. It provided a fundamentally broader base to the preparation for a performance and made actors search within themselves for inspiration, though she admitted that at times it could be frustrating. She gave me the following, and typical, example. The anecdote has a tangential connection with Sean Connery, but more than that it gives an amusing insight into the kind of intensity that was around at the time as actors struggled with the 'organic revolution'.

'We were doing a film called *The Fugitive Kind*,' Stapleton recalled, 'with Marlon, Joanna Woodward, Anna Magnani and myself. We were sitting around a table reading and Marlon was talking very, very quiet, because that's how he had decided he was going to play it. Actually, he didn't want the job in the first place, but they were paying him a fortune but that's by the by. So he was talking quiet and everyone else talked quiet; quieter and quieter because that's the way Marlon was playing it. In the end, I thought it incumbent upon me to mention it, and I said, "Marlon, will you tell me what you are doing? I cannot hear a goddamn word you are saying. Am I going deaf or what?" Well, he fell about. Anna, who hadn't dared say a word, kissed me. So did Joanna. Tenessee Williams, who was sitting off somewhere, chirped up and said, "Thank goodness you've spoken up, darling. I haven't heard a bloody thing all week." So that's what over-methodising can do to you.'

The point of the story is that Brando *did* talk quietly in many of his performances, even in situations which under normal circumstances would have demanded noisy intervention or a raised voice; both he and Dean were often accused of mumbling, but the students of this school of acting did not stand there, as normal convention demanded, and speak their lines loudly and with a clarity that would ensure those sitting in the gods heard every word. It wasn't going to be like that any more.

Connery, on whom Brando was an influence along with Cary Grant and Spencer Tracy, discovered that Brando's style matched his own Scottish burr which he had apparently no intention of changing for anyone. Brando's early films obviously made an impression. His interviews in later life are littered with references to Brando's *On The Waterfront* and *A Street-car Named Desire* in which he noted Brando's underlying style of almost tenderness. Connery spoke softly and, like Brando, was the same person in everything he did. As Joss Ackland pointed out, he developed the knack of bringing the part to him rather than the other way around, though it did not happen without considerable forethought and practice. Spencer Tracy was the same, so were Cary Grant and Clark Gable. But what Connery had realised earlier than many others in the British school of acting was that the trend was towards realism and to more down-to-earth acting than in previous generations.

It was he who said that in Britain in the late-1950s there was still a concept of the actor being somehow divorced from real life – even though he was attempting to portray it; that acting was associated with being statuesque and striking poses and declaiming with lyrical voices. It did not mean he would not appreciate Olivier's *Othello*; far from it. Spurred on by Cilento, Connery was seeking parts and projects that appealed to him and which he could have contact with at a grass-roots level. His quest for realism took him to the study of newer styles of acting, though it would not necessarily mean he would follow them.

He clearly noted the developments in America and, like a writer making notes for a novel, saw all of this as a part of the scholarship of his craft, sucking in information and spitting out the pips and the bits he did not feel worth digesting. 'I have nothing but the greatest admiration for him,' said Joss Ackland, 'and that is not any exaggeration. He realised very early on that he had to go on learning; that is the very essence of our craft.' The learning process was a crucial factor in Connery's development and direction. What he gained in this vital period was more than an ability to challenge his own work and question what he was doing, how he was doing it and how best he could improve upon it. He also established what would become a hallmark of his career: he taught himself not to accept the word of others that a particular part would be right for him. If he did not like it, he would not do it. He also learned to analyse scripts, studying both the character he was playing and the lines he was expected to speak. He would want to play a character his way instead of being told how, and later – when he had the power – make his own amendments to the scripts. 'It was a marvellous ability,' Eric Sykes confirmed.

As we will discover, this very aspect first attracted from directors and actor colleagues a certain apprehension that he should have either the capacity or the cheek to do such a thing; eventually it turned to admiration when it was realised he had an abundance of both.

During the summer and autumn of 1959 Connery had plenty of time to study. After the *Tarzan* adventure, 20th Century Fox failed to come up with a single acceptable suggestion for his next film. It wasn't entirely their fault, for Connery was not the most co-operative of contract players on their books. Of all the topics friends and colleagues included in their assessment of Sean Connery, the actor, most mentioned his resilience, if not downright stubbornness, in being able to resist parts which he was not convinced would suit him, or if he thought the script overall did not work and might drag him down.

There were other reasons why 20th Century Fox executives were growing wary. One complained about his manners and his dress, the sign those days of a rebel. 'Even if you did manage to persuade him to wear a suit for a business meeting, you were just as likely to discover that he had no socks on. It didn't do, not then.'

Days rolled into weeks and then months. He was still being paid under contract, but that was no satisfaction. Connery had just had his 29th birthday. Work was spasmodic and the studio people responded to his telephone calls with unfulfilled promises and mediocre offers.

Television and the theatre continued to appreciate his talents more than big-screen producers. He appeared in a TV play, *Riders To The Sea*, for the BBC and took second billing in another boxing story, Ralph W Peterson's *The Square Ring* with a youthful Alan Bates, which was broadcast on ITV in June. He interspersed these appearances with some DIY improvement work at his home in Wavel Mews, converting a garage into living accommodation which was altogether more vital than putting a roof over his little Fiat.

He returned to the Oxford Playhouse in 1959 to appear in a Pirandello play, *Naked*, but then curiously turned down two promising offers. First Joan Littlewood, who had seen him at Oxford, wanted him to join a Macbeth workshop she was taking to Russia, and director Anthony Mann offered him a decent speaking part, though not huge, in *El Cid*. The illness of Diane Cilento, who was suffering from a chest infection, may have had something to do with these refusals, although few were aware even then of Connery's friendship with her.

It was television again which sought his services for a series of respectable roles in the New Year of 1960, with notable actors and prestige productions. The BBC had commissioned an extensive and epoch-making series, *An Age Of Kings*, of 15 hour-long history plays of Shakespeare beginning on 10 April 1960, and shown every other Thursday until November. A description of it in *The Times* as an astonishing achievement was fairly typical of the reception. Connery appeared in the first four episodes, which represented a serialisation of *Henry IV Part I*, playing Hotspur to Robert Hardy's Prince Hal.

They were lively and robust productions which contrasted strongly and surprisingly with the normal BBC presentation of Shakespeare. This was largely due to the courage of producer Peter Dewes and the interpretational skills of director Michael Hayes, who were prepared to experiment in the face of possible establishment criticism. The idea was to attract an audience from the masses, people who would not normally go to the end of the street to watch Shakespeare. It was also something of a challenge for Connery, though Robert Hardy – who had understudied Prince Hal to his friend Richard Burton and had altogether far more experience with Shakespeare – was full of praise for Connery's work. There was the advantage that the role of Hotspur was not in verse, and Connery gave a relaxed, almost dashing portrayal.

'In my view his was a fine performance,' Hardy said. 'I don't recall what the notices were like but I think he was pretty well lacerated for being incomprehensible – it was the accent. It was a problem at that point, of that there was no question. I did not pay much attention to it because I knew the words anyway, but the whole point about Hotspur is that he is supposed not to talk like other people, and Connery certainly qualified in that regard. I suppose it was courageous casting, but I felt it worked. He was pretty strong but I think the amazing thing was that he then went on to pursue his entire career only mitigating his accent very slightly and never consciously, I think. Sean has achieved this thing of bringing the part to himself quite wonderfully. It is something we all think we can do; some of us are more chameleon. Most actors actually bring the part to themselves much more than they realise. With Sean, he does manage the ultimate which is to suspend disbelief.'

Connery returned to television again in the autumn for Giles Cooper's *Without The Grail*, broadcast by the BBC in September. It was an odd sort of play in which he had to investigate the activities of a character played by Michael Hordern. As with many of his roles, he had to learn something new; in this case it was the game of Mah Jong, which he was taught by one of his co-stars, the Chinese actress Jacqui Chan.

The television work had become quite vital to Connery. It paid him, that was true, but film work had all but dried up and if he was to retain his confidence and determination the kind of work television was offering him – albeit on an irregular basis – was important. His next gave him a particular boost; it was a significant and acclaimed play by a leading writer, and a quality production which – though he did not know it then – would prove to be the one that moved him to the launching pad of superstardom.

He was cast as the leading man in *Adventure Story*, Terence Rattigan's version of the life of Alexander the Great, for which he had to wear a blonde wig filled with curls more suited to Shirley Temple. It was a substantial part and, obviously taken by the appeal of the role itself and the implications of it as far as his career was concerned, he gave it the full treatment, playing with an enthusiasm and strength which was recognised and reflected in most of the reviews.

The Rattigan script portrayed Alexander through the ages, from young adventurer to eventual tyrant, and the transition provided Connery with considerable scope. The reviews were especially pleasing in one outstanding respect: *The Times* noted that 'certain inflections and swift deliberations of gesture at times made one feel that the part had found the young Olivier it needs'. He had been compared to Brando, he had been compared to Cary Grant, but perhaps no other single sentence in his entire career could be so gratifying.

Connery had forced himself into national stardom and was achieving recognition simply through these occasional outings rather than his appearances on the silver screen: he was sufficiently well thought of for the *Radio Times* to put him on the cover the week the Rattigan play was transmitted in June 1961. The play made such an impression that the BBC hierarchy immediately approved a hefty budget for producer Rudolph Cartier to begin work on a television version of *Anna Karenina*, and Cartier offered Connery the male lead to play opposite Claire Bloom in what many consider to be her most significant television role.

To capture the talent of Claire Bloom was one thing; to have given her a co-star of unequal talent would have been an insult but in fact it served as recognition by television, at least, that Connery had come a long way from the early raw, basic style which had earned him the description of a rough-cut diamond.

The edges had been smoothed, and his performances were polished. The individuality remained in almost every other way, and especially in his speech and movement. *Anna Karenina* was to be a giant production by television standards. For one thing, David O Selznick's original big-screen version starring Greta Garbo and Fredric March in the leading roles of Anna and Count Vronsky was still within living memory, and was notable for its supporting cast which included Basil Rathbone, Freddie Bartholomew and Maureen O'Sullivan. Even fresher in the public mind was the British version, Alexander Korda's 1947 production with Vivien Leigh, Kieron Moore and Ralph Richardson. Connery, cast in the role originally taken by March, was caught by the mood of it – concerned, excited, tense and a number of other adjectives – more so probably than anything he had done for two or three years.

Claire Bloom represented something of a challenge to him; she was a star of films and theatre who had performed in all the classics at the Old Vic; she was one of only two actresses whom Richard Burton said he enjoyed kissing, the other being Taylor. Her most recent major success was in the 1959 big-screen version of *Look Back In Anger* co-starring Burton, Mary Ure and Edith Evans.

Though the film had not been well received, it was nonetheless a personal triumph and beside her Connery's CV looked modest. But he was gathering a head of steam. Cartier recognised this and Michael Hayes, who had cast him in *An Age Of Kings*, also saw it. So did Robert Hardy and just about everyone else who had worked with him.

There had been a running discussion for months in the trade press and the entertainment columns of the national news as to why Connery had not been selected for more important screen roles. He was one of the most under-rated and underused actors on the British scene. True, the film business was facing many problems. Evaporating audiences had meant that increasing numbers of Odeons, Gaumonts and Granadas, often housed in those huge 2,000-seater high-street cinemas built for pre-war audiences, were being converted into bingo halls. It was happening all over the country: cinemas were being forced out by sheer economics to become the poor relation of a gambling craze, shunted into single-storey 400-seater halls, sometimes even smaller.

Film development money was also drying up in Britain, and those producers who were able to raise it seemed unsure of their direction. Because of the scarcity of cash and the nervousness of investors, projects which departed from the norm seldom made it to the drawing board. Too often film producers had to settle for old-fashioned, worn-out plots and twee, banal comedies verging on Whitehall farce or tired old gangster plots that had been Britain's lot since the war. America had moved on into the socio-docu-dramas and on again to break new boundaries in sexual awareness. The emphasis was on youth and young actors.

Connery was trapped in a time warp. He had missed the back end of one era and was now too old for another. Britain's answer to Brando he might have been, but the film industry had never recognised him as such – and especially not his employers, 20th Century Fox, who had failed to cast him in one single film since he had signed an exclusive film contract four years earlier.

Not a single film.

True, he had rejected some roles and Fox had taken money for loan-outs to other companies, though neither they nor Connery derived much benefit. Since appearing in *Darby O'Gill And The Little People* he had not gone back to Hollywood to work for Disney, Fox or anyone else, and had been cast in only two British films of no particular note or merit. The first was a Soho gangster movie, supposedly cashing in on interest in the British gangland scene dominated by such villains as Billy Hill and Jack Spot Comer who were the nearest the UK could get to the American Mob. But as a story of our times the scenes had already been played out in the columns of the Sunday newspapers and *The Frightened City* made little impact. Connery's role was fairly hefty, playing a tough crook employed by Alfred Marks to collect money from clubs and cafés in a protection scheme masterminded by a corrupt financier, Herbert Lom. It was filmed on an eight-week schedule from early December 1960 at Shepperton Studios while the streets of London's Soho, with its strip clubs, sleazy nightclubs, clip joints and jazz clubs, could not be bettered for the location work.

Much was made of the fact that a former Scotland Yard flying squad detective who had arrested a few villains in his time acted as consultant. It was thought that *The Frightened City* might do well, and the prestige location of the Odeon, Marble Arch, was selected for its opening in September 1961. Today it might be better viewed as a piece of social history, a record of crime at a particular moment. There were some decent performances, especially from Connery and Lom, but as a showcase for his talents *The Frightened City* did nothing for Connery, and certainly carried nowhere near the weight of the forthcoming television production of *Anna Karenina*.

His only other major film appearance during this unsatisfactory relationship with 20th Century Fox was another typically British movie entitled *On The Fiddle* with a line-up of familiar names for cameo roles, including Cecil Parker, Wilfrid Hyde White, Kathleen

Harrison, Eleanor Summerfield, Eric Barker and John Le Mesurier. The American comic Alan King was flown to England especially for one day's filming as the token Yank. There had to be an American angle in everything. This time Connery was a rogue who reluctantly joins the RAF, fills his time devising schemes of deception and, in the end, becomes a hero. It was predictably pleasant and uninspiring, and not the kind of material Connery wished for. This mediocrity must have made him wonder if he was destined to a life of occasional television performances.

His relationship with 20th Century Fox deteriorated further. Not surprisingly, Connery was angry and every telephone conversation with the studio people developed into a row. They came up with one small role at the end of 1961, a mere two pages of script in Darryl F Zanuck's otherwise massive, multi-million-dollar film *The Longest Day*, which also had the longest list of stars ever to appear in a Hollywood movie – John Wayne, Richard Burton, Richard Todd, Rod Steiger, Henry Fonda, Robert Mitchum et al. From a year's filming and 80 hours of film footage, Connery's part in this epic was minute – an amusing cameo shared with Norman Rossington and Kenneth More.

It was the one and only time he worked for Fox while under contract to them and thereafter they agreed to his ever-more pressing demands to be released so he could go his own way. By the time *The Longest Day* was shown in the cinemas Connery was a star and Fox must have been kicking themselves.

Much would rest on the screening of *Anna Karenina*, and while he was waiting for that event Connery was cast in a new West End play entitled *Judith* which opened at Her Majesty's Theatre, which brought him some localised notoriety for appearing on stage wearing only a small loincloth. This was a glimpse of things to come. The intended short run of *Judith* was cut even shorter because of poor houses, although one who attended was the director Terence Young who, years before, advised Connery after directing him in *Action Of The Tiger* to keep on swimming.

Various people have been given credit for Connery's selection for the role of James Bond. The topic had been debated in the newspapers for months, since the American producer Albert 'Cubby' Broccoli and his partner Harry Saltzman announced they were looking for a male lead for their series of films based on Ian Fleming's bestselling books. It may well have been an altogether non-orchestrated collective of people who were to come up with the name but none was as influential as Young, the director of the first Bond movie, *Dr No*. In that sparsely filled West End theatre, he sat watching Sean Connery in *Judith* and remembered his promise.

If further confirmation was needed that Connery was indeed a talent to be reckoned with, it would come with the viewing of *Anna Karenina* in which the skill of director Cartier had brought a completely different Connery to the screen than had been seen before. It was the result of much hard work and many, many retakes, more than he had ever done, so that his performance matched the superb portrayal by Claire Bloom in that difficult role of one of fiction's most average women. Critical acclaim was excellent and *The Times*, which had become an unintentional campaigner for Connery's seemingly unwanted abilities, adjudged *Anna Karenina* a most satisfying experience, worthy of praise on several fronts, especially 'Mr Sean Connery, a headstrong, passionate Vronsky'.

Terence Young had made up his mind. But there were several strong rivals and a backing studio in Hollywood and the co-producers themselves who might demand a better name. Not least of the difficulties concerning his approval for the role was Connery himself, who would not change his image or alter his style for anyone – and that included Ian Fleming's all-English, Eton-educated, Bentley-driving spy named James Bond.

5

BRINK OF
OBSCURITY

In an American television studio in 1954, actors prepared for the first film ever made of one of Ian Fleming's James Bond novels. It was to run for an hour and the setting was supposed to be the South of France, where the action begins for this adaptation of *Casino Royale*. But in the days of live black-and-white television, when nothing was pre-recorded, the facilities to exploit the drama and excitement of Fleming's stories were somewhat limited. The palm trees were cardboard cut-outs leaning against painted backdrops of the rue des Anglais, and the rest of the sets looked as if they had been borrowed from *Bilko*. Microphones hanging from moving arms occasionally got into shot; scene changes were limited and a mere week of rehearsals was frantic, especially as one of the stars, Linda Christian, was otherwise engaged – getting divorced from her husband Tyrone Power.

Naturally, Fleming's all-British hero has been Americanised for the duration. Now he's Jimmy Bond, complete with crewcut. He drinks Bourbon, not shaken or even stirred, and wouldn't know a Bentley if it knocked him down. Peter Lorre has him in a jam and with eyes rolling threatens to torture him to the edge of madness by pulling out his toenails with a pair of pliers.

'Tell him what he wants, Jimmy,' screams Linda Christian, also bound and prepared for torture …

But while Peter Lorre is preoccupied with his threatening behaviour, Jimmy Bond (alias actor Barry Nelson, fresh from 113 live episodes of *My Favourite Husband*) manages to extricate himself from his bondage, grabs his opponent's gun and shoots him, though not fatally.

'Kill him, Jimmy,' screams Miss Christian.

'No,' Jimmy replies. 'Send for the police.'

Cut.

The show is completed and Barry Nelson, 34, wonders if it might provide him with another long-running series that could rival *Lassie* or *Dragnet*, those other big television attractions of 1954. It did not. For the time being Jimmy Bond passed quietly into television history.

Seven years went by …

It is easy to be retrospectively astute and say Sean Connery knew that one day his ship would come in. Diane Cilento was as convinced as he was that it would and helped him prepare for the occasion. Restrospective thoughts and stories are usually devoid of doubt because they are tinged with the knowledge of reality and truth, and thus when he said he felt within him that the break would come we must believe him and accept that it was probably true. His time would have come whether or not he had been selected to play James Bond and there were plenty in his sphere who support that claim, though also with the benefit of hindsight. We could throw in some clichés about making his own luck or being in the right place at the right time, but there is little merit in discussing the alternatives of what might have happened to his career had Ian Fleming's Bond not thrust him on a fast track to stardom at the very time when it seemed he might disappear.

Stardom. It is the most overused and underdiscovered word in the actor's dictionary.

What does it mean? Is it great acting? Great popularity? Great wealth? The recognition of being very good, like Olivier or Gielgud or Brando or Tracy? Is it torment, as with Garland and Clift? Is it the door to habitual excess, like Burton and Taylor? Their patchwork of lives was laid bare for all to see, and for a thinking man there were obvious pitfalls to avoid – like the excesses and the throwing away of hard-earned wealth on unhealthy materialism and dubious business ventures. Quality control, either in work or life itself, was never going to be a guaranteed ingredient, as Connery would discover to his considerable anguish when the reality of stardom turned him into public property. But who would take account of that when reaching for the moon?

Stardom is what an actor strives to achieve. It has to be the first goal and the driving force, surely, is to play the leading role in a play or film, and then to be selected again and again until you are giving great performances and everyone in the world knows your name. Take away the dream and you destroy the initiative. Sean Connery had left it late and was very close to the point at which it would have been easy for him to have been passed over, cast by the wayside to content himself with second-string work and at best a decent career starring in television or theatre; at worst it would have dried up completely as it did for many actors around the mid-1960s.

Sean Connery was 31 years old when it happened and already drinking in the last-chance saloon. He had turned away earlier stardom and rejected major roles he did not think suited him. He had had a deep affair with the classics, had appeared in ten films and was still virtually unknown among the international film set. His moment arrived at a particular time in British movie history. A clutch of plays and films had already pointed the way – notably *Lucky Jim, Room At The Top, Look Back In Anger* and *Saturday Night And Sunday Morning*. Keith Waterhouse, then in writing partnership with Willis Hall, recalled, 'It suddenly struck home that people would listen to, and understand, regional accents.

Two young directors, Richard Attenborough and Bryan Forbes, came on the telephone and asked us to write something with a northern accent.'

Waterhouse, a northerner himself, naturally obliged. He found it amusing, as it certainly was for actors who had been brought up in the north of England and whose accent had been smoothed away by their dramatic training and elocution lessons. Harry Saltzman, a little-known Canadian film producer, had formed a company called Woodfall Films with John Osborne and director Tony Richardson. They produced *Look Back in Anger* in 1959 followed a year later by Laurence Olivier in *The Entertainer*, both written by Osborne and directed by Richardson. Woodfall finally struck a gold seam with *Saturday Night and Sunday Morning*, set in Nottingham and starring Albert Finney, Rachel Roberts and Shirely Anne Field, which the *Evening Standard* decided was 'at last the chance of our own new wave'.

Saltzman's interest in gloomy portraits of British life in the raw was waning, however, and he set his cap more positively at the lucrative international market. Looking to new horizons, he dreamed of an international blockbuster that would translate into every language in every country, and in 1959 began to pursue the rights to Ian Fleming's hugely successful James Bond novels which had done exactly that in the book stores. Even so, many hurdles and complexities were to be encountered and overcome and the events leading up to the Bond films are worth recalling briefly to show how close Connery came to *not* making a Bond movie at all.

In 1961 it was eight years since Ian Fleming's first James Bond novel had been published. He added to his list almost annually and the books had become bestsellers the world over, published in 11 languages. By the mid-1960s they had sold more than 50 million copies and inspired a rash of scholarly debates on campuses supposedly examining their sexual and social implications.

In a sense, Fleming had started a diversionary new wave of his own which was the exact opposite to the theories of the realism school and the intellectual theatre of Britain. Whereas Osborne and company trod the path of abject normality in colourless, dismal settings, Fleming took his readers on exotic, action-packed journeys of make-believe with thrills, spills, violence verging on sadism and a multiplicity of sexual encounters in far-off paradisal locations.

The James Bond character in the books, as opposed to the more sexy film version, was said to be modelled upon himself, and Fleming was the model of an upper-class Englishman – a snobbish sophisticate, Eton-educated who had done intelligence work during the war, unmarried until his 40s and, like many of his counterparts, he turned to the written word to set down stories inspired by his wartime activities. His attempts through the remainder of the 1950s to transfer his novels to the screen were dismally unsuccessful.

His first book, *Casino Royale*, was published in 1953 and the best offer he received for the screen rights was a deal with CBS for the one-hour 'Jimmy Bond' screenplay. 'It was an absolute disaster,' Barry Nelson remembered in 1992. 'The show was done in haste with cardboard sets, the exotic nature of the story and the whole point about the character of James Bond just vanished in the screenplay and was never heard of again. It was so bad that it killed off any thoughts CBS might have had of turning the Fleming books into a series.'

In those days tapes were not always made or, if they were, seldom kept long. But the hour-long special survived. Someone in Chicago, a devotee of Fleming's first novel, filmed the show off television. A print surfaced at the height of Bondmania in the mid-1960s and was made into a video – proof of who was the first man to play James Bond, the one before Sean Connery.

Others toyed with the prospect of making a film and then discarded the idea. The settings and locations required Hollywood-style backing. Britain's Alexander Korda showed some interest in Fleming's second novel *Live And Let Die* but decided not to make an offer. Rank bought a six-month option on *Moonraker* in

1956 but did not proceed, and CBS came back and talked vaguely about producing a Bond series for American television.

Fortunately for Fleming nothing came of any of these early fishing expeditions. Had the rights of his books been sold to television, or piecemeal to film producers at that time for what was in effect a pittance, the James Bond movie series that would span the next four decades and earn billions of dollars would have been dead in the water.

Fleming persisted and, having failed at bringing James Bond to the screen, wrote a thinly veiled pilot screenplay for a new television series entitled *Commander Jamaica*. After many meetings and much discussion that, too, failed to get off the ground. Fleming refused to waste his effort and turned the plot into another Bond novel, which he called *Dr No*.

In 1958 Ivar Bryce, a close friend of Fleming's from childhood, introduced him to the Irish director Kevin McClory who had just completed his first movie, *The Boy And The Bridge*. McClory came highly recommended and impressed Fleming sufficiently for him to agree to collaborate on the production of a Bond movie, a decision he would come to regret greatly. It was agreed that Bryce would produce, McClory would direct, Fleming would write the screenplay and the movie would be launched in the wake of the anticipated success of *The Boy And The Bridge*. The latter part of the equation collapsed; the McClory film was mauled by the critics and Fleming's agent, Laurence Evans of MCA, advised that he should disentangle himself from McClory and find a more experienced director.

Before that could happen, the three of them had formulated a plot and outlined the script. McClory later engaged screenwriter Jack Whittingham to give a final polish to Fleming's screenplay, provisionally titled *Longitude 78 West*, which eventually formed the plot for the next Fleming novel, *Thunderball*. The McClory film project was scrapped but the novel was published. McClory sued, claiming part ownership of the copyright. Lawyers had a field day. Fleming suffered a heart attack and lost his case.

Thunderball was conceded as having been based upon the film script, and thus McClory was entitled to part ownership of the screen rights to the story and the characters contained in the book, a ruling vital in allowing Sean Connery to return as James Bond in 1983 – ten years after he had said he would never make another Bond movie – in the aptly titled *Never Say Never Again*.

Meanwhile, Fleming was weak from his heart problems, exacerbated by his heavy drinking. He was anxious to make a deal on the sale of the screen rights to his books and provide a trust fund for his wife and son. It had been delayed for more than two years by the legal tussle with McClory. The court case attracted a great deal of publicity, aided by the revelation in the spring of 1961 that *Thunderball* was among President John F Kennedy's top ten favourite books.

Producer Harry Saltzman, now desperately seeking excitement and escape from the squalor of those so-called kitchen-sink dramas set in the north, paid $50,000 for a six-month option on all the Bond books, with the exception of *Casino Royale* which was sold earlier for a paltry $6,000 and then sold on again elsewhere.* At the same time another independent producer, the American Albert 'Cubby' Broccoli, a former Hollywood agent who once looked after Lana Turner and was co-founder of Warwick Films, was also looking for excitement. He, too, was interested in the Bond books, but discovered Saltzman had an option.

One afternoon Saltzman received a telephone call from a third party, a mutual acquaintance of himself and Broccoli, asking if he would be interested in a business partnership. He was, and out of their meeting came the formation of Eon Pictures and the most successful sequence of films in cinema history.

Broccoli and Saltzman had to find backing since both employed the cardinal rule never to use their own money. This meant they would have to interest a major studio. In the meantime,

---

* The rights were acquired by Charles K Feldman with Jerry Bresley and, funded by Columbia Pictures, they produced *Casino Royale* in 1967 as a spoof Bond film starring David Niven as Sir James Bond.

preliminary hype was instigated by some inspired press management concerning the search for the actor who would be Bond. Many names were put in the frame, some not even being considered, but it gave the British newspapers a running story and lots of famous faces to speculate upon, like Cary Grant, James Stewart, James Mason, Peter Finch and Richard Burton.

Ian Fleming was said to have favoured his good friend and wartime compatriot David Niven while other redoubtable stalwarts of the English acting fraternity, including Michael Redgrave, Trevor Howard and Rex Harrison, were all mentioned. It seems now barely credible that such names were even being considered but the inability to place them in such a scenario is largely because of the manner in which Connery eventually played Bond. And perhaps this was the point: no actor around other than Connery or, perhaps, Patrick McGoohan would have played it with an almost satirical perspective compared with the more archetypal portrayal that could have been expected from most of the British candidates.

Whether or not Saltzman and Broccoli would ever have cast any of these names remains unanswered. Broccoli has since said they were window dressing, because he was convinced from the outset that a relatively unknown actor should be cast in the role. The character was famous enough and to have him played by an equally famous actor might cause a conflict which could actually damage the success of the pictures. Broccoli said, again retrospectively, that he wanted Bond to emerge as a totally new screen personality and that meant that the actor playing him should also 'emerge' at the same time, so the actor *was* Bond and, possibly, vice versa.

This crucial element became one of the most aggravating aspects of the whole Bond series for Connery, and the one that caused him most grief when the media called him Mr Bond and not Mr Connery.

There was another consideration. Stars of any calibre did not come cheaply, and Saltzman and Broccoli were not exactly throwing fistfuls of dollars into the air. Furthermore, there would be obvious difficulties in getting a major star to commit himself to a long-term contract on such an unproven project which at that point still had no firm backers.

Columbia Pictures had said they might be interested if they could sign Cary Grant for three pictures. Grant read the script and said he would only commit himself to a one-picture deal. James Mason said he would make two but no more, and he, too, was ruled out (not least because of the money he wanted). Saltzman and Broccoli were certain in their own minds that the Bond films would run and run and they wanted to be sure of picking the right man, for the right price, who would go under contract for a series of five or six pictures, maybe more. All this scared Columbia who backed out anyway, even before negotiations for a star had become serious. Their refusal must rank only second to Decca Records turning down The Beatles.

As the two producers began to revise their budget plans downwards, more realistic possibilities came into the frame, names such as Roger Moore, Richard Johnson and Patrick McGoohan. All were being mentioned in the newspapers. The *Daily Express* even ran a poll for readers to vote on who should play James Bond, but the result was as inconclusive as the producers' own deliberations and anyway, as yet, it was all academic. Slowly Saltzman and Broccoli waded through their list of contacts. They had more or less ruled out finding an American backer when Bud Ornstein, who ran the London office of United Artists, was caught by the mood of the moment and agreed to finance the first Bond picture. It was confirmed in Los Angeles 24 hours later with the very definite instruction that the budget should not exceed a million dollars, which itself placed restrictions upon the money available for the actors and hardly showed much confidence in the project as a whole.

This was the year when Elizabeth Taylor had asked for and got the first ever million-dollar fee for any actor anywhere on earth by agreeing to star in *Cleopatra*; Warren Beatty, virtually unknown before *Splendour In The Grass* in 1961, was asking a $300,000 straight fee for his next; and United Artists had just signed Natalie Wood for $250,000 plus a percentage, along with a host of other names, for a multi-million-dollar production of *West Side Story*. The overrun costs on any of these productions was higher than the total amount allotted to that little British picture, *Dr No*.

The Bond film to be made in London was clearly not high on the list of priorities, and for the producers it was a rather forlorn hope to expect the signature of a star player – if, indeed, one was wanted. There were other problems to be overcome, too.

Terence Young was a busy director and was about to start work on a film for Paramount starring Ava Gardner when he found himself suddenly unemployed. The project was cancelled after a trivial row between Paramount and Gardner over her refusal to give up one of the two limousines she wanted at her personal disposal for the duration. It was a typical example of how old Hollywood was clinging to the past as the new independent producers were pushing their own projects along on a shoestring.

Young returned to his hotel to start packing his bags and discovered a message urging him to call Cubby Broccoli as soon as possible. Young made contact and Broccoli asked if he would direct the Bond movies. Apparently the choice of director was almost as difficult as finding a star and Young, who had something of a following in continental Europe, was third or fourth choice. Bryan Forbes had already said no, Guy Hamilton, who directed a later Bond film, had accepted and then pulled out for reasons unknown, and when Broccoli heard Young was free he cabled him. Young agreed, on condition he could choose the movies he would direct – *Thunderball*, *From Russia With Love* and *Dr No*.

Young very quickly nominated his own candidate, Sean Connery, the young actor he had directed in *Action of the Tiger* and who he had recently seen on the West End stage in *Judith*. 'He was so good, he acted the play itself off the stage,' Young reported. 'He has a good voice and, more importantly, splendid presence, and a quality that I have seen in only one man previously, Clark Gable.'

There was a good deal of chin scratching. Connery's accent put them off. There were also four other serious contenders, with Moore and McGoohan the front-runners. That left Young pretty much on his own as a backer for Connery, although he had also been suggested by Patricia Lewis, a columnist on the *Daily Express* which had been serialising some of the Bond books. Young said he believed Connery had never been fully extended in any film role he had undertaken and few people had witnessed his memorable stage performances, especially in the classics. Terence Young's point was that Connery had been busily learning to become an actor and not a film star, but he had all the attributes demanded by the Bond character: toughness, a good physique and sex appeal.

A private screening of *On The Fiddle* was arranged for Harry Saltzman in London while almost simultaneously Broccoli viewed Connery in *Darby O'Gill And The Little People*. Saltzman moved Connery to the head of his short list while Broccoli was undecided between the Scot and McGoohan. The latter eventually ruled himself out by stating he didn't like Fleming's fictional character and was especially concerned about the moral aspects associated with the overtones of sadistic sex.

Screen testing of a dozen or more possibles was going on, more or less as a formality. In the meantime Young arranged for Connery to meet Saltzman and Broccoli, along with the United Artists' people, at their office in South Audley Street. Young telephoned Connery and suggested that since this was the most coveted film role on offer in England for years, he might consider helping the situation along by resolving to give a good account of himself, not be excessively demanding and, overall, create a good impression. Perhaps he might also consider wearing a suit for the occasion. At that time everyone wore suits, even Bill Haley and fledgling stars of the emerging swinging sixties. Connery mumbled a reply which did not, in Young's view, augur well. In fact, he turned up in clothes which were the exact opposite of those suggested – a casual, tieless shirt, slacks and one of those

1950s lumber jackets. It was as if, said Young, he had decided that wearing a suit would be a sign of his subservience and conformity to the rules, as if he deliberately wanted to antagonise the two men who had it within their power to make him rich and famous.

Broccoli wasn't antagonised, but he remembered the odd clothes, the baggy, unpressed trousers with a brown shirt without a tie and suede shoes. Connery's impression of the two producers was one that remained with him for years. Cubby was a large and generous man; Harry was small, curt and explosive. There was an apocryphal story later that Cubby would give you a cigar and Harry would come along and take it out of your mouth.

As discussions progressed Connery made a bit of a fuss. He thumped and pounded the desk, according to Broccoli, and told them what he wanted and how he saw the character of James Bond being created on screen. This impressed the two producers for, as one of them said, 'It shows he's got balls.'

Saltzman mentioned that they were testing a number of people for the role. Connery refused to participate in what he described as a meat market on the grounds that it would be impossible for him to convey in a few minutes how he would interpret the part and the way in which he would inject what he believed to be subtle but essential comedy. He said they could hire him if they wished – or not, as the case may be. If they did, it would be a question of taking him as he was and not as he might become. He also demanded a non-exclusive contract which permitted him to do other work, outside the Bond movies. The producers did not like that one, but eventually agreed to a one-for-one situation.

Connery left the office, and as he departed the film men rushed to the window to watch him striding across the road below their window. Broccoli observed that it was true, he moved exceptionally well, like a panther, and later used another analogy, stating that the difference between Connery and several other young actors they had seen was like comparing a still photograph with film.

Saltzman thought the man came alive when he moved and

possessed an impressive litheness for one so tall. 'He bounced across the street like he was Superman,' said Broccoli.

Broccoli, however, remained worried about Connery's accent and, worse, he looked more like a bricklayer – matching Jill Craigie's first impression – than the upper-class, champagne-sipping extrovert he was being hired to portray. His general demeanour did not fit the part they were selling. They were concerned, too, about whether he would be able to handle the dialogue. 'Don't worry,' Young reassured the two producers. 'I will deal with that when the time comes.' In fact, it was being taken care of; Diane Cilento was already coaching him for the role.

They screen tested almost 20 actors; they walked potential Bonds up and down in restaurants but Connery gradually climbed to the top of the list. Ian Fleming was not consulted about the choice of actor who would bring his hero to life, but his reaction to Connery was said to be fairly lukewarm. Kingsley Amis, a friend of Fleming's and a fan of the Bond books, said in his *James Bond Dossier* that Connery might well be entirely convincing as a Glaswegian businessman but not as Fleming's public-school adventurer. He later admitted in a television interview that Connery was probably the best Bond anyone could have wished for.

Once the news broke, though, there was a good degree of consternation, verging on unbridled anger and astonishment among establishment fans of Bond books. They could not understand why a Scottish-accented, virtually unknown actor more used to pints than Dom Perignon '57, which he had probably never tasted, had been selected and, more to the point, how on earth would he play the role? In a kilt?

Sheilah Graham, the Hollywood columnist, came to London to investigate and wrote immediately that he was desperately wrong for the role. She said that Ian Fleming thought so too, but wouldn't say it in public. Like Amis, Graham subsequently had the good grace to admit she was entirely wrong, and that a few slips in the social airs and graces department were less important than the hugeness of the sex appeal which Connery displayed.

Graham was one of many pundits who dismissed Connery as a has-been before he had even moved into first gear. Hindsight brought a multitude of accolades: that it was an inspired piece of casting, a courageous decision by the producers and an equally courageous one by Connery himself. According to Cilento, in a 1964 magazine interview, she encouraged Connery at a time when he was thinking of declining the Bond offer. He had already turned down involvement in two Hollywood-produced TV series, and was dubious about taking on this type of role.

Connery had agreed to a fee for the first film, *Dr No*, of £6,000 plus expenses for location filming, a small fortune at a time when you could buy a nice house for £2,000. In the grander scale of film-making, however, it was nothing to write home about. Fleming, thrilled though he was that his books were at last to come to life in the cinema, still had reservations about Connery. So did United Artists, only they made their doubts known in no uncertain terms. Connery was tricked into a film test on the excuse that they wanted him to appear with an actress who was being tested for a leading role. UA executives back in Los Angeles, who had been apprehensive about him all along, saw the test and suggested that perhaps Saltzman and Broccoli could do better. Luckily they were ignored.

Fleming was also now aware that his first major production had been entrusted to a director whose work had been patchy and who was himself coaching a virtually unknown ex-coffin polisher. 'They've decided on you to fuck up my work,' Fleming off-handedly said to Young on their first meeting. Young replied tetchily that he did not think anything Fleming had written was immortal, whereas the last picture he made won a Grand Prix at Venice. They shook hands and agreed to start from an even base; once filming began, Fleming came and watched, and was impressed.

Terence Young was a driving force in the shaping of the first Bond film, creating the blueprint for the future, and that included the shaping of Connery – though he conceded that Connery brought the humour along himself. It was he, after all, who had wanted Connery in the role and there were those on the set who were of the belief that Young was going to have a Bond more in his own mould than in Ian Fleming's, in which case he needed the rough-diamond quality of Connery – the description, it will be recalled, which he originated – as a counterweight to the upper-class snobbishness of Fleming. If Fleming's Bond was the one on the pages of his books, Young's Bond was the one that would bound out of the celluloid.

Young was described as 'a bit iffy' as a director, but an absolute gent who could turn nasty on occasions; he certainly had the ability to be tough when required. He was born in Hong Kong in 1915, the son of a police commissioner, educated at Harrow, then in Switzerland and Cambridge where he gained blues in boxing and rugby. He served as a Guards officer during the war and worked occasionally on War Ministry films.

One who was close to the production of the first four Bond films said he was certain that Young was intent on reflecting his own image and he did not like Richard Maibaum's scripts. 'First of all, there were three or four scripts already in existence when he came on the scene. He virtually ripped them apart. One thing the previous writers had done was to stray too far from Ian Fleming's own words in the book and both Terence and Cubby felt that was ridiculous. Having put Ian's words back as the main thrust of the script, Terence, who was a brilliant script technician, then managed to re-create Bond in his own image, as played by Connery. It was a marvellous piece of writing that managed to achieve all that was required, not merely satisfying his own, and eventually Connery's, whims but dealing expertly with Cubby's desire for plenty of sexual innuendo, double entendre and an abundance of exceedingly classy tit and bum. He injected lots of one-liners, too, that were never present in the book.'

Young dined in fine restaurants, stayed at the Dorchester, ordered good wines and knew their vintage and pedigree. His suits were carved from the finest Savile Row cloth and his shirts and shoes were handmade. James Bond was to be a mixture of Ian Fleming's upper-class ideals, Terence Young's love of the good life and Sean Connery's tough, mean streak and abounding sexuality. All of this was somewhat overwhelming for Fleming himself who apparently found it difficult to accept these interpretations of the character, although when he saw the image on screen he thought it well done. Later still the author said that if he had to write the Bond books over again he would do so with Connery in mind. At the time, though, before seeing the final film, there was always going to be a problem about interpretation. Young believed Fleming sought some kind of fulfilment from James Bond, creating a character he would have liked to be, so he took Connery to his own tailor for the fine suits, to his shirt-maker for the kind of shirts Bond would have had and then to his shoemaker for handmade leather shoes. Connery also needed some more hair. He was already going thin on top and so a toupee was necessary from the word go. He was ambivalent about such an addition and unlike many of his contemporaries who continued to wear wigs into old age he disposed of it as soon as possible and allowed his natural baldness, when it eventually arrived, to shine through.

In the meantime, he was thinking himself into the role. He had carefully analysed it, taken Young's advice on board and decided he was going to play it with his tongue firmly in his cheek, with a kind of sarcastic humour, pushing the words out of the side of his mouth with an insolence that suggested he was engaged on a giant send-up of everything English. 'It was a massive piss-take by Connery,' one insider observed. 'If you look at the film now with that thought in mind, you can see it. The books themselves were written without that kind of humour; where there is humour in Fleming's work it is black comedy. The jokey kind of insolence that Connery introduced could only be achieved by someone standing outside of it all and looking in which is what he did and it was a hundred per cent successful. That was Connery's doing.'

It was a curious place to find Stanislavksi, in a James Bond film. What Connery had taught himself was the ability to analyse the script, dissect the character and quite clinically add a new dimension from his own thoughts and so draw the character inside himself. His long, studious preparation for a role and, as he became more powerful, his adjustment of scripts to suit himself, became a crucial part of his work.

What came out, when he played the role of James Bond, was a character of *his* making, not Fleming's, or Terence Young's. Young's contribution, however, cannot be understated and Connery was generous enough to admit that he learned much from his director – perhaps more than he realised. Those close to both in the early days discovered in Connery's Bond a sophistication mimicked from Young and, although some of his nuances and acting tricks were inspired by Young and to a lesser degree by Fleming, at the end of the day it was Connery who pulled all the things he had learned together. He was the creator of the Bond who became so much larger and athletic on screen than was ever possible to portray in the written word. In the end, it was his adjudication of the role, regardless of the advice he was receiving from everyone else connected with the picture. What he did was invent a piece of celluloid history, and he did it in a way that could never be copied by any of those who followed.

Connery was the core of the film around which Terence Young built this first excursion into escapism, egged on by the demands of Cubby Broccoli for an array of pouting women in scant attire. Fast cars. Exotic locations. Women. Baddies. Action. More women. Plus some attitudes that were Connery's own. These images coincidentally exploited all the things that Connery, dressed in his Savile Row suits and silk shirts, was able to achieve. Broccoli, Saltzman and Young made Connery a star but conversely, Connery himself claims a very great deal of the credit for making the producers into multi-millionaires. Even before the picture had finished shooting a row was brewing about who was exploiting whom.

Of course, the outcome and success were unknown at the time that final preparations were being made to begin filming. Fleming told his friend Noel Coward that he was very happy, and when the production unit went out to Jamaica for location work in January 1962 Connery had the opportunity of meeting Coward, who had a house there not far from Fleming's.

At the time, very few people on the set of *Dr No* believed they were involved in anything particularly special. Connery and those members of the crew who were needed on location had travelled to Jamaica tourist class, and there was nothing to suggest it would be anything other than a run-of-the-mill thriller. His co-star, Ursula Andress, who joined the unit towards the end of January, certainly did not think so either, even when she had completed the film. She flew into Kingston at the end of January with her husband John Derek and met Connery, she recalled, under a mango tree. 'We became good friends and he is still my friend,' she said. 'He is one of the very few people I know whom success has not changed.'

Connery eyed her pensively when he first saw her in her bikini for rehearsals of the scene in which she appears on the beach collecting shells. He thought she had rather strong shoulders and thighs, almost like those of a female body-builder, although she was not especially muscular. She looked entirely feminine and she and Connery made an excellent pair in every respect. The moment when Andress, as Honey, emerges from the sea in her white bikini wearing a hip knife is one of those classic scenes for which Bond movies became renowned and memorable. There was Connery's Bond, exhibiting blatant lust with a false nonchalance covering his smirking lechery, as if the girl had just walked naked across the dance hall of the Palais at Fountainbridge.

It would not be remembered for the quality of acting, but who was looking at the finer points? Chris Blackwell, future head of Island Records and a young friend of Fleming's at the time who worked on *Dr No* as a location scout, said, 'That scene was absolutely stunning, and when it was done everybody behind the cameras applauded.'

What was happening here was new to British cinema. The staid heroes of the past had had their day and were going to be very quickly killed off. The hero of the Fleming books was not, by and large, a particularly pleasant man and was especially noted for his sadistic sexual tendencies.

Connery toned down the sadism and played it for laughs. He gave Bond more style, panache and a good-humoured heroism that appealed to an entire audience. He was thoroughly male chauvinist, grabbing girls at every – but every – opportunity; he littered the countryside with corpses without so much as a twitch of remorse. But Connery's James Bond was a parody of what was intended in Fleming's two-dimensional character, with Connery adding the extra dimension himself. The moment, for example, when he watches the evil Professor Dent empty his gun into Bond's bed pillow, thinking he has killed him, was masterly handling of a potentially offensive scene. He confronts Dent with an almost apologetic superiority and says, 'That's a Smith and Wesson and you've had your six,' and thereupon fires two smart bullets into Dent's heart.

He gives a half smile. Connery was telling his audience that they did not have to believe what he was doing; all they had to do was sit back and enjoy the fantasy and the illusion. He had discovered a way to involve his audience so they were virtually cheering him, just as kids did the good guys at Saturday morning pictures.

Young had to keep a close eye on Connery for fear that any social errors slipped through, and one or two did. There were complaints about the way he buttoned his jacket, for example, and it amazed him that people would carp at him for that. There were more pressing problems for Young, however. Andress's accent was so strong and patchy that she had to be dubbed.

When a final print was ready, United Artists sent executives from New York to view their investment in a private cinema in London to decide what publicity campaign should be mounted. Upon their judgement rested the exposure the film would be given in America, a crucial market as far as Saltzman and Broccoli were concerned. If distribution was limited returns from

Dr No would be so small as to threaten the whole future of the Bond series.

Initial reaction was not good. Connery had provided an unexpected humour verging on derision for the whole picture, and the Americans did not see the joke.

They trooped out of the viewing room muttering words of criticism and consolation. The film would not do well in America. In fact, they would be surprised if it did much business anywhere. Lucky for them that they had only put up a million dollars; losses would be minimal. Furthermore they recommended that United Artists should spend nothing on promoting the film in America: let it open quietly somewhere at the back of beyond, put it into the drive-in movies and small-town theatres, a route normally reserved for the many speciality low-budget movies, and allow it to pass peacefully into history.

Broccoli and Saltzman would not accept the film was a dud. Nor did Connery. The summer months, while he waited for the premiere in October, seemed incredibly slow in passing. The producers launched a promotional campaign and Connery made himself available for interviews, though there were few takers. The first stirrings of success began at the London premiere, at the Pavilion on 6 October 1962. *Dr No* was received with encouraging notices. There were exceptions such as Ian Cameron in the *Spectator*, who described Connery as a superannuated Rank starlet trying to act sexy and criticised his sartorial sloppiness. Later Connery could ram the words down his throat, but the bad reviews were sufficiently outnumbered to boost the movie's chances and there were even glowing tributes normally reserved for major multi-million-dollar films from tinsel town. Though small in circulation, the influential *Films And Filming* said, 'Dr No is the headiest box office concoction of sex and sadism ever brewed by a British studio. This is one of the X-iest films imaginable ... a monstrously overblown sex fantasy. There hasn't been a film like *Dr No* since ... when? There's never been a British film like *Dr No* since ... what?'

The film offered a newness in techniques cheaply achieved (less than £14,000 was spent on sets at Pinewood's Stage D), sexuality and exciting fantasy. Audiences began to flock to *Dr No* in surprising numbers and soon it was doing as well, ironically, as Darryl F Zanuck's hugely expensive, star-studded *The Longest Day*, in which Connery had a small part and opened in London at around the same time. The box office receipts for *Dr No* clocked up over a million pounds within four months, and by the time it was due to open in America United Artists were forced to revise their plans for a quiet disposal job.

The film was given a New York premiere after all, and such eminent critics as Bosley Crowther of the *New York Times* found themselves in the somewhat embarrassing position of having to sit through a jumped-up little film from England full of sex and violence; not the thing at all. However, at the end of the show, Crowther deemed it worthwhile reviewing the picture and said snobbishly pleasant things about it. *Time* magazine, not known for its coverage of trivia or the inconsequential, decided that the arrival of James Bond on film was of sufficient merit to warrant a leading article: 'Agent Bond ... sure does titillate popular taste and at last this scarlet pimpernel can be seen on screen. As portrayed by Scotland's Sean Connery, he moves with tensile grace that excitingly suggests the violence bottled in Bond ...'

Dr No provided the foundation stone for an enormously successful run, which would make Broccoli and Saltzman exceedingly rich. This first film earned $6 million in box-office receipts in America alone, which was then an outstanding sum for a British film. Sean Connery was 32 years old, had more money than he had ever seen before and stardom had grudgingly settled on his doorstep. Whether he would actually want it remained to be seen.

6

ONWARDS AND
UPWARDS

D^r *No* changed Connery's life, but then everything was changing in 1962. It was the year before the swinging sixties was officially christened as such yet attitudes were still being challenged. Pointers to the stances which were to follow in a tumultuous decade were everywhere. *Life* magazine would soon declare London as the city of the decade. President Kennedy was shoring up the government of South Vietnam. Nelson Mandela was arrested and sentenced to five years' imprisonment. Andy Warhol exhibited his painting of a can of Campbell's soup. David Frost caused uproar with his satirical BBC television show *That was The Week That Was*. Spies abounded in the Cold War, the Berlin Wall provided scenes of terrible killings and the world came to the brink of nuclear war with the Cuban missile crisis from which Khrushchev fortunately backed away.

Out of these events the Age of Aquarius, and an era of uncertainty, was born. The realities of the world were stark. Escapism became not just a matter of imagination, reading books, watching movies or listening to the vibrant new music. It soon became an actuality by dropping out, hitting the road, dodging the draft and experimenting with all manner of drugs from marijuana to magic mushrooms. Young people were searching for new icons to replace the ageing demigods of the last generation, a search which would benefit Connery's status beyond imaginable proportions. It was the beginning of a revolution across the board, from the way people spoke to the way they dressed, travelled and had sex. Everything was changing.

Connery's contribution, and the benefits he derived, were significant. Whereas on the one hand John Osborne and others were creating new themes and the likes of Albert Finney were acting them out, Connery was blowing out at the other end of the scale of popular escapism, and he wasn't sure if he liked what he was creating.

In spite of some college people anxious to make more out of it than really existed, Connery could not believe that Bond was an important aspect of the developing sociological trends. It was just different, spectacular and sexy. Success with *Dr No* was to be built upon in *From Russia With Love*, which was cynically stacked with sex, voyeurism and violence. The film series, specifically with Connery's insolent humour which caught the aspiring mood of young people, was merely part of the jigsaw, an element of the eruption of total change.

It became a model and focus from which other actors and film-makers subsequently benefited. A whole new genre of tongue-in-cheek spy thrillers produced opportunities for actors such as Michael Caine, David McCallum and Patrick McGoohan in Britain, but realistically that was the extent of the influence of Bond films on art and society. It was Connery himself – not the character – who attracted an iconoclastic following, unrivalled anywhere in the acting profession at the time and virtually unmatched until Dennis Hopper, Peter Fonda and Jack Nicholson moved it on further when they rode up on their bikes in *Easy Rider* in 1969.

Life-changing developments were occurring in the Connery

household as well as on the professional front. His association with Diane Cilento was known only to friends. It had been an exciting relationship, with fiery scenes and periods of separation, and remained volatile and unpredictable. On Connery's part, there were occasional dalliances alleged by gossips – after he had become famous, of course, because no one was especially interested in his love life before that.

In the preliminary publicity to the Bond films, Connery had even given a press interview in which he extolled the virtues of bachelorhood and having no one permanently around to run his life. 'Let no man say that a red-blooded Scot turns away from a beautiful woman's shape – beyond that I am being discreet,' he said. In other words, his private life was private, a fact which inquiring reporters would discover with a resounding certainty in the months and years ahead. 'What no one knew in the early summer of 1962 was that Diane had been expecting his child since April,' said a close friend of both. 'Her marriage to Andre Volpe existed in name only and had in effect collapsed in 1960. Sean and Diane became very close and between their fleeting periods of volatility they were together as often as their work schedules permitted. There was no such thing as a quickie divorce and the due process of law took two years or more before Diane was free, although even then the prospect of remarriage never seemed to us a certainty. She was a model of the forthcoming 1960s woman, independent minded, and would not have been at all scared by the thought of being on her own with two children. In fact, I think the prospect even appealed to her, and she had said often enough to those of us who were prepared to take her seriously that she did not want to marry again.'

Sean and Diane had been to Fountainbridge that summer, presumably to impart the secret news. On her very first visit Diane walked in, put herself inside Connery's childhood territory and the tenement where he was born and drew in the atmosphere. Brother Neil recalled that Diane flopped down into an armchair and kicked off her shoes as if she had lived in the place all her life.

The first night she was there, she sat up talking to Effie and Joe until two in the morning.

With Cilento's pregnancy confirmed, Connery began to think of marriage, an inbuilt instinct, one might imagine, from the working-class morality of Fountainbridge. His security was greater than it had ever been, and though the Bond launch was yet to happen he was convinced it would be a success. He proposed several times but Diane did not give him a definite answer. She was still talking in terms of a relationship in which they could lead their separate lives in a sort of togetherness.

Cilento had not quite worked out the details and he remained equally certain that they should marry which, he reminded her, was the normal course for two people in love. He had already moved towards securing the trappings of a successful family man by acquiring a large house. With typical Connery disregard for conformity, he had purchased a rambling Victorian property in London's not-very-fashionable locale of Acton, at the time being used as a convent by 25 nuns of the Order of the Adoratrices. It was a four-storey building set in large gardens in a cul-de-sac off Acton High Street; he paid £9,000 for the property and said he intended to spend several thousand pounds renovating the stark interior.

The remodelling work included turning the nuns' 37-foot-long chapel into an L-shaped sitting room, which was the focal point of the new house. The work proceeded that autumn to the point where there was an illuminated sign over the front door spelling the ultimate legend of suburbia, Acacia House, and Connery was nearing the realisation of two major events: the launching of James Bond followed immediately by marriage. Diane set some pre-conditions and talked about them both retaining a fair amount of freedom. She would naturally resume her own career as soon as the baby was born. She said she objected to 'ownership' in marriage, especially when it referred to people, nor did she place importance on promises because she knew too many friends who found them impossible to keep.

The wedding, which they hoped would take place before their child was born, depended upon her divorce from Volpe being finalised. Her decree absolute was received in October on the grounds of his desertion, the judge having exercised discretion about her admitted adultery. In the meantime, Connery had become famous and had a press pack in tow, a new experience altogether. James Bond and Sean Connery had rapidly become, in the eyes of the press, one and the same and a London wedding would have been a circus with the new star under microscopic examination. For the producers of the Bond movies, however, the personal developments in Connery's life could not have been better timed.

But Connery wasn't playing. He avoided the press and a London wedding. The focus would have been turned towards Cilento, in any event, once the news leaked out. In 1962 pre-marriage pregnancies among the rich and famous, and especially film stars, were still portrayed in terms of a scandal. Sex meant scandal, as Elizabeth Taylor and Richard Burton had discovered to an outrageous degree that very year, and cabinet minister John Profumo and Christine Keeler would the following one. Connery was for the time being not in the same league, of course, but a newly famous British icon with a heavily pregnant actress whose baby was conceived while she was married to someone else had all the makings of a good run in the British press. Connery was already being headlined for far lesser incidents: four lads under ten managed to get into Acacia House and stole a few things; thus, BOYS ROB JAMES BOND.

They decided upon a 'secret' wedding in Gibraltar. Cilento was staying with friends in Europe away from prying cameras, and she and Connery arranged to meet at the local register office on 29 November 1962, where a rapid completion of the formalities allowed them time to escape the anticipated battery of flashbulbs. Connery managed what he set out to achieve and caught the reporters on the hop.

Co-operation at some level with the publicity requirements of

Harry Saltzman and Cubby Broccoli was contractually necessary, and also important in that the second Bond film, *From Russia With Love*, was soon to go into production. United Artists, still tentative that *Dr No* might have been a one-off miracle, and with its success in America still to be achieved, had cautiously doubled the budget and allotted $2 million to the next film – though this was no big deal when compared with the budgets of films being produced in Hollywood at the time. Connery's share increased dramatically, but only after heated exchanges with Saltzman.

During the ten weeks of work on *Dr No*, Connery had been promised £100 a week expenses while working abroad and a lesser amount to cover disbursements in London. According to Sheilah Graham, 'Harry tried to knock the expenses out of Connery's total pay … and of course Connery naturally objected, as well he might. For Sean everything is black or white, and there are no grey areas. He expected others to be the same and that row was just the start of what developed into a feud.'

Connery was sure in his own mind – and said so publicly a year or so afterwards – that Broccoli or Saltzman would have played Bond themselves if they could have, to save the expense of paying him. It would develop into a slanging match and tempers flared easily and often. There was a certain pride attached to his professionalism, but equally he wanted what he believed was a better share of the pot. Quarrels were overcome, albeit temporarily, and the show went on, with preliminary work on *From Russia With Love* scheduled to begin in February 1963.

Meantime, it became necessary for Connery to indulge the publicists as the hype for *Dr No* merged with the pre-publicity for the new film. Just such an opportunity delivered itself in the casino at St Vincents in northern Italy on the evening of 9 January 1963 when Connery was at the roulette table. According to the story in the next day's newspapers, he had won £10,000 playing a system apparently devised by Ian Fleming for James Bond, and at the time he just happened to be surrounded by three starlets hoping to be selected for roles in the new picture. The consolation if they weren't was that they were getting a free trip to Italy and had their pictures taken with Sean Connery.

If the publicity was to be believed, the casino apparently paid out the ten grand without the slightest concern that such a system had been used, and Fleming was contacted for a comment. He had used the system himself, he said, but had never managed to achieve that kind of success. Did Connery win the money or did he hand it back to the owners in the car park? We shall never know.

The Bond roadshow moved on to Rome where the starlets were supposedly going to do a screen test with him, and more publicity resulted from another scam: they were all kidnapped by students and held for three hours. And then a touch of real-life drama was introduced when Diane, also in Rome awaiting the delivery of their child, duly gave birth to a boy they called Jason on 12 January. It is never hard to be cynical when discussing the antics of film publicists, and Jason's arrival ultimately became part of the press package.

Like Beatlemania, Bond fever developed a momentum of its own. It was on a roll and nothing would stop it, and for the true devotees who emerged after two or three Bond films and went to see them often, analysing every aspect, *From Russia With Love* would figure as a classic. The plot was stronger than *Dr No*, and it also stands out as the most menacingly violent of the Bond films, the one in which the humour was blackest. This time there was nothing casual or accidental about the construction of the movie, which was altogether different from *Dr No*.

Having seen the public reaction to *Dr No*, the producers were able to draw up in order of importance a list of ingredients which they would build upon. First and foremost, Connery's own position was strengthened both on and off screen. The basics, like his wardrobe, were given priority and £1,000 was allotted for a new selection of Savile Row clothes. More importantly, from the detailed audience reaction notes the producers, along with the director and scriptwriter, had to adjust to an interesting discovery. *Dr No* was made with due seriousness and the humour was often accidental: although there were jokey one-liners the audience had also laughed in the 'wrong' places, often at some aside or added nuance by Connery. They were very quick to spot this, and used it in the development of *From Russia With Love*. The producers were more confident of their position and, given an increased budget and a wider scope from one of the best Bond plots written, they were able to extend themselves into finding decent, realistic actors to set against Bond.

Terence Young, meanwhile, was engaged casting the other essential ingredients, female accompaniment from photographs of 200 possibles from across Europe. The principal choice was the runner-up in the 1960 Miss Universe contest, Daniela Bianchi, about whom much was said at the time in that pre-feminist era.

Dick Maibaum, writing the screenplay and developing the humour, still retained much of Fleming's own dialogue surrounding the basic plot involving the criminal organisation SPECTRE, which must kill Bond and take possession of a decoding machine to gain the upper hand over the intelligence community. Bianchi was the Russian lure, Tatania, and the character actress Lotte Lenya was Rosa Clebb. Connery, meanwhile, found a superb match in the dyed-blond Robert Shaw as one of the best Bond adversaries ever in his portrayal as the psycho-assassin who scared the audience half to death in a pre-title scene in which he appeared to kill James Bond.

It was, of course, a lookalike, and he was just practising for the real thing. This ploy was the invention of Harry Saltzman who was also instrumental in upping the violence level and introducing a spectacular fight between Shaw and Connery on the Orient Express, which was in truth filmed on two stages at Pinewood with both actors undertaking a remarkable amount of the stunt work themselves. It ended with Bond strangling his nemesis with a cord from his trick wristwatch. Connery's excellence often revolved around these areas of the script; he displayed a cold viciousness which he usually capped off with black humour, a one-line remark that would release the tension that had been built up during the scene.

Michael Caine, who was mere months away from creating his own screen character, Harry Palmer in *The Ipcress File*, felt that this was one of the elements which contributed to Bond/Connery's success. Caine believed Connery had made Fleming's Bond far tougher than had been originally intended, and that he had been given the lines to take the edge off the scenes through humour, or rather hamish dialogue that immediately sent it up and informed the audience that it was all one big joke.

The best example of this, in this second Bond film, was perhaps displayed by the smirk on Connery's face when he returns to his room to discover Tatania in his bed, apparently naked except for a black bow around her neck. He tells her she is the most beautiful girl he has ever seen, proceeds to get into bed with her and when she says, 'I think my mouth is too small ...' his response has the yob element cheering: 'No, it's the right size. For me, that is.' There was only one way of delivering the line without getting arrested, and Connery managed with the same considerable skill that he had shown throughout. Even on the brink of the permissive age, *From Russia With Love* went beyond established boundaries of voyeurism, including a touch of the taboo topic of lesbianism.

In between location filming in Turkey, Spain and Scotland – the latter giving him a chance to return to his old stamping ground as a 'star' – Connery was contracted by director Basil Dearden, who had been hired for a movie called *Woman Of Straw* with Gina Lollobrigida and Ralph Richardson. It was the first major role offered to him outside of Bond and, in view of the personalities involved, was especially appealing. To Lollobrigida, who had already peaked but was still a major star, the idea was less appealing and she needed convincing. As with the Bond movies, United Artists were the backers for an independent company producing the film. Lollobrigida recalled later,

'When I was engaged for this picture, UA treated me like a

queen. Great days, hah! They gave me all kinds of approval. Script approval. Director approval. And, of course, actor approval. Now they wanted very badly Sean Connery. Sean who? I asked. So several of them came to Rome to talk to me, try to convince me. They didn't say to me that he was not very well known, that he was a very good actor, or that he was handsome. No. Nothing of that. No, they said to me, "He's a re-e-e-al man." A real man? Hah! I was so astonished I accepted him immediately.'

Connery's star was undoubtedly waxing and would be further enhanced by the double-quick release of *From Russia With Love*. The premiere was staged less than two months after completion, director Young and editor Peter Hunt having burned the midnight oil to get a final edit by September, less than six months from the time filming actually began. Again the comparisons with Hollywood show an incredible disregard for the bureaucracy that surrounds the making of any film. For those who are able to spot the mark of good editing, Hunt would become something of a hero. With the additional backroom people of John Barry writing the score, Lionel Bart producing the title song and Matt Munro recording what became one of his biggest hit singles, another spectacular opening was in view. One slight hiccup came with the otherwise captivating first-time performance of Daniela Bianchi. Like Ursula Andress, her accent was too thick and her voice was dubbed over.

There were a few complaints about the 'A' rating which, it will be recalled by older readers, was the classification for family audiences with parental approval. It was the forerunner of the current PG, with 'X' being the adult band. In that sense, it could be said that Bond helped push back the boundaries of permissiveness. There was even debate in *The Times* about it. Sandy Wilson questioned the moral rectitude of allowing children to be confronted with the kind of violence displayed in *From Russia With Love*, to which a mother replied indignantly that she would have been ashamed to be seen at the cinema without a child accompanying her because in her view James Bond was pure slapstick and in fact contained less sadism and reality than a *Tom And Jerry* cartoon. All of which rather summed up the phenomenon of James Bond.

The critics on the serious papers, more used to grappling with the social or artistic merits of a film, found themselves faced with a product that was almost impossible to define or criticise in the normal way. They either had to castigate the whole production, including the meritorious technical effects, as a terrible excursion into violent fantasy or enter into the spirit of the film, laugh at it and record the excellence of those responsible. The *Daily Telegraph* hesitatingly chose the former path and spoke of *From Russia With Love* being a reflection of an ugly, totalitarian world with what looked ominously like approval. It was a good point, not easily dismissed.

Connery knew this and in early interviews deflected the question with replies about humour, and how he had personally managed to give the Fleming character its extra dimension. He had, and fortunately it pleased Fleming. For Connery personally the premiere at the Odeon, the foremost cinema of Leicester Square, marked a special triumph, confirming his arrival as a noted force in the cinema which he was apparently keen to mark by bringing his family to London to join himself and Diane at the opening. Parents Effie and Joe were nervously overawed by the whole occasion.

The crowds were remarkable, and elements of British cinema history were about to be rewritten. *From Russia With Love* became the first film to play at four major West End theatres at the same time and the film went into the black with its British box office receipts alone.

Accolades for Connery included his promotion from number ten to number four in the list of Top Ten actors. Oxford University joined a growing band of Bond fan clubs and the Variety Club of Great Britain gave Connery a special award for the way he had created the character of James Bond, and in doing so had helped restore some of the lost glory to the British film industry.

Externally, Sweden insisted on cuts in the violent scenes before the film could be shown, some countries banned it altogether after the Russians had announced a certain displeasure, and it also became the first film since those featuring Disney characters to inspire a merchandising operation.

As far as Connery was concerned this, according to close observers, may well have been what he considered the point of making it: the realisation that he had, hopefully, passed the point of no return and a rather exciting future could be in prospect. He was again being pursued by Hollywood, entering a phase where work offers came often. He had a fearful workload of five pictures in less than two years, though the consolation was that it would earn him a sum of close on three quarters of a million pounds.

His colleague Robert Hardy had judged £6,000 for the Bond film to be a small fortune for a struggling actor, but two years on he had achieved an even larger advance in his personal situation; it was sufficient to provide the base for a kind of confidence that only men who reach this point in life are able to describe.

In Connery's case it was to be portrayed in the gossip columns as big-headedness. Money became a topic he quickly placed behind his 'private' door, which only heightened the discussions and innuendo later on when his financial affairs came to the public eye. He was known to be a tough bargainer, and was getting a press reputation for taking the normal bounds of Scottish meanness too far. But who could blame a man who, having come this far, showed an enthusiasm for holding on to what he had?

There were a few dark clouds, that November, in an otherwise blue sky. The media and the public seemed more than ever incapable of separating him from his film character, which he found intensely annoying. Fact was merged with fiction. He *was* Bond, and in many ways the character he had created had in a perverse sort of way reciprocated. But other more pressing problems disturbed the afterglow of a successful opening.

He was by then well into the filming of *Woman Of Straw*, and all was not well; not well at all. In the interviews with journalists he had always made the point that the reason for insisting on a deal which gave him the opportunity of alternating the Bond films with other movies was so that he would never be typecast. He was fond of telling the story of the time he went for an audition and walked out because the casting director asked him, 'What type of actor are you, Mr Connery?' The thought of being typecast riled him. That was why he was making pictures like *Woman Of Straw*, in the hope that audiences would accept him in other parts. This was not necessarily so; it placed upon him a pressure to be better in the 'other' films. *Woman Of Straw* should have been one of those vehicles – to employ Hollywood parlance – which would aid this turn-and-turn-about sequence of almost Dr Jekyll and Mr Hyde proportions. The film was shot with remarkable speed at Pinewood. It was a small cast, and a play that could be performed with ease on the London stage. It is the story of a rich old man's nurse, played by Lollobrigida, who is persuaded by the nephew (Connery) to marry the sick uncle, Ralph Richardson, and thus inherit and share out the uncle's fortune.

The nurse actually begins to grow fond of the old man, but when he dies prematurely she is convicted of murder. The Connery character had tricked her and murdered the old man to get all the money for himself. The ending is rather predictable, and the whole is rather lacklustre. Richardson snorted along amusingly, Connery presented his credentials in confident, though somewhat colourless style, while Lollobrigida never could invoke much sympathy as the wronged nurse.

Connery was realistic enough even while filming to know that his first major non-Bond movie was not going to be the success he had hoped. Lollobrigida sensed this and was ill tempered on the set. Connery in part blamed himself. He had read the script for *Woman Of Straw* between takes on *From Russia With Love*. 'I won't make that mistake again,' he said afterwards. 'I did not have time to concentrate.'

There was also a problem that he had perhaps not anticipated, in that everything he did now would be compared with his performances as Bond and that situation was to arise time and again in the coming months. When filming finished in December he flew to Los Angeles to begin work on *Marnie*, an Alfred Hitchcock project which appeared to offer considerable promise and prestige, and whose schedule he could fit in before starting work on the next Bond, *Goldfinger*, in March 1964. It was a tight squeeze and by the end of filming *Goldfinger* he would have worked without a break for virtually 14 months.

The confidence derived from financial security, and the misfortune of having worked on two scripts which he had accepted without the deeper analysis he would have preferred (*Another Time, Another Place*, and *Woman Of Straw*), led him to approach *Marnie* with caution. He did not give an unqualified yes to an offer which came out of the blue from Alfred Hitchcock, which rather surprised the master; in fact, he was apparently taken quite aback when Connery asked to view the script.

'No one,' said Hitchcock's London agent, 'ever asks to see a Hitchcock script. Not even Cary Grant did that ...'

'Well, I'm not Cary Grant,' Connery replied. 'And I would like to see the script.' He insisted that he had been forced to play in so much tripe in the past he now felt it incumbent upon himself to read the words in advance.

Without further ado, Hitchcock duly obliged and, by the way, approved the leading man fee of $200,000 plus 5 per cent of the film's profits, which put Connery right among Hollywood's highest male earners for a single picture. Only the likes of Burton and Brando were getting more. It was an odd fact that Hitchcock, well known to dislike actor ego, complied with every request after a private viewing of *Dr No*.

The story had been on Hitchcock's desk for a long time. He had bought it specifically for Grace Kelly from *Poldark* author Winston Graham in 1959. Universal Studios were involved and had offered to back the film financially while Joseph Stefano, who had written the screenplay of Robert Bloch's *Psycho*, adapted Graham's novel with Kelly in mind. Universal and Hitchcock, presumably with

Kelly's approval, announced her return to the screen with a press statement on 19 March 1962 that after a six-year break from the movies she would begin filming for Hitchcock in Hollywood that summer. Her husband Prince Rainier of Monaco, whom she married in 1956, would accompany her. Graham's story was a psychodrama involving aspects of rape, crime and sex that might not have been especially compelling to the elder statesmen of Monaco, by whose laws and traditions the former Miss Kelly was now bound. There was so much public disquiet about her return to the screen in such a role that she backed out and Hitchcock shelved the project until he could find another leading lady.

That turned out to be his recent discovery Tippi Hedren, the 26-year-old New Yorker whom he had cast for 1963's *The Birds*. He was so taken with her that he cast her for the lead in *Marnie* and had the script rewritten by a woman, Jay Presson Allan, to accommodate the style of his new young star.

Hitchcock believed Hedren and Connery were the perfect combination. They were two of a kind, in his view, and both would be influenced and moulded in the way he wanted. If Connery suspected this, and held out for script approval and the right fee, then the master had also done his homework and knew it was exactly the kind of role Connery was seeking. The story was filled with a kind of perverted eroticism, Hitchcock exploring the premise that everyone was perverted in a different way.

Marnie is a compulsive thief and sexually frigid, brought about by psychological problems resulting from an uncaring, man-hating mother, a prostitute whom she had witnessed killing a man. Mark Rutland, her employer, played by Connery, is a young, attractive, rich widower and company executive who discovers his junior is a compulsive thief and develops an obsessional infatuation for her, wanting her because – rather than in spite – of her compulsion to steal. Below the line exists the theory that Rutland hopes to catch Marnie in the act of kleptomania and rape her on the spot; that was the essence of the fetish with which Hitchcock motivated Rutland.

The sub-plot may have come as something of a surprise to Connery and Hedren since it was not in the script, and during the preliminary discussions on characterisation and motivations it seems Hitchcock failed to mention the idea to either of them. It was just in his mind and something which would come out in the fullness of time. He had been known to use the ploy on several past occasions for crucial scenes.

Connery found Hitchcock an immense joy to work with. He seemed to have been anticipating a mass of directional hints from Hitch but hardly received any. The director's theory seemed to be based upon the fact that he was paying Connery an enormous sum for his services and if he could not do the job then it was his own, and not Connery's, fault. Connery was at times literally open mouthed by the whole experience. Hitchcock had noticed he had a tendency to allow his jaw to hang loose when he was listening to someone talking to him. 'I don't think people are interested in your dental work,' he told Connery one day. It was one of two lessons Connery learned from Hitchcock's sparse direction of him. The other was to slow down; he often spoke too quickly. 'Just sneak in some dog's feet,' Hitch said, and Connery knew he needed to slow down his delivery.

It was, however, Connery's misfortune to be involved in yet another production where there was trouble on the set. It arose between Hitch and Hedren during the shooting of a highly charged and emotional part of the film, the tensions so strong that they were almost visible. The blow-up came three quarters of the way through shooting when Hedren asked Hitchcock if she could have a weekend off to attend a charity function in New York. He said without a moment's hesitation that it was not possible and that he thought the break would damage her concentration and affect the intensity of her performance. There was a nasty shouting match. Harsh words were said, and Hitchcock was wounded by a reference to his weight. Thereafter, and for the rest of the picture, he would only speak to her via a third party: 'Tell Miss Hedren ...' To which Miss Hedren replied in similar vein.

Top: Still in the military, Sean shows off his muscles with wrestler Chopper Howlett.

Right: Who would have thought that the fresh-faced sailor would turn out to be the biggest star in the UK?

Above: International stardom beckoned when Lara Turner personally chose him from 300 other hopefuls to star as her love interest in *Another Time, Another Place.*

Right: Sean with his own leading lady, first wife, Diane Cilento. The couple secretly married in Gibraltar in 1962.

Top: Connery with his wife Diane and his proud parents Joe and Effie.

Bottom: It was happy families; Sean, Diane, their son Jason and Diane's daughter Gigi.

Top: Ian Fleming (right) initially worried that Connery wouldn't be able to bring the fictional hero of Bond to life. His fears soon disappeared as Sean made the role his own.

Bottom: His old friend Roger Moore stepped into Sean Connery's shoes to play Bond. In 1983 they were rivals on the silver screen with each playing the 007 character in different movies.

'The name's Bond, James Bond' – Sean in the unmistakable pose.

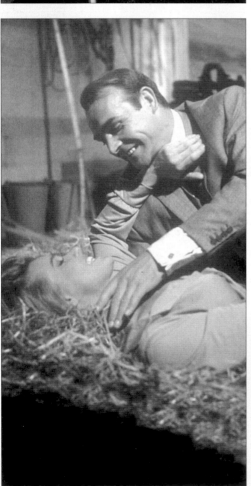

Sean Connery with a selection of the many famous Bond girls. Clockwise from *top left:* with Ursula Andress in *Dr No*; in *Diamonds Are Forever* with Jill St John; receiving plenty of attention in *You Only Live Twice* and wrestling with Honor Blackman in *Goldfinger*.

Although the press were eager to keep referring to Sean as 007, he was keen to establish himself in other varied roles. With his friend Michael Caine he starred in *The Man Who Would Be King*.

Connery has tackled a
vast range of roles
throughout his career,
making each and every
one his own. Here he is
seen in *Zardoz* (*top*)
from 1973 and *The Hill*
(*right*) from 1965.

Connery was stuck in the middle of this, and there were those who believed it had been part of Hitchcock's technique to keep the actors on their mettle. If that was the case, the reviewers were not at one in judging that it had worked with great success. Regardless of what happened on set, and given that this was nowhere near Hitchcock's best, it provided Connery with a unique insight into the man and his method of working. What he experienced was quite unrepeatable, because it was the end of an era for Hitchcock. It was to be the last Hitchcock film photographed by Robert Burks, edited by George Tomasini, with a score by Bernard Herrmann. Soon after it was completed Robert Burks, Hitch's devoted cinematographer since *Strangers On A Train* in 1950, died with his wife in a fire at their home, which caused deep distress to Hitchcock. A little later, George Tomasini died. Bernard Herrmann remained for a time but not long enough to work on any other Hitchcock film. Tippi Hedren, badly shaken by her experience, remained under contract, but was never cast again by Hitchcock.

There was also disappointment among Hitchcock devotees about the film itself. Even the old master felt the final edit deflated some of the highly emotional and neurotic drama. There were undoubted problems with the Connery character. The part originally called for a much older man and someone had suggested (too late of course) that Olivier would have suited it better. Hitchcock agreed and admitted that perhaps Connery did not make the most convincing Philadelphian businessman he had ever met. On reflection, he saw the story as requiring a 'gentleman' as a foil to the unsophisticated girl, an elegant man, one much more elegant than Connery. This was not necessarily a criticism of Connery, but more of himself for choosing him. Connery had done well in a complex role and, as was to be standard form on many of Connery's pictures, the technicians on *Marnie* agreed, especially for the way he had helped them during difficult times. They presented him with a thousand-dollar gold watch at the end of it.

When *Marnie* opened that summer reviews were mixed, but it attracted a reasonable trade at the cinemas for which some credit must have been due to James Bond and *From Russia With Love*, which had swept America in April. Comparisons, as always, were made with past Hitchcock masterpieces and disappointments were expressed. Even so, *Marnie* has stood the test of time and has reappeared at regular intervals down the years.

Connery's Hollywood experience failed to turn his head towards the more extrovert trappings of stardom normally associated with those on half-millionaire salaries, and there was considerable comment in gossip columns and among his Los Angeles contemporaries that he simply refused to comply with the rules of the glitzerama game. He turned down the traditional studio limo in favour of a self-drive runabout, preferably, he said, a VW. He shunned the proposal to house him at a fashionable apartment-hotel and said he would prefer the motel he stayed at some years ago which was cheaper and more convenient. The presence of James Bond in Hollywood also brought a crop of party invitations which he generally turned down, and it was noted that his off-duty clothes were usually sloppy jeans and shirts. America, by then well aware of the success of James Bond, simply could not understand the man's attitude.

The only concession to the studio publicity department was to give rather brief interviews on location in Maryland, allow himself to be photographed with actress models and filmed having a chat with Hitchcock about the merits of British and foreign women which received rather more attention than it truly deserved.

Diane Cilento added to the publicity prospects when she arrived in Hollywood in the second week of January, bringing her two children and their cook. If the Universal people were expecting to get husband and wife together for a major publicity bash, they were sorely disappointed. Cilento had her own show to promote, having just completed her co-starring role as Molly, the gamekeeper's daughter in the film version of Henry Fielding's ribald novel, *Tom Jones*. In that regard, the Connery family had at least to be thankful to Harry Saltzman – well, he thought so! – for having put both Sean and Diane into orbit in his major productions. Woodfall Films, in which he was partnered by angry young men of the British scene, had provided the production backing for *Tom Jones*; John Osborne wrote the screenplay and Tony Richardson directed. It was the same team that brought us *Look Back In Anger, The Entertainer* and (minus Osborne, but plus Alan Sillitoe) *Saturday Night And Sunday Morning*. When she arrived in Hollywood Diane learned that she had been nominated for an Oscar for Best Supporting Actress and she was 'hot'.

The *Los Angeles Times* was among those who made the most of her arrival and soon discovered that she did not, indeed would not, talk about her husband. According to Sheilah Graham, Diane refused to be interviewed with Sean, and vice versa. Their professional lives were separate and self-contained, and furthermore they did not wish to discuss them. In a thousand-word article on Cilento in the *LA Times*, Don Alpert made only one mention of her famous husband … 'and is married to Sean Connery', which, considering the fact that he was currently in Hollywood starring in a Hitchcock film and enjoying great success as James Bond, was a bit of an understatement.

Cilento met Hedda Hopper, too, and even Hopper herself mentioned Connery in a single sentence. Hopper wrote in her notes that Cilento had arrived for the interview 'wearing a very smart white tweed double-breasted coat, topped by a smashing hat in sharp orange felt. For a girl who likes deglamourised and off-beat roles on stage, she has a marked flair and high style for private life.'

For the duration they rented a thousand-dollar-a-month Bel Air hotel-apartment with a private swimming pool. It was not hugely demonstrative in Hollywood terms. The whole thing was almost a see-through plot of deliberate ordinariness verging on inverted snobbery, with Diane delivering what had become the standard line for herself and her husband: 'I consider myself to be a very private person when I'm off screen. I like playing parts, but I do not like playing that part off screen. Acting is a profession and something you should be professional about. I've been acting a long time and it's the only thing I know how to do. Most actors wonder why they went into it but they couldn't stop doing it.' Don Alpert said that in one respect he found Cilento a joy to listen to, but felt she was a very inhibited young lady.

Inhibitions aside, she was right at the centre of Hollywood attention. *Tom Jones* had secured ten Oscar nominations, a remarkable feat for a British picture. In the event it won four, which included Best Picture against the outstanding competition of *Cleopatra, How The West Was Won, America, America*, and *Lilies Of The Field*. It also won Best Director (Tony Richardson), Best Screenplay (John Osborne) and Best Original Score (John Addison). Unsuccessful nominations included Albert Finney (Best Actor), Hugh Griffiths (Best Supporting Actor), followed by three nominations in the Best Supporting Actress category for Diane Cilento, Dame Edith Evans and Joyce Redman. But though none won, they had the joy of seeing it awarded to that greatest of British eccentric characters Margaret Rutherford, who won the Oscar for her role in *The VIPs*, the Terence Rattigan story in which she co-starred with Richard Burton and Elizabeth Taylor.

Other great British performances were also recognised, with nominations for Best Actor and Best Actress for Richard Harris and Rachel Roberts respectively for *This Sporting Life*. And also in the running was Leslie Caron, nominated for Best Actress in Bryan Forbes's low-life melodrama, *The L-Shaped Room*.

All the realism of the British scene had come together, finally, for a takeover bid in Hollywood on a scale previously unknown. The British successes at that year's Oscar presentations were all part of the euphoric 1964 invasion of America by British entertainers.

Beatlemania was sweeping the country after the Fab Four arrived in February to tumultuous greetings everywhere. Three weeks later Connery's second Bond film *From Russia With Love* opened across America to a tremendous reception, while other

British-made movies such as *Tom Jones, This Sporting Life* and *The L-Shaped Room* all made their respective impact. London truly was the city of the decade.

It was a great and hugely successful period for British talent and, after The Beatles, none was more successful in terms of mass appeal than Connery himself.

7

WANTING A
BIGGER SHARE

No one knew, in 1964, how close the Bond bubble came to being harpooned by a curious mixture of avarice, ambition and acrimony apparent only to those at the hub of what had quickly become a slick operation. When Honor Blackman arrived at Pinewood Studios in the spring of that year to begin work on *Goldfinger*, for example, she was struck by the professionalism and enthusiasm of the whole outfit, especially Connery. Yet he most of all already harboured severe misgivings about the role of Bond and the detrimental side effects that it had bestowed upon him.

Blackman told me, 'Sean was always there, on time, meticulous and careful. He was keen on looking at the scripts and in my view was an extremely intelligent actor who always seemed to be in total control of what he was doing.'

But the outward efficiency of the Bond set masked an undercurrent of discontent which would erupt like a succession of mini-volcanoes. The runaway success had caused a good deal of moodiness in the Bond camp and Connery came back from America to discover that his first director, Terence Young, had parted company with the producers in a dispute over money even though he had already begun pre-production on the film. He understandably wanted to renegotiate his position (as Connery had successfully done). There were also unresolved discussions about the direction the Bond movies were to take. What had started out, in the eyes of United Artists at least, as a small-time movie venture had grown into a major business and several of those who had contributed to the success thought they deserved a greater share of the financial rewards that were, by March 1964, taking on rather promising proportions.

Dr No had already netted more than $3 million and the production costs of *From Russia With Love* had been virtually covered by box-office receipts in Britain alone, a feat which was being talked of in the way one would talk of miracles being performed. Whatever the film took in America and elsewhere would be a bonus – a $10 million bonus, as it turned out. Connery was unhappy on two key fronts – professional and financial – although looking at the cold black-and-white statistics of his situation it would be difficult for anyone to whip up sympathy for him. One aspect had been temporarily, but by no means unreservedly, resolved. His up-front fee for *Goldfinger* had been raised to £50,000 plus a percentage of the profits. There remained a chasm of unhappiness between himself and the Broccoli–Saltzman partnership.

The professional disquiet was as irritating as the money problem. Bond in media terms had taken over his life and – after only two pictures – he was already disillusioned and talking about getting out. There were those in his circle who posed the question, 'What will it take to satisfy this man?' One close to Broccoli had suggested, once it was obvious the Bond series was going to rake in the money, that they should make Connery a partner in their production company, Eon, so he could be persuaded to stay on and join in the promotional and marketing ventures by the sheer value of the deal.

Broccoli and Saltzman would not consider such a step, nor were they ever likely to; they made the point that it had been their venture from the start, they had found the money, risked their credibility and literally forced the Bond pictures on to the screen when once they seemed doomed to a mere book readership.

Connery was being pulled in several directions, and while he may have been sure in his own mind that ultimately he wanted to spend his life working on film or theatre projects that appealed to him, and be a success in the process, it wasn't that easy. The direction of his career, and life, clearly remained a matter of personal and private debate as well as public speculation. For the time being he was inextricably linked with Bond. He might not even do another Bond film, regardless of the money. Bond had brought him recognition and given him security. He could go on playing it for ever and, as Cubby kept pointing out, make himself very, very rich in the process.

The actor, meantime, struggled to claim space outside the Bond arena and to show he was not a one-act wonder. Unfortunately, nothing he had done so far matched Bond's commercial success and there was always the inherent fear that if he ditched the character completely he might slip back into oblivion.

While all this was going on, there was a massive image-making operation orchestrated by Broccoli and Saltzman to build up their investment. Bond was the keyword – not Connery. Broccoli was the pursuer of that emphasis: push James Bond first and Sean Connery second; the character was the star of the show so that, in the event of a change, it would lessen the impact. But the two became one.

Connery had experienced two years of that kind of exposure, of being prodded and poked and pursued by all and sundry, facing an increasingly hostile press who believed – or were led to believe – that he would give in and let them into his life so everyone could discover that he really was James Bond. What dozens of magazine and newspaper editors the world over would have liked was a picture spread on Connery, at home in his super-de-luxe London pad filled with electronic gadgetry, driving at least a Mark II

Bentley Continental, dressing himself in handmade silk shirts, Savile Row suits and fine tweeds, suitably cut to accommodate his Walther PPK in a Berns Martin holster, and splashing out nightly at a casino dressed in his white tuxedo with girls on his arms and winning thousands of pounds with his system.

None of that matched. He still lived in his converted nunnery with Acacia House over the front door. His everyday clothes were a mixture of old trousers and sloppy shirts which he bought at discount stores. His car was a Volkswagen camper whose special equipment was a washbasin and portable toilet until the recent purchase of a second-hand Jaguar. The only weapon he had ever carried was a 12-bore shotgun on a rabbit shoot once, and if he ever gambled it was for pennies during between-takes poker on the set. Evenings were seldom spent out on the town. He preferred to go anonymously to a cinema or the theatre and invariably ate at home.

So what happened?

One magazine ran an eight-page spread with words and pictures on the James Bond phenomenon, with Connery as Bond in every conceivable pose – yet Connery's name was not mentioned once. Not a single mention. And under the photographs, the captions began 'James Bond ...'

Sean Connery had ceased to exist.

When he began to reject the advances of the publicists and the reporters they turned nasty. Like all movie stars, he quickly became regarded as public property and had the same kind of focus that was being directed at the likes of Elizabeth Taylor and other grand stars, who at times wallowed in it but were equally driven to distraction. The difference with Connery was that he did not match their excesses in his personal life, and thus it became necessary to find an angle. Because of the stars' riches, which were considered to be bestowed upon them by their adoring public and not through any special skills, very little sympathy was gained from moans about voyeuristic exposure and the demands of the media.

There were many who felt the same as Connery. Albert Finney grumbled about his fate after his appearance with Diane Cilento in *Tom Jones*. Following the palaver over the epoch-making sexual freedoms expressed in *Saturday Night And Sunday Morning*, he believed he was being exploited as the creator and key figure in this sexual revolution. The rumbustiously blatant sex of *Tom Jones* is what sold the movie, of course, because as a production it was riddled with flaws and after the novelty value had worn off was generally put away. Finney groaned, 'I just felt I was being used. I wasn't involved. I was bored, most of the time.'

The exploitation of sex and Connery's (or Bond's) prowess was the key factor in the Bond hype. Life, in that regard, was already full of pressures, although many in his profession would have gladly faced such misfortunes. They had doubled of late because of the media interest in Cilento. The rows with his producers, the continuing discussions about what he considered to be fair pay, his search for professional satisfaction outside Bond, Cilento's pushing to see that his status was raised and his running battle against a press onslaught were really only just beginning …

Terence Young who, some said, had been the originator of so many of the quirky qualities that made Bond successful, was gone and Guy Hamilton, best known for *The Colditz Story* which he wrote and directed, was in the director's chair. Writer Dick Maibaum had been replaced by veteran Paul Dehn, a former London film critic and versatile screenplay technician who was ready to build upon his predecessor's work. With two such key roles switching into other hands, it would not be unreasonable to expect changes on the Bond set. Even as he took over the pre-production work, Hamilton began making a daily trip to Dehn's apartment in West London, where Maibaum's script for *Goldfinger* was being rewritten, and having 'ongoing discussions' with Broccoli and Saltzman about content. Both men had very firm ideas about what aspects they wanted to build up; but firm ideas have a habit of changing. They were moving away from the underlying realism of some of the scenes of the first two films and more into the realms of comic-strip fantasy, and there was further reappraisal after the release of *From Russia With Love*.

Two directors who worked for them confirmed with certainty that the two men were often poles apart. They argued about who had the best idea, and not which idea would be best for the film – if either.

Decisions might be waited upon for hours, but it was their movie and their money, in a manner of speaking. They were still making notes, ticking the inclusions they liked and felt brought most commercial benefit while deleting others which had not worked. Saltzman enjoyed the idea of extending Bond's range of techno-toys like the gadget-filled Aston Martin, and using modern devices to bring Fleming's original writing up to date to take account of modern developments in warfare, aviation and so on. For Harry it was the addition of the expectedly unexpected that mattered – the exploding suitcase in *From Russia With Love* or the ejector car seat in *Goldfinger*. The audience was carefully let into Q's secret and then sat waiting for the event to happen, as they knew it would.

Broccoli had his own ideas about the popularity of Bond. The sexual content had been increased in amount but downplayed in value, so as to reduce any risk of attack by people concerned about public morals. As far as the girls themselves were concerned, not much had changed since the first female lead to play opposite Connery in *Dr No* was cast. Terence Young had suggested a young, exquisite but then unknown actress named Julie Christie. Broccoli thought she was sensually beautiful but no good for a Bond film because she was lacking in one essential department, which Broccoli summed up in two small but telling words: 'No tits'.

So far the women in Bond movies had largely conformed to Fleming's idea that they should complement the Bond character, be his playthings and attractive adornments, there for Bond's sexual gratification and the titillation of the audience. The list of leading ladies in Bond movies who had their speaking parts dubbed over – Ursula Andress, Daniela Bianchi, Eunice Gayson (in both *Dr No* and *From Russia With Love*), Shirley Eaton (in *Goldfinger*) and Claudine Auger (*Thunderball*) – is perhaps the best illustration that the inclusion of several well-known actresses was specifically and cynically for their visual quality and not for their acting prowess.

Hamilton changed the perception of Bond's women quite dramatically and, moulding his and Dehn's ideas with those of Young and Maibaum, produced what became the formula for virtually all future Bond films. The sexuality remained as it did throughout the series, swaying back and forth into situations above and below the line, though largely above and pushing to the limits the certification requirements for the widest possible audience. Violent sex should not be inflicted *upon* women; in fact the reverse happened, and for the first time much of the sensuality and sexual interest was to be discovered in female adversaries who were very capable women, matching the emerging 1960s female, not necessarily succumbing to male advances and able to fight back. Hence the arrival of Honor Blackman as Pussy Galore, fresh from her famous television role in the highly popular series *The Avengers*, in which she appeared as the leather-suited Cathy Gale. It was she who disarmed the Bond charisma immediately with the line, 'You can switch off the charm, Mr Bond. I am immune.'

Connery reacted to this new situation with pleasure, if a touch uneasily. The standard bedroom scenario of submissive women, to which Bond reverted and became so staid and repetitive under Roger Moore's tenure, at least remained fresh and appealing with these changes of pace, and for Connery personally it provided the opportunity to add another dimension to the role.

The basic sexual overlay did not change, merely the way it was portrayed, and Connery achieved it with style. 'He was exceedingly handsome, virile and sexy and that really was the tenor of what the script was always trying to display,' Honor

Blackman told me. 'I think we both appreciated that the script was especially good at that and he made everything look deceptively simple, anyway. Personally, I always thought he was an inspired choice for the role and as an actor I would rank him alongside Spencer Tracy and Cary Grant. They were very much in the same mould; they were of that school who have this remarkable ability to be particularly competent at the job, and yet give the impression that they were really being themselves. And this is what Sean did.'

The side effect was the continuing erosion of Sean Connery as both a person and a serious actor. 'I know very well that he was an excellent actor by then, and could easily have been a very good classical actor. He had already done lots of superb theatre work,' said Blackman. 'And on *Goldfinger* I could see quite definitely another Connery trying to get out, but he never let on.'

By devouring the fictional character within himself, as Blackman, Robert Hardy and Joss Ackland have all noted, there was an added danger that the outside world would see nothing but Bond. Connery was alert to this problem almost from the word go, but never imagined it could reach these proportions. Just as the soap stars emerging on television were to become known by their character names, Connery was facing being locked in the most high-profile role in the world.

His new director had observed the difficulties. Hamilton remembered seeing him a mere five or six years earlier as a film extra and later as a struggling actor, and not being impressed. He was the first to agree that Connery had improved beyond measure, learning all the time. Even between the first Bond film and the second he had jacked up his performance with considerable skill. Hamilton could see Connery's problem, though, and appreciated his desire to do things other than Bond – easier said than done because, as the Bond industry grew, the films were getting bigger in terms of production and taking far longer to complete.

Bigger budgets and a higher content of technically difficult stunts and location filming added weeks to the overall timespan. Connery was nailed down for longer periods of time and the producers were naturally reluctant to give him release for other work until a picture was wrapped up. That's what the contract said and they were sticking to it, especially now that they were paying him more money.

Other considerations cropped up during the early summer of 1964. The physical demands of *Goldfinger* were increasing. Connery liked to do as many of his own stunts as possible. Much of the judo interlude with Honor Blackman was performed by them; a great deal of the fight with Robert Shaw in *From Russia With Love* was done by the two men and it saved days of production time, not to mention the benefits on film.

Apart from meeting his own performance criteria, Connery also discovered Hamilton to be a man he could do business with. He was impressed by the casting for *Goldfinger*, too. Honor Blackman hardly fell into the glamour-puss category of some of the Bond girls, and she knew it. So did Broccoli, who mused for some time over her suitability. She was nonetheless an equally inspired choice for this strange Fleming character who was inclined towards lesbianism. This was downplayed (apart from a couple of barely noticeable jokes) and she was turned into a sexy adversary for Bond, a role which enabled Blackman to bring weight and strength to what is often considered to be the liveliest and most amusing of all the Bond films.

Gert Frobe, the substantial German actor playing Auric Goldfinger, was another great character Connery enjoyed working with and both he and Blackman would be called back later to team up for a less successful rematch in *Shalako*.

Connery became very angry during questioning by a female French journalist brought on to the set one day by the film publicists. When told Goldfinger was played by Gert Frobe, the journalist asked, 'Who's she?' Connery's rage boiled over and he walked off the set until the woman had left, and was later castigated for being rude. It was incidents like this that eventually led him to discourage his publicity people from bringing journalists and photographers on to the set – then a traditional method of pre-publicity. Showbusiness journalist Kenelm Jenour recalled that sometime later, when he was London writer for the *Hollywood Reporter*, he had been taken on to the set at Pinewood. Connery came in and the two of them stood chatting amicably for several minutes until Connery discovered he was a journalist and walked off. Jenour was subsequently ushered away. Before long, Connery invariably chose to work on a closed set.

The Connerys were darting between work like mad things. Diane Cilento had been signed for Carol Reed's much-hyped but ultimately dismal extravaganza *The Agony And The Ecstasy*, which allegedly cost $12 million and took a lot less at the box office. Bosley Crowther described it as an illustrated lecture of a slow artist at work. However, to Cilento it appeared to be – and was – a prestigious role starring with Charlton Heston (somewhat mis-cast as a man who was supposedly a homosexual dwarf), Rex Harrison and Harry Andrews. Cilento looked for this kind of artistry in scripts, and the subject matter was appealing to her own Italian heritage. She spoke the language fluently and in between films regularly undertook major literary translations. Cilento flew to Rome with her mother and children in June for the start of filming while Connery himself was still deeply involved with *Goldfinger*, which was eventually wrapped up in July 1964.

He left the *Goldfinger* set sweating, puffing, angry and mumbling something about 'never again', and flew to Rome to join his wife for his first holiday in two years. She was seldom to be part of it because of her own commitments, though they did have some fun with Rex Harrison who enjoyed the local cuisine and wines whenever on location.

Connery got straight down to some serious reading. He had taken with him a screenplay for a film based on Ray Rigby's unproduced play *Breaking Point*, which he co-wrote with RS Allen, based upon true-life events. It could not have dropped into

Connery's lap at a better time, while he was still filled with the frustrations of playing Bond. It was a powerful story, retitled *The Hill*, which required a tough, all-male cast and was stacked with stark brutality as a group of prisoners rebel against the harsh discipline of a British military stockade in North Africa during World War Two.

Pinewood producer Kenneth Hyman had bought the rights some years earlier, but could not find a studio to back him. The blood, sweat and cruelty of the play went against the grain of British war films which generally glorified the returning heroes. The men in the stockade were heroes, but imprisoned largely for failing to obey the rather silly orders of some daft officers. Their spirit had to be broken before they could become soldiers again, and the central feature of this mental and physical torture was a large hill of sand and rock which the prisoners were forced to undertake at the double, in full kit and in the boiling sun.

Initially Connery wanted the role of the cruel and psychologically disturbed RSM eventually played by Harry Andrews, who came to the film straight from his role with Diane Cilento in *The Agony And The Ecstasy*. Connery was cast as Joe Roberts, one of the instigators of the men's rebellion. It was a role containing all the ingredients that he sought to help him get away from the typecasting aspirations of producers who could see him only in the glitzy world of Bond. It was the complete opposite: real, gritty and completely unglamorous, and minus toupee for the first time. Hyman was also seeking the services of Sidney Lumet, the renowned American director probably best known then for his 1957 film *Twelve Angry Men*, starring Henry Fonda and Lee J Cobb, for which he won an Oscar nomination.

Connery's agreement provided Hyman with the confidence he wanted, but there was one matter of financial importance still outstanding – Connery's fee, a straight payment of $400,000 which was almost as much as the aggregate salaries paid to the remaining line-up of excellent British actors, including Andrews, Michael Redgrave, Ian Bannen, Ian Hendry, Jack Watson and

Alfred Lynch. The latter had been the star of Connery's last film before Bond, *On The Fiddle*, a mere three years earlier and for which Connery had received nothing more than his weekly salary from 20th Century Fox. That he could now command such a figure – which matched the fees being demanded, and achieved, by leading male actors anywhere in the world – was a measure of the rise in Connery's international status.

But he had to pay for it. Fame and popularity, sought and courted by actors and film stars – even by those who deny it – as being the goal of every thespian ever to walk in front of an audience, hit with such force that Connery and Cilento were wringing their hands in despair. And, hate it though he might, Bond had suddenly become a crucial part of the support mechanism for the ailing cinema industry the world over.

8

BONDMANIA

'The sweet and troublesome smell of success hung like a huge, fluffy cloud waiting to turn black and rain on everyone's parade ...' So read a quotation in an American magazine, and contrived though it was it seemed to sum up what was going on in Sean Connery's life in 1965, a year of mixed feelings. With the passing of time, we forget what it was like when Bondmania took off. It was not quite on a par with Beatlemania, but not far off and the arrival of *Goldfinger* signalled the onset of some rather dramatic scenes in this gathering tide of popular acclaim.

Sean Connery was still in Spain, filming *The Hill* in a Spanish desert where he and half the cast had gone down with dysentery, when 5,000 people – the largest gathering of cinema fans in London since Elizabeth Taylor married Michael Wilding – crowded into Leicester Square on the night of 17 September 1964 for the premiere of *Goldfinger*. They were naturally disappointed that James Bond wasn't present but Honor Blackman was feted – in a way: 'Honor Blackman? Who's she? We're here to see Pussy Galore.' She had a whale of a time but found it a touch scary. The fans screamed and pushed and shoved and pulled until the large glass door at the front of the Odeon smashed under the pressure and police had to force everyone back, using loud hailers to warn of the dangers of someone being crushed to death.

The only sadness was that Ian Fleming, the creator, had died a month previously after collapsing while visiting the *Goldfinger* set earlier in the year, and did not survive long enough to see the final emergence of this cultural phenomenon and the character now set to become a legend.

Across the country, records were broken. Front-of-house managers were saying, 'Not since *Gone With The Wind …*' and trying to think of other comparisons, because no film had made such an impact in years, and certainly no British film. Furthermore, no British film in history created such a stir in America where United Artists finally decided that Bond was a success and drew up a massive promotional campaign for the opening in December 1964.

All around the US, and throughout Europe and the Far East, *Goldfinger* was playing to packed houses and those gross figures that are charted in *Variety* and other trade papers as the mark of success or failure of any film began ticking away like a machine gone haywire. *Variety* reported it was the fastest money-making film in the history of motion pictures, a grandiose claim that had been applied to many others, before and since, but in the case of *Goldfinger* was barely an exaggeration. It took $10,374,807 in 14 weeks on the circuits of North America and Canada. The money men at United Artists were rubbing their hands in delight and congratulating themselves that they had backed a winner, even if it had taken them two years to realise it. The cash tills were still ringing away, until the clock rapidly reached 20, 21, 22, 23 million dollars, on an outlay of $2.9 million. Connery was to receive 5 per cent of the net profits.

Life magazine put Shirley Eaton, the gold-painted girl, on the front cover, *Playboy* adopted James Bond as its hero and said Connery was the man of the decade, *Newsweek* talked of Freudian undertones, and the *Saturday Review* said Connery had got the role off-pat now. Meanwhile, the John Barry music album of the Bond soundtrack knocked The Beatles off the top of the charts, college professors began to write theses about Bond and campus groups argued until late into the night on why it should be so.

As the roadshow travelled, the momentum increased. In Paris there were scenes which someone said had not occurred since Marilyn Monroe visited in 1960. At the press conference and premiere women were weeping, crowds were bruised and battered in the crush, ribs were broken, chairs were overturned, cameras were smashed and stars were jostled. 'It is frightening,' said a member of the local gendarmerie. 'All this over one fictitious English detective. They did not make such a fuss over Maigret.' Nor would they, and in a way Sean Connery and his mounting anger over media attention merely added to the whole business.

He was being dubbed Britain's answer to Marlon Brando, Greta Garbo and Cary Grant all in one go, the two males for obvious reasons and Garbo because he was adopting a reclusive air, refusing to meet the press for any other reason than to talk about the production of the new film *Thunderball*, while the publicists muttered on the sidelines, 'That's all the thanks we get for making him a big star.'

Press conferences turned into scrums, and very few journalists were now allowed into a one-to-one interview with him. Such were the requests, such was the volume of interest, that eventually he had to call a halt and even well-known writers and authors discovered that getting past the guards was more akin to attempting an interview with a senior member of royalty. Those who were permitted into the inner sanctum of his thoughts at this time were given a long briefing from his minders on the subject of James Bond: the character should not dominate the interview. He was disappointed when other aspects of his career were ignored: that he liked to act in the theatre; that his best roles were in Shakespeare's *Macbeth* and Giradoux's *Judith*; that he was first rate in Ibsen and Pirandello ...

All of these things had been lost, forgotten and trampled into the dirt in the clamour for the projection of Sean Connery as James Bond – which was, after all, exactly how the films were now being publicised by the producers: 'Sean Connery *is* James Bond' was the message bellowed from the posters and hoardings.

It made him angry even to talk about James Bond because quite often the interviewers could not differentiate between the actor and the character and posed questions which ultimately sought to roll the two into one. The search for Connery the man became merely an adjunct to the discussion of some of James Bond's more reprehensible habits. Film publicists, always single minded in their task, considered him to be rather ungrateful as they wheeled in one eager writer after another who, more often than not, left empty handed.

Before long, adjectives like unapproachable, rude and irascible were being used, and an image of Connery – as opposed to Bond – was being painted in unflattering terms. Those adjectives began to be poured out in tirades, usually by newspaper people who did *not* get an interview.

One who did was Italian journalist and author Oriana Fallaci, whose previous interview subjects had included Hugh Hefner, Dean Martin, Alfred Hitchcock and Norman Mailer. She reported that in Connery she was confronted by a giant with a 'firm face, yet marked with lines deep as scars, large, mild, defenceless eyes, the eyes of a lamb flung down between the hyenas and the tigers of the world under pretext of doing them a favour'. This, she said, was the first thing that struck her about him; this truly imposing size, dramatised by excessively large shoulders. She was also struck by his shyness, a shyness overlaid by a gay, careless air, ingratiating smiles, the shyness of an adult who was discontented with himself and probably very alone, very uncertain.

The Italians have good insight, and a fine perception in assessing the hidden passions and desires of a person, and this came through as Fallaci continued her mission, finally achieving what she sought, to get Connery into the interview mode. It became one of the few occasions in his very public life that he opened up. From an almost hostile beginning, he progressed to the point where it is almost possible to visualise him slowly relaxing, becoming more comfortable and, in the end, joking and even mildly flirting with her. But her interview was quite definitely the exception rather than the rule.

He confessed that he hated talking about himself because it embarrassed and bored him. He could not see why on earth a man should have to explain himself publicly, or open his home to journalists to allow them inside to judge how one lived. The fact that he had become a star – he used the words 'money-making machine' – was all the more reason why he should refuse the degrading compromises of publicity.

He admitted that the image people had of him was that of a fellow devoid of intellectual capacity, boorish, aggressive – the image created in newspapers. When he read such words, it angered him to the extent that he contemplated physical harm to the writers. He was at a loss to see how to combat it, except hire someone to go around saying, 'Listen … he has a brain, too …' The moment success became monstrous, facilitated by James Bond, it ran out of control.

He complained that in the great welter of publicity over Bond his own personality had been subjugated, though he could offer little reason why it should not have been. He was a man, by his own account, of 'few faults and few virtues'. Among the latter he included a sense of humour, a sense of morality, a sense of truth. He never told lies. Never. His defects included his egotism, temper, anger and vanity. He also considered himself to be very vulnerable, but would rather slit his throat than show it.

Diane Cilento, who had just arrived in Paris for the premiere of *Goldfinger* and with whom Oriana Fallaci spent a good deal of time, admitted her surprise that Connery had opened up with his private thoughts. The Bond image rankled with Cilento, too. She felt persecuted by the secret agent, and to them he had become a monster. Thereafter Fallaci became good friends with the

Connerys and they would visit her in New York where she had an apartment. During one of Connery's lone missions to begin talks about a new film, and while waiting for Cilento and the children to arrive, he and Fallaci went to the cinema. Fallaci reported that she met him at his hotel – a small and modest place – but even so they had to leave by the service entrance because a large crowd of fans had been keeping a watching vigil at the front.

They walked all the way to the theatre where the new John Schlesinger movie, *Darling*, was showing, starring Dirk Bogarde, Laurence Harvey and Julie Christie, who might have been his own co-star in *Dr No* had Cubby Broccoli not ruled her out on account of her diminutive bust measurement.

A long queue of people was waiting at the cinema, and Connery took Fallaci to the end of the queue, and proceeded to wait. She was astounded. Why didn't he just call the manager and get the best seats in the house? He refused, and insisted on standing in line, just like everyone else. In the end, it was all to no avail. When they arrived at the ticket office he was recognised and they let him in for nothing, which rather spoiled his fun.

After the theatre she suggested supper. He agreed, but said he did not want to go into a restaurant because people were constantly coming up to him and asking for his autograph. So they went to an all-night deli and took away some sandwiches. Fallaci was bemused and ended the evening pondering how difficult it was for a man *not* to be corrupted by 'the fame, the money, the stupid adulation'.

The Hill was adding to the adulation, though in this case it was not stupid and pleased Connery greatly. The film received excellent reviews and Connery's notices were especially satisfying because he was at last recognised on film for what he considered to be decent work: 'A bold, agonising and proudly human experience' … 'disturbingly effective' … 'psychological masterpiece'.

It was chosen as the British entry in the 1965 Cannes festival, in spite of its controversial nature which had drawn criticism in the news columns for its supposed besmirching of the good name of the British military. *The Hill* undoubtedly contained some of the finest performances in recent times on the British scene, especially from Harry Andrews and Ian Hendry. But there was a basic flaw which was particularly aggravating to American audiences. The sound quality, through Lumet's bid for realism, was unfortunately quite poor, and this was a distinct disadvantage in America where the natives had difficulty in translating British accents, Scottish brogues and Army slang at the best of times.

The American version was equipped with subtitles after Hyman had refused to allow MGM to dub the entire picture with American voices. And so, when it was unsurprisingly a box-office failure and MGM pointed to this flaw as the cause, it was withdrawn from the American circuit and filed under commercial failure.

Back home, *The Hill* collected six nominations for British Academy Awards, but won only one – for Oswald Morris's photography. It had mixed fortunes, but proved the point that Connery had been trying to establish for some time, and had so far failed to present a totally convincing argument to his critics, that his abilities on screen went beyond the boundaries of Bond.

In the meantime, Harry Saltzman had opened up a second spy front with Connery's good friend Michael Caine, having purchased the rights to Len Deighton's novel *The Ipcress File* in which Michael was going to play the lead. Caine had been under contract to Saltzman after exactly ten years in the business. He was at the point of make or break. He had made 37 television appearances, most of them in roles so small that he wasn't even listed in the *Radio Times* credits, and had made a similar impact in all but the last of the 15 films he had been in, the last being *Zulu* in which he had finally secured a starring role alongside Stanley Baker.

But Harry was going to make him a star. Sheilah Graham heard him make the promise, and true to his word the wheels had been set in motion. Saltzman bought Deighton's novel, cast his boy as the cheeky, chirpy Cockney agent whom he called Harry Palmer (the character was unnamed in the book) and placed him at the cheap end of the spy spectrum where the agent wore glasses, had holes in his socks, rode on buses, lived in a seedy flat, shopped for his dinner in the supermarket and had sex between grubby cotton sheets. With Palmer, Saltzman had covered the market at both ends, and pulled off a remarkable feat from which Connery and Caine both ultimately benefited. There was no precedent to what happened to the two working lads with no formal training and little education and certain members of the British acting hierarchy looked on with restrained horror as these two upstarts proceeded to take the world by storm with their cheek and their faults and their absolute uniqueness, enlarged and magnified on the big screen. For Saltzman to do it a second time, with Caine, was something of an achievement, and between them they killed off once and for all the last lingering image that the outside world retained of British actors, that they were polite, middle-class chinless wonders.

Another interesting development came out of this age of making it. Connery and Caine overtook and left standing a whole bunch of other 'name' actors, if they will pardon the comparison, and made the leap across the Atlantic, where it counts, into international stardom in double-quick time while most of the rest, who had been around at the beginning of the so-called new wave, travelled less well. Certainly none made it so big.

Only Peter Sellers and Richard Burton of that era became total stars, although Robert Hardy says regretfully Burton wasted his chance and the *Daily Telegraph* obituarist said he threw away success like an old sock. Connery became the absolute idol of the age and Caine established himself within seconds as the new Britisher, the international Cockney. No one else made it in quite the way they did, even though their early work was comic-hero stuff and, in the intermediate period, quite patchy.

But fame was a double-edged sword. In April 1965, Connery was obviously not even sure he wanted it, as he sat waiting to take off from London airport bound for Nassau, followed by 102 actors and technicians and twelve and a half tons of assorted film gear for the commencement of location work on *Thunderball*. The fourth Bond movie got underway in a strained atmosphere and with Connery smarting from press headlines speculating on the state of his marriage. To rub salt into an open wound, a *Daily Express* headline failed to recognise that it was Sean Connery's marriage they were talking about: a large banner screamed out 007 PARTS FROM DIANE CILENTO, with a strapline stating that Bond had left their home for a trial separation.

Inquiring reporters laid siege to Pinewood Studios in the week before Connery flew to Nassau; any who managed to penetrate the security ring were escorted from the set and Connery refused point blank to talk to journalists, which merely heightened the ardour of their editors.

Meanwhile, in Nassau, work was well ahead on the biggest list of Bond toys and accoutrements yet, the budget having been doubled yet again to $5.5 million, including a life-size Vulcan bomber which was, in the film, hidden under the sea. There was a small fleet of sleek futuristic two-man submarines moored offshore, and a huge 95mph hydrofoil camouflaged in the shell of a luxury yacht. Tiger sharks were being caught and placed in the Olympic-sized swimming pool of a nearby villa, rented for the duration. Reels and reels of film were being loaded and flown in; the white sandy beaches were littered with power cables and sound booms.

As they rehearsed the spectacular techno-scenes, the calm blue waters of the Caribbean were awash with masked men in orange and yellow scuba suits armed with spear guns for the climatic scene where 25 American aqua-troopers take on 20 villainous SPECTRE frogmen, while ashore, press agents in their shiny suits, starlets in their minuscule swimsuits, bit-part players, extras, technicians, make-up people, set designers, electricians, cameramen and a breathless assortment of additional staff were preparing for the moment when director Terence Young – having made up with the producers and back in harness – called, 'Action!'

The rush was on after a slight legal complication involving the role of Kevin McClory who, it will be recalled, had proved in an earlier court action his joint ownership of the story and was appearing for the first time as producer.

By the time Connery arrived in Nassau the communications scene, as *Look* senior editor Gereon Zimmermann described it, was 'historic'. Reporters and photographers had flown in from all over the world, and nearly every major publication from America, Britain, Europe, Canada, Australia and Japan had sent teams out, joined by television crews from the BBC, ITV, ABC, NBC and assorted other speculative voyeurs.

Glenn Rose, a Hollywood publicity man attached to the *Thunderball* unit, perspiring in the humid tropical heat of the Bahamas, did not know which way to turn. He very soon discovered that initially they were not, as he described it to Connery, all 'two-bit gossip hacks'; among the press pack were at least 14 senior editors and writers of the world's leading magazines – like Zimmermann himself – all clamouring for a top-notch spread on the biggest Bond extravaganza to date, hyped by the added excitement of rumours of Connery's marital problems.

It was a publicity man's dream and the possibilities were immense. Rose knew very well he was staring at a promotional opportunity of incalculable value. And now, of course, they weren't just talking about the promotion of a movie. The massive marketing operation of James Bond products was in full swing, with shoes, toys, T-shirts, cards, posters, perfumes and toiletries. Jay Emmett, chairman of the Licensing Corporation of America, which controlled the copyright of Bond-linked goods, confidently predicted sales of $40 million in 007 products. He underestimated. More than $60 million worth of licensed merchandise went on sale in America alone.

Press or no press, Connery wasn't talking. The likes of Zimmermann came and went with articles devoid of even a quote from the star of the show, and had to make do with a one-liner from Terence Young who trotted out the familiar fact that Connery also played a very fine Hotspur. He gave only one lengthy interview, to a team from *Playboy* who had been courting him for months for 'The *Playboy* Interview', recognised in Hollywood then as the mark of a man who had made it. A few weeks before beginning work on *Thunderball*, Connery had met them in a pub near his London home for a preliminary chat.

He arranged to meet them again on the set of *Thunderball*, and kept his word when they arrived. There, the interviewers from this last bastion of male chauvinism cautiously threw at him their carefully calculated and typically loaded questions aimed at extracting his views on a wide range of topics, especially his own attitudes to women as compared to the image he had acquired through Bond – a subject they had been warned in advance that he would not care to discuss.

Was he masterful with women?

Connery replied that he was, and that he had had a certain amount of experience in that field. But he had never been a womaniser, as Fleming had called Bond. 'Of course,' he added, 'one never loses the appetite or appreciation for a pretty girl even though one does not indulge it. I still like the company of women but then I like the company of men too. They offer different sorts of fun, of course, but I do not have a retrospective appetite for women in my past.'

The *Playboy* interviewers pressed him on the subject, pointing out that there were critics who claimed that Bond's appeal was based solely on sex, sadism and snobbery and his defenders, most notably Kingsley Amis, found Bond a repository for such admirable qualities as toughness, loyalty and perseverance. How did Connery see him?

Connery: 'He is really a mixture of all that the defenders and the attackers say he is. When I spoke with Ian Fleming about Bond, he said that when the character was conceived Bond was a simple, straightforward, blunt instrument of the police force, a functionary who would carry out his job doggedly. But he also had a lot of idiosyncrasies that were considered snobbish … but the virtues that Amis mentions – loyalty, honesty – are there too. Bond doesn't chase married women, for instance. Judged on that level he comes out rather well.'

Playboy was leading up to a point. Did Connery think Bond was sadistic?

Connery: 'Bond is dealing with rather sadistic adversaries who dream up pretty wild schemes to destroy, maim or mutilate him. He must retaliate in kind, otherwise who was kidding who?'

And now came the crunch … How did Connery feel about roughing up a woman, as Bond sometimes had to do?

His reply, taped and recorded for posterity, was one he would come to regret, not so much for having said what he said but for the way it became repackaged and rewritten out of context down the years thereafter.

'I don't think there is anything particularly wrong about hitting a woman – although I don't recommend doing it in the same way that you'd hit a man,' he said. 'An open-handed slap is justified – if all other alternatives fail and there has been plenty of warning. If a woman is a bitch, or hysterical, or bloody-minded continually, then I'd do it. I think a man has to be slightly advanced, ahead of the woman. I really do – by virtue of the way the man is built, if nothing else. But I wouldn't call it sadistic. I think one of the appeals that Bond has for women, however, is that he is decisive, cruel even. By their nature women aren't decisive – "Shall I wear this? Shall I wear that?" – and along comes a man who is absolutely sure of everything and he's a godsend. And, of course, Bond is never in love with a girl and that helps. He always does what he wants and women like that. It explains why so many women are crazy about men who don't give a rap for them.'

As always, the line between fact and fiction, the actor and the character he is portraying, became blurred. Connery was talking about his own views as they related to James Bond. But the quote returned time and again to haunt him. Taken out of the context of a discussion of the character he had created on screen, the one single sentence that Connery would not be averse to giving a woman a slap was picked up and represented as a news story around the world. Year after year, it was to be rediscovered and rewritten. Years later he made one of his rare appearances on a television chat show, agreeing to an interview with Barbara Walters in America. Primed by her researchers and with his quotation to hand, Walters challenged and chided him. Once more he had to explain the context in which he made the comment and that it was not his normal practice to go around slapping his women. Connery's anger was apparent, as was the glee with which Walters took him to task.

In 1992 the quote resurfaced yet again, this time in an Australian magazine article on Connery – and once more it was republished with all the appearance of being a recent observation when in truth 23 years had passed since he said it. As before, it again bounced around the world, seemingly as a new fact.

There was nothing new or surprising in that, of course. It has always been the fate of famous people, whether entertainers or politicians, that their past pronouncements and observations may be rediscovered and used again and again by profile writers, authors and newshounds. Connery saw it becoming something like a dripping tap and this kind of media exposure where his words were snipped and cut and used in all the devices common to newspaper and magazine journalists in the end merely encouraged him to redouble his efforts to protect his privacy and even his thoughts.

Others had tried, without success, torn between a contractual need to help promote and publicise the film yet retain some control on personal data. Before long, he became something of a trendsetter in the privacy game, though it took colleagues in Hollywood a decade or more to catch on to his technique of giving interviews in which he said nothing of a controversial nature about himself, other than comments which related specifically to his work.

The message was that he, Sean Connery, was an introvert. James

Bond and Sean Connery, the actor, were extroverts. He clearly anguished over his situation in the Bahamas and it showed when the *Playboy* interviewers neared the end of their questioning. 'As a non-extrovert,' they asked, 'does it make you uncomfortable to be the object of so much world-wide press coverage and public adulation?'

Connery: 'To be quite honest, yes. I find that fame tends to turn one from an actor and a human being into a piece of merchandise, a public institution. Well, I don't intend to undergo that metamorphosis. This is why I fight so tenaciously to protect my privacy, to keep interviews like this one to an absolute minimum, to fend off prying photographers who want to follow me around and publicise my every step and every breath. The absolute sanctum sanctorum is my home which is and will continue to be only for me, my wife, my family and my friends. I do not and shall not have business meetings there or acquaintances or journalists. When I work, I work a full stint ... I have no idea how I'll feel or what I will be doing five years from now ... I have always moved around and been prepared to raise my middle finger at the world. I always will.'

Connery had made his position abundantly clear. It was a statement of intent; a declaration of his feelings which were to be built upon and reiterated with even greater resolve at a later date; and as the *Playboy* interviewers left the set of *Thunderball* Connery let it be known that there would be no more interviews for the time being. The remaining writers and editors, hoping for a conversation with the world's most sought-after actor were in the main unlucky. He said no to most of the rest – including a television crew working on a one-hour special, entitled *The Incredible World Of James Bond*. Even Joan Crawford, somehow financially involved with this project, could not get him to change his mind.

Connery was working and nothing would get in the way; he was quiet and lonely, in spite of the crowds who had been enlarged by a contingent of American students over for the Easter break who were plaguing the surrounds of every film location. He managed a good-humoured smile when a group of them swam out to the boat and cried, 'You are our leader. Speak to us!'

One person on the Bond team said she thought that inwardly Connery was badly affected by his troubles but, apart from his anger at the press horde, did not show it on the set. He telephoned Diane daily and after he had been in Nassau for two weeks she flew out from London with her daughter and their son Jason to join him. Naturally, the balloon went up again. Connery innocently fuelled the saga by acquiring a 'hideout' at a place called Love Beach in the Garden of Eden, which of course had the headline writers wetting their proverbials.

Pursued by additional planeloads of press, Connery and Nassau itself was now overpoweringly at the mercy of the gossip hacks and newshounds – as opposed to the more 'serious' writers and interviewers – and the publicity people were showered with unanswerable questions about the couple's love life. By late April the Bahamas was under siege: Were they staying together at Love Beach? Did they share the same bed? Had they made it up? On and on it went, with speculation that Diane, who had been more famous than her husband when they married, could no longer stand the pressure of playing second fiddle to James Bond. Cilento told her friend David Lewin, 'This industry can take hold of you and wrap you up like a piece of meat. But I can tell you, we are not going to let ourselves be merchandised. Sean and I have our own lives to lead in our own way.'

This plaintive cry of intent, the cry of those who become public property, was barely audible in the mad scramble that surrounded them. The semi-beatnik she had married had become the world's 'hottest' star. And this was confirmed at the end of the year when the annual poll of cinema managers conducted by the New York *Motion Picture Herald* voted Connery the most successful money-making star of the year. Elvis Presley was in second place, followed by Julie Andrews and Sophia Loren. Way down the list were Richard Burton (7), Peter Sellers (8), Peter O'Toole (9) and John Wayne (10).

Thunderball was scheduled to open by the end of the year, and May was the deadline for the location work. It was his fourth Bond film, and he was contracted to do two more. He was already talking about calling it a day.

9

NEVER AGAIN (1)

Like a king who did not feel inclined to attend his own coronation, Sean Connery sat at home with his family on the night *Thunderball* opened in London's West End with a double premiere at the London Pavilion *and* the Rialto one after the other, leaving his co-star Claudine Auger to take the bows. Some fans, presumably suffering from withdrawal symptoms at not having caught a glimpse of their idol in the flesh, unscrewed the frames of half a dozen photographs of him on the cinema wall and took them away. Madness was in the air, and Connery was reading an aptly titled script. He was to co-star with Joanne Woodward in *A Fine Madness* (coincidentally Diane Cilento had been offered a part in *Hombre* with Joanne's husband, Paul Newman).

A Fine Madness was about a rebellious poet and, though it was as far removed from Connery's present situation as he was from the seedy bedsit in Chelsea of a decade earlier, the title rather summed up his surroundings, and life in general. It was mad. The money. The adulation. The rows with Cubby and Harry. The fans climbing over his garden wall. And especially the day he went to the toilet in Japan and looked up to discover a camera pointing down at him through an open window. It was *all* mad.

Newspapers never take account of personal feelings. The fine old British tradition of building people up and then knocking them back would eventually allow him to experience the downside. Meanwhile, inside the profession, his friends and colleagues looked on with conflicting degrees of envy and horror. The money was a crucial element, for everyone was talking about it and how much Bond (and/or Connery) was making and how much the latest movie had grossed in the last five minutes, or in the last week or in the last year. But anyone trying to get to the bottom of what had clearly become a continuous, rumbling, rambling row between Connery and the producers is met with contradictions and a complete polarisation of views.

A typical example occurred soon after the opening of *Thunderball*. Kevin McClory who, as a former boy wonder with Mike Todd, had seen his chance and taken it, stood one evening in the American Bar of the Dorchester speaking in a manner which demonstrated that he was rather pleased with himself, having received news that *Thunderball* had taken $1,130,000 in one week in New York alone.

When someone asked if he was getting his 2.5 per cent, he responded gladly that they must be kidding and that a multiplication of that figure by ten would provide a more accurate assessment of his expectations. If McClory was taking such a substantial cut from his one film, how much were Cubby and Harry taking? A calculator wasn't necessary to work out that it was a tidy sum; to arrive at the exact figure would be tiresome, and envy would set in. When *Thunderball* eventually grossed – it is an awful word, but there is no substitute – $28 million in America in one year and as much again elsewhere, it could be seen that McClory was set up for life.

To project this further, the total take so far on the four Bond films was $150 million or more, excluding the merchandising, for an outlay of less than $10 million. Such boasts and speculation were upsetting for Connery. Even though his own pay packet had increased substantially with each new picture, he still did not feel that he was getting his fair share of the huge pot that was being generated by his face while he was taking all the flak.

The million or two so far guaranteed was superbly silly money for an actor to be paid for four months' work every year or so and, true enough, he felt guilty about it initially, especially since his mum and dad were still in their two-roomed tenement flat and refused his offers of a better house. Each picture began to eat more and more into his time, putting pressure on his other work, and the fact remained that the money was being raked in by the producers more quickly than by a croupier on a rigged roulette wheel.

Connery was certainly in an enviable position financially. It was possible to count on one hand, and still have a finger to spare, the number of stars in the entire world who could turn to a producer and say, 'I'll do it for a million dollars. Take it or leave it.' He did exactly that when Charlie Feldman, owner of the rights to the only Bond book that wasn't in the Eon library, called him one day and said, 'You've got two more to do for Cubby. Will you do *Casino Royale* for me after that?'

Connery quoted his price. One million. Feldman winced aloud and said his budget wouldn't run to it. So Connery said he was sorry but he could not do it for less. Feldman then proceeded to pack his production with a host of compensating star names, including David Niven, Woody Allen, Orson Welles, Ursula Andress, Deborah Kerr, John Huston, Charles Boyer and William Holden in what film critic Leslie Halliwell described as 'one of the most shameless wastes of time, talent and money in screen history'.

Connery may well have gained some small satisfaction when he saw Charlie Feldman in a London club not long after *Casino Royale* had been made.

'How did it go, Charlie?' Connery enquired, knowing full well that the producer had been wringing his hands as costs ran into millions.

'I tell you what, Sean,' he replied. 'I wish I'd paid you the million. It would have been a whole lot cheaper.'

The other three actors in the same position were Taylor, Burton and Brando. In fact, the year Connery was making *Thunderball* MGM paid a million dollars (plus a percentage) to Taylor and $750,000 to Burton to appear together in *The Sandpiper*. Straight after that Burton was persuaded to join the current in-vogue genre of spy thrillers when Paul Newman and director Martin Ritt in Hollywood acquired the rights to John Le Carré's classy novel *The Spy Who Came In From The Cold*. His agent asked for and got $750,000, in spite of Paramount's considerable reservations about his drinking; Burton was at the peak of his earning ability, partly because – as he complained bitterly – 'Elizabeth is more famous than the Queen'.

These were the only people who could be compared to Connery's earning power at the time, but there was a difference. As the Scot knew by a check on the box-office receipts in *Variety*, *The Sandpiper* – for all its international hype and with the two most talked-about stars of the decade – took $14 million worldwide and, since Taylor was on 10 per cent of the gross, she collected another $1.4 million on top of the million she had already been paid. Burton received straight fees for *The Sandpiper* and for *The Spy* (amounting to an aggregate of $1.5 million). Jack Warner then signed the pair of them for *Who's Afraid Of Virginia Woolf?* with Taylor receiving $1.1 million and Burton another $750,000 plus perks, such as living expenses and limousines, plus a percentage each.

The point about these telephone numbers was that, as Connery would surely argue, he was doing better business than the Taylor-Burtons together and better business than Brando, who did not finally exceed the guaranteed million-dollar earnings mark until 1966 when he was signed to co-star with Elizabeth Taylor in *Reflections In A Golden Eye*.

Even before he started filming *A Fine Madness* Connery was talking about renegotiating his deal for the next Bond, *You Only*

Live Twice, due to be filmed in the early summer of 1966. He was quietly hinting that it would be the last Bond he would do. Sheilah Graham got wind of the possibility that Connery was on the verge of pulling out and tried to see him. She said it was always more interesting to talk to Sean Connery about James Bond because she knew beforehand that he was going to complain. The prosaic producers, on the other hand, knew the star was unhappy and tried to make it harder for her to see him. So it became a challenge, she said. At the second time of asking, she got to see him.

'What's going on, Sean?' asked Graham. 'Are you quitting or what?'

'This is the last one,' he replied. 'The sooner it's finished the happier I'll be. I don't talk to the producers. It's been a fight since the beginning. If they'd had any sense of fairness, they could have made me a partner. It would have been beneficial for all. It could have been a very happy thing if they had been fair.'

When Sheilah Graham approached the Saltzman–Broccoli camp, they merely reiterated what they had said all along: that they had taken the risk in the first place by buying up Fleming's books which had been around for years with no takers, and they had put their financial muscle behind Connery, an unknown. Anyway, in their view it was Bond not Connery who was the star. Further, Saltzman insisted, they were not ungenerous and pointed to the fact that he personally had just put Michael Caine under a 12-picture contract and had paid him 'most of the $400,000 I get for loaning him out for a picture'. According to Graham, they were not the greedy monsters that Connery saw them as. 'And think of this,' she added, 'when he makes other films, he proves he is a good actor but they are not as successful as his Bonds. He should relax and enjoy his success and good fortune.'

It wasn't just a question of money. There were endless meetings and conferences about the content, more girls and more far-fetched techno-toys. Saltzman remained the ideas man, churning out suggestions so quickly and furiously that his success rate was rather low. However, what they had already decided for *You Only Live Twice* was that a number of the behind-the-camera regulars in the Bond team were to be replaced, according to Saltzman, to keep it fresh.

Director Lewis Gilbert, just completing *Alfie*, which confirmed Michael Caine as a major international star in a film that was made for under a million dollars, was to direct the next Bond. He had turned it down twice because four had already been made and a pattern was being established. Exactly, said the producers; they wanted to keep injecting new ideas, and the budget had been increased to around $6 million. Gilbert accepted. There was also to be a new editor, a new cinematographer and, most interestingly of all, Roald Dahl had been hired to write the screenplay. Even so, it was not a happy ship, at least not as far as Connery was concerned. Personal aggravations apart, the whole Bond concept, he believed, was moving even further towards a comic strip and he had reached a stage where he was simply not talking to Harry Saltzman.

The rumbles rumbled on. Among the problems uppermost in Connery's mind was where his family was going to live. The house at Acton had become so well known that there was a constant group of people lingering nearby hoping to catch sight of him and his family. Fans had taken to roaming the gardens, there had been two burglaries and, all in all, a worrying situation had developed to the extent that he decided to sell, and furthermore announce publicly that he was selling so that perhaps the pestering would stop. He placed an advertisement offering the house for sale at £17,950 under the heading, 'Sean Connery, the motion picture actor, offers for sale ...' In its place they bought a property in Spain and sought anonymity in London, with a Victorian house in Putney.

A Fine Madness was the name of the film, and it offered a temporary haven, an arty, with-it film that gave Connery the opportunity of taking in the comparatively relaxing air of

Greenwich Village. It was a complete change of pace and setting and it was a wonder, in many respects, that he managed to psyche himself into such a vastly different role while his head churned with the demands being made on him elsewhere. The film was to be shot on location in New York, and Cilento was filming at the same time in Phoenix, Arizona, with Paul Newman on *Hombre*. She took the children and their nanny with her and there was some weekend commuting for a couple of months until both had finished their respective projects.

The role in *A Fine Madness* came close to Connery's own heart. The underlying connotations of the present, along with echoes from his past, were similar, if exaggerated, as he played an out-and-out rebel sacked for rudeness, haunted by his poetry that no one listened to and seeking freedom and peace. It gave him the opportunity to at least suspend his audience's notion that this was just James Bond taking a breather. The screenplay, adapted by Elliot Baker from his own novel, provided Connery with a character which in the wrong hands could have come out as an unappealing no-hoper.

The critics recognised his achievement in turning the character into an interesting and funny man, one with whom American audiences could identify because of his ability to repel authority and cut through pretentiousness. The reviews in America were good and *Films And Filming* magazine made an interesting observation about his voice and accent: '[Connery's] accent becomes more and more engaging with every film. When you hear him you can trace the story of his life … of metropolitan Scotland, the showbiz drawl of London, the transatlantic snarl of New York; without losing any of its origins, the accent gets richer and more delightful with each new venture.'

Connery produced one of his best non-Bond performances so far, though he found the British audiences, and more especially the British media, less inclined to accept him in any other role than James Bond for the time being. *A Fine Madness* did nothing to alleviate that situation.

By the time filming began on *You Only Live Twice*, word was about that Connery had somehow managed to persuade Broccoli and Saltzman to release him from his contract, leaving him free to negotiate one-off deals for each remaining picture he did for them. There was talk of an almighty bust-up, especially between himself and Saltzman, which seemed to be borne out by the fact that there was absolutely no contact between them, even on set. They had apparently agreed terms for the movie currently in production and the producers were hoping Connery would have a change of heart and continue on after that; it was a notion that certainly did not accord with Connery's feelings at the time.

However, the crazy circus that surrounded the whole proceeding was building up to another crescendo as they headed to Japan for the first location shooting. Roald Dahl had written his script with remarkable speed, though there were changes to be made and he was warned he would be needed in the Far East for revision. This and Connery's disquiet proved to be the least of their problems as the usual planeloads of technicians, actors, equipment and sets were on their way to Tokyo.

The vital ingredient of the girls, always a difficult and laborious task – pawing over mountains of photographs, calling them in for a walk-past and so on – had become even more of a problem. It wasn't just a case of arguing amongst themselves who they should hire. This time the Japanese government was involved because permission had to be sought for filming at various locations. An order came down from the highest level that, as this was a major international movie to be shown in pretty well every country in the world, there should be some Japanese girls among the cast.

This stipulation was communicated to Broccoli while they were still working at Pinewood and several Japanese girls were brought in for auditions. None suited. Most had lost that natural bloom of youthful innocence in the process of becoming westernised. The producers decided not to use them, but the Japanese insisted and at that late stage they could not argue. Finally several Japanese girls were flown from Tokyo but the two leading contenders, Mie Hama and Akiko Wakabayashi, could not speak English and a crash course had to be arranged. Mie had difficulty with her lessons and Lewis Gilbert could wait no longer; they decided to drop her.

One of the other Japanese members of cast was asked if he would mind explaining to Mie why she had been dropped. Cubby gave him some money and told him to take her out to dinner and explain their problem – that the film was being held up and that cost money.

The next morning the actor went to Cubby's office to report on the events of the previous evening.

'Well, did you tell her?' asked Broccoli.

'Yes,' replied the actor, 'I told her.'

'And how did she take it?'

'Oh well, you know how it is with the Japanese, Mr Broccoli,' the actor responded quietly and without a flicker of emotion. 'She could not return to Japan and lose face like that, not after all the pre-publicity back home. James Bond is king in Japan, and she's got the big role opposite him. She would look very silly.'

Cubby stirred himself quickly and looked around the table where a meeting had been in progress.

'Well,' he said. 'I think you can say we are having second thoughts. She's not so bad. She can keep at it and we'll manage to find a role for her somehow.' Mie eventually accepted a smaller role as Kissy, the island girl who dives for pearls whom Bond falls for.

The Japanese girls were not the only problem. They had still not cast Blofeld, the central villain . Saltzman, who had been looking for a Gert Frobe type of actor, turned up one day and announced he had discovered a Czechoslovakian who fitted the role exactly. He was brought to Pinewood Studios to begin work, but he was not a success. Lewis Gilbert said he would have to go, and go he did.

Donald Pleasence, later to become a good friend of Connery's and a near neighbour in Spain, was quietly taking a breather when the telephone rang.

'They wanted me for Blofeld in a hurry,' he told me. 'They had already started work on the film and wanted me to read the script and create a character totally different to anything that had been done before, and I think we achieved that. Because of the rush, most of my role was filmed in close-up at Pinewood so I did not see a great deal of Sean, but I was aware of what was going on. It was something of a turning point for him, because he came out and said he would not do another Bond movie; this was going to be the last. I did not discuss it with him at the time but I could tell it was a delicate issue. So I did my three weeks of intensive work, and took the money and ran, as it were. I could see, though, it was a difficult decision for him and it took a good deal of courage to turn his back on Bond, a lot of people would have stayed with it until they died or got the push. But it was the correct decision, of course, because he made a great success of his career after Bond and I admire him very much for that.'

With talk abroad that Connery was quitting, the press pack descended upon Tokyo in another great horde, mingling with the even greater crowds of Japanese fans to whom James Bond was seen as some kind of god, this tall, striding, mysterious figure towering above most of them by a foot. Rather less intrusive than the rat pack was Alan Whicker, who had arrived with his own camera crew ready to follow the Bond production unit around the country for a documentary on the making of *You Only Live Twice*, which was shown on BBC2 in March 1967.

Connery and Cilento journeyed to Japan via the pretty route through the Philippines, trying to miss the travelling roadshow, but even in Manila they were soon recognised and mobbed. The local police force was summoned to rescue them from the crowds who surrounded them within seconds.

In Tokyo it was worse.

The Tokyo Hilton was under siege 24 hours a day, not merely from the dozens of press but also from hundreds of fans, every one of them anxious to get a photograph of their idol. It would have been amusing if it wasn't so annoying, but even so the story of Connery's bodyguards must bring a smile. As the crowds surrounded and surged at his every move, he had been provided with the services of 12 heavyweight Japanese security men who were to encircle him as he made his way to work each day, just as they would a visiting president or Frank Sinatra.

On their first morning the guards were lined up to form a human corridor down which he should pass. As he did so, almost without exception, the men reached inside their pockets as if going for a gun, pulled out cameras and snapped pictures of the great man at close range. After that the guards gave him ultimate protection when he went walkabout, though there were occasions when it was simply impossible.

In several sequences Connery was required to walk alone through the streets of Tokyo, and a quiet period was chosen so that the crowds would hopefully not be a problem. On their first attempt, however, hundreds of Japanese appeared from nowhere and within 15 yards of beginning his stroll Connery was virtually lost. All that could be seen of him as Guy Hamilton and his crew began to film was his anguished face as he stood head and shoulders over a huge mass of black-haired heads.

Eventually, the Bond film unit moved to the village of Akime, in the south-west, to which they travelled by bullet train. It was such an out-of-the-way location that they did not expect any crowd. When they arrived, however, they discovered that several thousand Japanese sightseers had beaten them to it, and an enterprising bus company was already taking bookings for excursion tours around the film locations. The local police had to send for reinforcements and it took three days before they were able to get the crowds under control. Alan Whicker and his crew kept at a discreet distance, recording the continuous mêlée. In his commentary Whicker said he would never have believed what was happening had he not seen it with his own eyes. He thought Connery was a hero to withstand such pressures, although he noted that he seemed tired and ruffled. Diane told Whicker, 'He's been pushed beyond normal limits because everywhere you go someone's following him, or hanging out of a tree.'

They were trapped for hours in their hotel, and spent many off-duty moments playing table tennis. Connery also agreed to a number of press interviews, which pleased publicist Glenn Rose after the trouble he had experienced getting Connery to talk to the media in the Bahamas. In fact, he agreed to give 11 fairly major interviews.

It was only later, said Tom Carlisle, the six-foot eight doom-voiced publicity director for the early Bond films, that they realised some of Connery's comments displayed his eagerness to see the last of 007. Carlisle said he did not harbour any grudges about Connery's reaction, and 'always understood' his resentment about the communications vacuum he had been led into by the popularity of the films, but there had been nothing in his professional background that could have prepared him for the onslaught that came with each Bond film.

'I know that in England,' Carlisle said, 'it is possible for the most successful male actors who avoid outright scandal in their personal lives to live out their entire careers without experiencing a half of the brouhaha that Connery had endured on any one Bond film. During the first five years, as publicity director of these films, I was the person most concerned with bridging the credibility gap between this legend and the honest actor who repeatedly described his involvement with it as "Frankenstein's monster". Mine was not a gratifying experience; in those five years we dealt with more than 10,000 members of the world's press – and yet Sean Connery's relations with them deteriorated to a state of armed truce. For the last two years of that period I was unable to convey to him the relative merits of a story in the *Birmingham Bugle* or *Time* magazine. As long as they concerned James Bond, he did not really want to know.'

As to the films themselves, Connery agreed with the critics who were complaining that the story and character of the Bond movies was being obliterated by the increased scientific content. *You Only Live Twice* was a further example: the budget allotted to designer Ken Adams was the equivalent of the entire cost of making *Dr No* and included the building of a volcano on the backlot at Pinewood 126 feet high, 400 feet in diameter, with 200 miles of tubular steel, 200 tons of plaster and 250,000 square feet of canvas.

Now the serious critics began to take the movies as a matter of course. All the things that made Bond original, a one-off, had either become commonplace through repetition or had been overwhelmed by the emphasis on technology. Connery knew he was playing second fiddle to gadgetry and everyone on the set knew that was the direction the producers had decided upon. They had gone for sparkling, way-out adventure, tinged as always with U-rated sex. Accepting that it was their decision to make, then *You Only Live Twice* may be viewed for what it was: Bond at its most expensive, lavish and spectacular, packed with local colour, noted for the superb creation of Blofeld by Donald Pleasence – proving there was still scope for fine acting – and the especially impressive sets which filled the screen for the explosive climax.

Anyway, Connery had made his decision – that there was no better time to go. He had made his mind up even before he started the picture and as soon as he finished *You Only Live Twice* he announced that he had made 'positively my last appearance' as James Bond. Money was not the reason for his departure. His friend Eric Sykes knew that it went much deeper:

'True, he was fed up with being Bond and with all the demands on him. When he became established, they still tried to make him behave like Bond and go around to all the parties and press receptions in the toupee and smart suits, and all the gear, and he said "Oh, bollocks" to all that. He just wasn't interested; he hated it like nothing else, in spite of the fact that it was a potential gold mine. But the key to it wasn't so much the money, or that Bond had become a comic strip or even that he was expected to play the role off screen as well as on. It was simply that Sean always wanted to stretch himself, and still does. Bond no longer stretched him; that's what was really getting to him.'

Connery confirmed that himself. In an interview published soon after he completed the Japanese adventure he said that Bond was 'bloody killing me as an actor'. He acknowledged his desire to break out because it had become increasingly difficult to plan other projects with Bond films taking longer and longer to produce. Whereas *Dr No* had taken little more than four months from start to finish, *You Only Live Twice* had taken six. 'It put me in a very vulnerable position,' he said.

It could have been so different, Connery mused in one interview years later, and thought it was quite feasible that in other circumstances the distributing studio, United Artists, could by then have been owned by Connery, Broccoli and Saltzman. Instead he was leaving with a bitter taste.

If there was some creativity remaining, it centred around the props and not the people. In comparison to *Dr No*, Connery the actor was no longer required as such, a fact made abundantly clear by the publicist Tom Carlisle. He was soon to be found projecting the Eon theory that James Bond would go on for ever, regardless of who played him. Naturally they would have preferred Connery to continue, if for no other reason than financial security, but if he had made up his mind not to do another Bond film then the producers were certain they would find someone with the same qualities that had come across when they interviewed Connery as 'an experienced nobody'.

The job specification as it had evolved since the beginning of the Bond series did not require a man of outstanding acting ability, Carlisle claimed. It would have been welcome, of course, but was not the overriding consideration. Looks, movement and superb athletic condition were more important. In other words, Eon was prepared to insert an advertisement in the Sits Vac columns: 'Wanted: A new 007. Must be tall, dark, handsome, virile and athletic. Acting experience desired, but not essential.'

All of which confirmed what Connery had been feeling for a long time.

But Connery was not alone in his discontent. The two producers were themselves beginning to think of splitting up. As they finished filming *You Only Live Twice*, *Variety* reported that the Eon marriage was crumbling. The complexities of the Bond partnership – which *Variety* speculated would require a United Nations council meeting to apportion the proceeds – was the only stumbling block to a break-up.

They were already going their own separate ways with other projects. Saltzman was producing film versions of Len Deighton's novels *The Ipcress File*, *Funeral In Berlin* and *Billion Dollar Brain*, starring Michael Caine, the new wonder boy of British acting and overnight star after ten years in the business. Meanwhile, their togetherness in the Bond empire – which apart from the pictures now involved the supply and sale of more than 100 different licensed merchandising items produced by 16 separate manufacturers and selling more than $50 million worth a year – would take months to unravel, though it was eventually achieved and Saltzman moved into management with a multi-million share-out from the partnership.

Connery did not leave an immensely wealthy man. He was comfortable, of course, but had nothing to compare with the bank balances of Cubby and Harry. Out of the shackles, he began to have more expansive thoughts of his own and these would include a desire which comes to all successful people from modest backgrounds: that they should return to their homeland and give something back.

It may well have been that some elements of the publicity surrounding him through those heady days of James Bond had found the mark, when so-called friends claimed he had turned his back on his old mates from the early days in the profession and forgotten about his roots; that he could no longer be bothered with Scotland and especially did not wish to be reminded of his upbringing at Fountainbridge.

This did not seem to be borne out by the film studio biographies, released with each picture. They invariably mentioned his poverty-stricken childhood and, in fact, he personally appeared more than anxious to continue to get the message across. In a studio press release for Warners Bros, he dictated the following statement for inclusion with his biographical notes:

> [Not long] ago, the establishment was in complete control. On stage and screen the monopoly was held by actors who reflected the fads and foibles of the so-called upper classes. An actor had no chance unless he was the stereotype gentleman. Ronald Coleman, Noel Coward, Rex Harrison and Leslie Howard projected this image. Great actors, I admit, but they hardly typified the average Englishman ... It wasn't until the rebellion against class distinction, which revealed life as it really is, that things began to change ... and audiences could identify with the non-hero.

As to his involvement with the proletariat in the place of his birth, it could hardly be said that he had, to date, been seen as a man actively concerned with his home ground; in fact it would have been easy to gain the impression that he did not wish to return there more often than was necessary for family commitments. A sudden surge in this direction was apparent, through the combination of having a secure future in terms of money, having more time available at the end of Bond and possessing a genuine desire to help.

In the years to come he quietly began to disprove the theory that he was simply not bothered. His interest materialised along diverse channels through which he eventually poured some creditable chunks of his personal fortune. In 1967, between movies, he became interested in a project to revitalise the Scottish shipyards and especially in the rather revolutionary proposals of the Scottish industrialist Sir Iain Stewart, whom he met at a golfing dinner in London. Connery was intrigued by Stewart's planned experiment in the shipyards involving a five-year deal to enhance management and worker co-operation, a scheme that received the backing of Harold Wilson's Labour government.

He was sufficiently impressed by Stewart's argument that he travelled to Scotland to look at the proposals for himself and talk to shipyard workers personally. He decided to finance and film a documentary about the problems of Clydeside, which he entitled *The Bowler And The Bunnet* (the bunnet being a flat cap). The film was to show Stewart's experiments with worker participation and the breakdown of restrictive practices and manning agreements that dogged pretty well every section of British industry in the 1960s. Connery wrote special scenes showing carpenters becoming painters and decorators when the need arose and he had workers and union officials in the boardroom – all of which was much talked of but, in practice, unheard of; they were interesting theories, but ahead of their time.

The film failed to get a national airing, although it was shown on Scottish television and was apparently liked in Moscow. Ultimately, Stewart's attempts to modernise labour relations in the shipyards failed. He resigned soon after his company merged with the Upper Clyde Shipbuilders the following year, and 15 months later the new company went into bankruptcy.

Connery's sortie back to Scotland was a forerunner of his involvement with the formation of the Scottish International Educational Trust a couple of years later, to provide scholarships and bursaries for underprivileged young Scots, and other charitable acts such as the establishment of a drama chair at Strathclyde University, financed through Connery's own enterprise and various fundraisers such as golf tournaments. Some poured scorn on this sudden upsurge of national pride, but in a major television show he reasserted his commitment to Scotland with such fervour that the Scottish National Party made an approach to see if he would be interested in standing for Parliament.

He declined but offered to help out whenever he could. His affiliation with the ScotNats became a developing aspect of his life, though not a mainstream activity. His politics were low key and his comments reserved for sounding off in private.

The Scottish diversion, however, was a mere detour from the job at hand, which was to re-create himself in the eyes of the movie-going public. The task was not that easy and, as later co-star and acquaintance Sir John Gielgud assessed for me, the key to future success in his acting was to widen his range sufficiently to 'escape the Bond image ... which must have been very difficult for him'.

Difficult, and never plain sailing. It would soon become apparent that going solo was filled with pitfalls and risks, and there were some high-blown but ultimately dubious projects that were to provide rather unstable foundations on which to base his future.

10

'HE'LL REGRET IT'

There were plenty around who said Connery would sink into obscurity without Bond, and there were some who would have *liked* him to fail. And yet the period immediately beyond what was being described as his final appearance in the role seemed filled with potential and possibility. In many ways it would also be a test of his acting strength and personal confidence in that he was working without a safety net, with the cushion of a task which he performed well and with ease replaced by the volatility of diversity. The late-1960s became a graveyard of high hopes in the film business, particularly in Hollywood where the climate of burgeoning independent producers and the nervousness of the money men had produced a scattergun approach to film-making. Connery would discover that he could not remain unaffected by the peculiarities of an industry where big names, big money and great expectations seemed at that moment to be foundering in a sea of mediocrity.

A big name was assumed to mean everything to the status and eventual success or failure of a film. Connery was a big name and the focus was directed upon him for different reasons. Dozens of scripts arrived for his perusal; directors and producers were calling with all kinds of ideas, some of them plain daft. One Italian producer even signed up Connery's brother Neil, who had never acted in his life and was still working at his trade in Edinburgh, to appear in a spoof Bond film with Daniela Bianchi (who co-starred in *From Russia With Love*). Although James Bond and Sean Connery were never mentioned by name, the implication was clear. Connery, angered by what he saw as exploitation of himself and Neil and about the small sum that the Italians had paid his brother, tried to stop it. When he failed the cheeky producer even asked him to help promote the film which, of course, he refused in Celtic fashion.

Meanwhile, his association with Bond seemed on the face of it to have been severed. The producers made a final attempt to hire him for the next in the series, *On Her Majesty's Secret Service*, with a payslip alleged to be approaching a million dollars up front and a percentage behind. Connery said no again, and then found his future being speculated upon as he became caught up in the backwash of the publicity and hype surrounding the hunt for a new Bond. The producers temporarily settled on the unknown George Lazenby, whose biggest starring role to date had been in a chocolate bar advert; they were intent on proving that Connery's departure would not affect the popularity of Bond.

Connery, determined and cautious, began carefully trying to pinpoint the work that would best suit his need to escape, as Gielgud put it, the James Bond aura as quickly as possible, and though scrutiny and caution were the key words they would not necessarily guarantee success. In fact, there followed a fairly worrying few years immediately after *You Only Live Twice* and, although financially rewarding, he was personally left dissatisfied and, some said, unsure of both himself and his future.

There was, however, no sign of that when he began filming *Shalako* early in 1968. 'He was cheerful and full of beans,' Eric Sykes, who was also in the film, recalled. 'We sang all the way in the back of the car taking us to work on location in Spain. It was a five-hour drive, and he couldn't have been happier. He was even more cheerful after we'd stopped at a roadside bar and the owner produced a dusty old half-filled bottle of Johnny Walker Black Label from under the counter which we consumed by the tumbler full at about thruppence a glass, and continued on our journey, singing all the way.'

This first project Connery accepted after Bond had a special appeal. Producer Euan Lloyd held the rights to the Louis L'Amour novel *Shalako*, about a former US cavalry officer turned guide who leads a party of European aristocrats through Apache country on a big-game hunt. The special appeal came in Lloyd's description. He wanted to make a Western that everyone would remember – like *Shane* in 1953, which Connery especially liked. That apart, he clearly enjoyed the prospect of a Western; not a cowboy as such, but with plenty of Indians and the chance to extricate himself from the Savile Row suite image.

Lloyd was full of enthusiasm. He said it would be Britain's first major Western and would contend for world recognition. Connery was offered an encouraging financial package reported to be worth a guaranteed $1.2 million to be paid over nine months. Lloyd had put together strong backing, largely from British sources, and had a budget approaching $5 million which would enable a good cast list made up of Brigitte Bardot, along with the top British line-up of Stephen Boyd, Jack Hawkins, Honor Blackman, Peter Van Eyck, Eric Sykes and the former American footballer Woody Strode. Furthermore, the director was to be Edward Dmytryk, the famed member of the Hollywood Ten and *film noir* era, which many would have seen as a plus sign for the project. Richard Burton, who worked with him a couple of years later, reckoned he was past his best, though the feeling was apparently mutual.

Connery was more doubtful about Bardot, whom he imagined would attract the same kind of trivialised press attention he had been trying to avoid, although that was surely the point: for Taylor and Burton, read Connery and Bardot. It certainly had the kind of commercial ring to it that would fire the imagination of the publicists, and Connery knew that better than anyone. But the idea never took off.

In June 1967 he flew with Lloyd to look for suitable locations in Mexico. Bardot, according to Sykes, did not fancy South America. She had filmed there previously and preferred a European site. There were also labour problems in Mexico and so they settled on Spain, around Almeria. Connery arrived two weeks early in order to be given horse-riding lessons by his former stunt arranger on Bond, Bob Simmons. As Sykes pointed out, Connery had never learned to ride and the role required him to spend half his time in the saddle. 'He was a very proficient horseman by the time we started,' said Sykes. 'He looked as if he had been riding all his life.'

Brigitte Bardot, still a major star, arrived on location in fitting fashion, speeding through a dust cloud in a white Rolls Royce pursued by a large posse of photographers and an entourage following on behind. She took over several rooms at the best hotel in the area while Connery rented a villa for Diane and his family to join him. The press had turned up mob handed again, spurred by extravagantly worded press releases which portrayed Connery and Bardot as the most excitingly cast twosome around starring in the most sensuous film Bardot had made. It was a gossip writer's dream encounter, but if hearts were fluttering Connery's was not apparently among them.

There was even a television documentary being shot entitled *Shalako Safari*, such were the expectations for the success of the movie. 'It was a brave undertaking, really,' said Sykes. 'A Western with an international cast seemed a good idea, and had wide appeal. The Germans used to do these expeditions in those times, the 1890s, always carrying their bone china and the crystal goblets. These things did happen. The most striking thing about the film, though, was to work with Sean Connery, and I am sure that anyone who does gets to know just how good an actor he is.'

It soon became clear that Connery was the driving force, in

more ways than as the male lead. Bardot, who came to the set as 'the star', expected to be treated as such. There was also a tenseness with her former friend Stephen Boyd and rows with Dmytryk almost from the outset. Honor Blackman said it was not an especially happy film; nerves were jangling and patience was stretched. At one point Bardot threatened to quit. It was either a mark of the problems they were facing with a somewhat turgid script, or of Connery's true ability to conduct his own on-set editing. Eric Sykes described it as an 'instinctive, almost intuitive quality' which Connery possesses:

'We were sitting side by side in the sunshine in Spain learning our lines. Mine were few compared to his, but I noticed that every so often he would tear half a page, or even a whole page, of dialogue out of his script and throw it on the floor. There was a pile of a dozen or more screwed-up pieces of paper, so I asked him why he was tearing these bits out. He said it was unnecessary crap that was not needed. He was actually editing his part as he went along, apparently without reference to the director Eddie Dmytryk. One scene in particular was with him and Brigitte Bardot, a long scene where they were sitting around a pool and he was required in the script to explain what he did about satisfying his sexual desires in the wilderness and she was reflecting on memories of Europe – it went on and on and on, for about eight minutes. Sean's editing, those pages that he was tearing out and throwing on the floor, turned it into a slick two- or three-minute scene, and much better for it. I had never seen anyone do that before, nor since. He did not even consult Eddie Dmytryk, a well-thought-of director. Sean had already done the thinking and ripped out the gash material. Eddie did not challenge it because when he saw what Sean had done he knew it was right.'

Discussing, in 1992, work on *Shalako*, and able to draw on a 25-year friendship with Connery, Sykes remained eager to expound on the qualities of the man and his generosity as an actor:

'Those of us who worked with him in those early days – and probably more so now – were able to get first hand his sheer professionalism. Everyone on the set of *Shalako* admired him, especially the way he sort of took over. Brigitte was supposed to be the star, but Sean was carrying the production on his back, and she recognised that; in the end, she admitted it was his picture and although some critics said it wasn't that good, that's a matter of opinion. Anyway it would have been a good deal worse without him. From a personal point of view, I can quote a specific example of how he helped me. I was in difficulty because of my hearing problem and wore a hearing aid which I had to take out when we shot a scene. We were doing the a scene in a barn, about eight of us sitting around in the hay listening to Sean giving a longish speech, and I had the next line to Sean's. Without my hearing aid I would have missed my cue, so Sean devised a simple answer. When he came to the end of his piece he rubbed his ear, which looked perfectly natural on screen, but it was his signal for me to say my lines.'

Connery returned from Spain agitated and fed up. The film had not turned out at all well, and he knew it. The final edit only heightened his fears. The mixed critical reaction could not have surprised him. His personal reviews were good, and the *Sunday Telegraph* acclaimed Connery's 'convincing portrayal' as being suited to take its place among memorable Western heroes such as James Stewart and Gary Cooper. *Shalako* was given a massive publicity build-up with premieres in Munich, London, Glasgow and New York. Bardot attracted a huge throng of fans in Germany and the London opening was accorded royal attendance, with Princess Margaret and Lord Snowdon. In Scotland Connery took his family to the Glasgow Coliseum and the crowds cheered their famous Edinburgh son. Thereafter, and with some mauling by influential critics in America, the film drifted disappointingly away, remembered only by his most ardent fans.

In the annual poll of the Top Ten box-office stars for that year Connery had wilted from number one to sixth and he did not even make the Top Ten in the US. It was too early to become nervous about the future, and perhaps he never really was, but lesser men might have considered that if his star status was to survive then he desperately needed a runaway success to push him back into pole position. In fact, promising though the immediate future seemed, it merely held two more disappointments.

Great expectations had been roused by, and in theory there ought to have been nothing wrong with, his next film, *The Molly Maguires*. It was a good story with good stars, it was in the hands of Martin Ritt (director of *Hombre, Hud, Edge Of The City* and *The Spy Who Came In From The Cold*) and was strongly supported by Paramount with a hefty $11 million budget. Connery set off for America for the four-month shooting schedule in May 1968 with high hopes of restoring his confidence and job satisfaction.

Richard Harris, then 34 and fiery, and Samantha Eggar were awaiting him at the other end to co-star. It was a good team of progressive young actors, as good a team as you could put together. Yet there is always the uncertainty. Have they made the right choice? Is the film suitable for their style? Will the film turn out the way they've interpreted the script? Will they, the actors, mess it up? Will the director lose his grip? Will the producers insist on some idiosyncrasy for commercial reasons and ruin it? Will the editors and the final cut take away its heart and soul? Nothing changes in the preliminary thoughts and there was a topical discussion between Harris and Connery one day while waiting to film. They had somehow or other got on to discussing religion.

'I am a very religious man,' Harris proclaimed.

'Oh, yeah?' said Connery.

'Yes, but I don't believe in God,' said Harris. 'If I regret anything I've done then I'll forgive myself … I'm not going to confess my sins to someone else.'

'I know the feeling,' Connery said, and they began talking about regrets.

There were a few, said Harris, largely about the films he had chosen to get involved in. *The Molly Maguires* – at that stage – was not one of those he regretted though it might become one; nor was

This Sporting Life which had been his carriage to stardom five years earlier and remained his favourite.

'I've been guilty of a lack of judgement in my choice of roles,' he admitted to Connery. 'I turned down *The Ipcress File* which went to Michael Caine; but I did *Caprice* with Doris Day. I once walked off an aeroplane when I learned that was being shown. *The Red Desert* was also a miserable experience. Antonioni completely misrepresented the project. If he had not made a career in the motion-picture business, he would surely have been head of the Mafia. And then there was *Mutiny On The Bounty* – it looked terrific with Brando, etc. and was a total fucking disaster.'

And so here they were again, hoping that they had chosen right, and on location in the town of Eckley, Pennsylvania, population 87, a godforsaken place not many years off becoming a virtual ghost town. The coal mines that used to support it were long ago closed, and the few residents who remained were mostly pensioners. But Eckley was a remnant of a piece of American history and the home of the true story on which the film was based.

The Molly Maguires was the nickname of a bunch of rugged Irish immigrant miners who formed a secret union in the 1870s to fight against the brutal exploitation of coal miners by the Pennsylvanian owners. They were a violent crowd who fought for their rights to such a degree that their local preacher warned them constantly of the adage, 'He who lives by the sword (or knife) shall die by the sword.' Director Ritt read an outline of the story by screenwriter Walter Bernstein and gave him the go-ahead for a full treatment.

He saw *The Molly Maguires* as the subversive start of the labour movement in America. There was a built-in sub-plot, with the story of the miners running as a sort of modern-day parable on civil rights, which had of course become a major issue in the 1960s. There was a similar thread to both stories and Bernstein and Ritt perceived the idea of using a documentary technique and initially wanted to film in black and white. Paramount did not think this was a good idea. Why go in black and white when all of those wonderful new colour facilities were becoming available? Everyone expected colour. So Ritt overcame that by spraying the buildings with coal dust so they looked grimy; it was black and white by design. It seemed like a good idea at the time.

Connery first discussed the script for *The Molly Maguires* with Ritt when he visited Diane Cilento while she was making *Hombre* with Paul Newman. As soon as the financing had been confirmed Ritt signed him up. The fee was excellent, reportedly approaching a million dollars and a share of the profits, and it must be said Connery was still riding on the crest of the Bond wave in terms of his value to a film.

The story also appealed to Connery himself, having just made his own documentary on labour relations, and he was happy to talk about his affinity with the character he was portraying and why he wanted to do the film. As always the actor rolled back the shades of time to liken the militant miner fighting for social justice with his own background, which was obviously a set piece for inclusion in any interview. 'Unless you give a man something aside from malnutrition,' he said, 'you're going to get retaliation, terrorism. I know what it's like. Members of my family worked in the mines.'

Ritt must have heard of the saying attributed to Jack Warner, 'If you want to send a message, use Western Union.' In spite of it, he seemed intent on sending a message in *The Molly Maguires*. As he ended the shooting, he enthusiastically told a gathering of newsmen, 'Last winter I visited an anthracite mine and suddenly my old radicalism began to flare anew. I don't intend to make a polemic, but I will bring to this movie my human bias for people who are being put upon. Having been through the McCarthy era, I will naturally bring a certain bias to a story about a police informer who came to be regarded as a hero in this country.'

The director dealt with a good deal of his bias in the picture, and the film had considerable merit. The Paramount people were not impressed, however. The editing was tampered with and Ritt claimed his film lost a lot in the final cut version. Paramount's answer was to shelve it for 18 months. It was not released until the early summer of 1970, to mixed reviews. Harris and Connery were both applauded but Connery admitted that the film just did not catch fire; the audiences agreed and it joined the ranks of the top ten biggest losers of the decade.

Though Connery and Cilento were settled in the new house at Putney, visiting friends said it had a kind of unfinished feel to it, as if they had not quite completed the furnishings. There was an emptiness, said one who was close, and even an impermanent feel to the place. This may have been explained by future developments. The marriage had undoubtedly been strained to breaking point by recent events and perhaps there was no route back to the way things were. Connery had joined Diane on a visit to Australia and they had spent some time at their homes abroad in Spain and the Bahamas. It was clearly a difficult, if not a fractious, time as if he were in limbo. Michael Caine recalled a scene of domestic non-bliss which occurred while he was staying with them in Nassau. Diane was cooking lunch and Connery and Caine went out for a drink. One thing led to another, recalled Caine, and when they returned for lunch two hours later it came flying through the air as Sean said, 'Darling, we're home.' The pair of them were covered in green beans and gravy. Diane had written a novel, aptly entitled *The Manipulators*, which was now published and she was working on a second. She and Connery were vaguely talking about working together on a film and Connery had discussed a number of theatre projects, including directing a play on Broadway. He was also working on a screenplay for *Macbeth* which he planned to direct. The project was abandoned a year or so later when he heard Roman Polanski and Kenneth Tynan had had a similar thought.

In spite of his marriage problems, Connery continued to work as hard as ever. In March 1968 he completed a rapid intervention in a film called *The Red Tent*, appearing as Arctic explorer Roald Amundsen. The film was based upon the true story of General

Nobile's 1928 airship expedition to the Arctic and, since Amundsen died tragically while trying to rescue survivors when the ship crashed, Connery's participation was limited to three weeks of filming in Russian locations.

The movie itself was a mammoth production, beautifully created against spectacular true-life landscapes, meticulously researched for exact detail, exceptionally well scripted and in production for 66 weeks in difficult locations almost regardless of cost. *The Red Tent* was being spoken of in epic proportions, one of those films that would go down as a classic. Even though his appearance was limited, Connery received star billing above Peter Finch, Hardy Kruger and Claudia Cardinale, much to the dismay of Finch, incidentally, but that was not Connery's doing.

The producers were merely exploiting his name, but the name, the budget and the great hopes were all in vain. *The Red Tent*, a joint venture between Russian and Italian producers, was shown in those two countries on its release in 1969. But Paramount, the international distributors, chose to shelve it for almost two years. It was not shown in America until the autumn of 1971 – the second of Connery's films in a row to be put on the rack by Paramount. It was eventually released to a limited circulation in Britain in June 1972. Reviewers were divided. The *New York Times* thought that director Mikhail Kalatozov had shown remarkable ingenuity in taking a situation which offered such potential and making it so dull. Others were less critical, offering acclaim for the visual effects which, as one suggested, were the best since *Dr Zhivago*. It crashed, however, and joined *The Molly Maguires* on the list of biggest losers in recent times.

It was one more example, if Connery needed to be told, that an interesting story and an almost bottomless pit of money did not necessarily add up to a soaraway success. In truth, *The Red Tent* was a movie out of its time. A new era had already dawned; battles with authority were being waged; students were rioting and getting shot. World leaders were nervous and civil rights issues were flaring again, along with the growing pains of women's rights and gay rights. Timothy Leary was extolling the virtues of turning on, tuning in and dropping out. It was another kind of time warp, with its own genre of films just as it had been a decade earlier with new ideas like *Dr No*, produced on a shoestring of less than a million dollars. And at that very moment, in 1969, another such film was to lead the way into the latest diversion. Dennis Hopper and Peter Fonda were putting the finishing touches to a small, unheralded road movie called *Easy Rider* which no one would back until they had squeezed $375,000 as a total budget out of Roger Corman and went on to make $34 million. This was the scene that Connery would find himself increasingly positioned against.

Unaware of the impending financial disaster of *The Red Tent*, he looked around for what to do next. A long period of apparent inactivity followed; nothing came along that he fancied. Diane was writing and preparing to work on a new film, he was writing and playing golf and talking to producers and directors. They alternated their living quarters between their homes abroad, and friends observed that their marriage was edging closer to the danger zones. Dubiously cautious of scripts, and perhaps subconsciously avoiding anything with a high risk factor, Connery turned his attention back to the theatre.

Both he and Diane had been impressed, or perhaps intrigued is a more accurate word, by an earlier work of the Canadian playwright Ted Allan Herman whose new play, curiously entitled *I've Seen You Cut Lemons*, was being mentioned as a possible candidate for the West End. It was a very 1960s play, attempting to shock with a taboo subject. Connery was offered the chance to direct and Diane was to star. Robert Hardy recalled,

'I hadn't heard from Sean for some time, and then he came on the telephone one day and said he wanted me to appear in a play he was directing, playing opposite Diane in what was basically a two-hander. Anyway, I read it and eventually agreed to do it, perhaps against my better judgement – it was a thoroughly complicated play. It contained long passages of tiresome dialogue.

To add to the difficulties, it was a play about an incestuous relationship between a brother and sister which was not the most inspiring of topics. Another difficulty which I did not realise at the time was that Sean and Diane were experiencing difficulties in their marriage, almost on its last gasps, I believe, and this play was some kind of attempt to stay together. I think Diane believed that by working together they could forge a new and better relationship. Sean had insisted that I went to live with them for the period of final rehearsal at their house in Putney; he seemed to think that I would get down to it more easily by rehearsing on the spot. So that's what we did. Anyway, we did the play and it received appalling notices largely because it was so complicated. But I have no regrets about doing it. I did my best for Sean and altogether it was a very illuminating experience because Sean turned out to be a very good director. It came at a time when he was in the doldrums, and was probably experimenting, and one must always experiment. He was extraordinary in that respect, but overall he is a kind man, a rewarding man to be with.'

The play opened in Connery's old stamping ground of Oxford in the autumn of 1969 and then went on a month-long tour of the provinces, to theatres in places like Newcastle and Manchester, where audiences did not show an especial appreciation of either the subject matter or the play itself. Nor was it any better in London, where it opened at the Fortune Theatre and drew the top-line reviewers because of Connery's attachment. The notices were bad and the show closed after five days.

'Sean seemed to take it reasonably well,' said Hardy. 'He had done his best, we all had, with extremely difficult and not very commercial material. He made a little speech, thanking us, and that was that.'

For the time being there was nothing more on the horizon, except a golf tournament in Morocco which Connery flew off to in the company of male friends. By now his marriage to Cilento was at rock bottom and the trip would have been welcome. During the competition he met an intriguing woman. Micheline Roquebrune, a Moroccan-born artist who lived in France with her husband, two sons and a daughter, the youngest, a son, slightly younger than Connery's son Jason. She spoke several languages. A year older than Sean and similarly passionate about golf, Micheline was a skilful player. Her then-husband was less happy about his game, played badly at Morocco and left early. Roquebrune and Connery met on the metal stands, both having won their tournament.

'I think I was madly in love with him from the first look,' said Micheline in 1989. Connery was also taken by the fact that she was singularly unimpressed by the name Sean Connery. She barely went to the movies and the name was only vaguely familiar. They spent a couple of days in each other's company, though Connery never once spoke of being unhappy in his marriage and Micheline eventually returned home convinced that she would never hear from him again. Then three months later he called her and said it was urgent that they meet: he could not get her out of his mind and was certain he was in love with her.

Connery moved out of the house at Putney and bought a substantial double apartment overlooking the Thames at Chelsea, in a block where Joachim von Ribbentrop had lived in the early 1930s. He put up a smoke screen about staying single, whereas remarriage was already in the line of possibilities.

With the financial failure of recent films, Connery's reputation and status as a major box-office attraction had slipped and he was glad to receive delivery of a script from his good friend and director of *The Hill*, Sidney Lumet, who was casting for a film called *The Anderson Tapes*. It was a strange story with undertones of Big Brother and illegal telephone-tapping capers by government agencies and others, but the plot was based upon a multi-million-dollar theft and was liberally spiced with sex and violence, masterminded by an ex-convict, the character to be played by Connery. It was a role which returned him, albeit temporarily, back into America's list of Top Ten stars. It was in many ways a story similar to the James Bond adventures, though a complete reversal for this time Connery was on the other side of the law. It differed in two other major respects: the plot was weak and the sub-plot mysterious and largely unexplained. Beneath the somewhat mundane story was supposed to be a thematic attack on what the publicity people described as a 'biting indictment on over-surveillance' in a society lurching toward Orwellian times. Francis Ford Coppola tackled the subject with a good deal more skill, though perhaps rather more starchily, in *The Conversation* in 1974.

While planning what he believes to be the perfect heist, the Connery character's movements are relentlessly recorded by microphones wherever he goes. The irony is that the surveillance was not directed at him, and the robbery is allowed to proceed unheeded until finally it traps him. The electronic devices are accidentally instrumental in his capture. Every type of the most modern bugging and surveillance equipment is stacked into the film, with video screens and tape recorders everywhere. It was the first thriller tackled in a kind of pseudo-documentary way, but in the final stages develops into an unintentional farce by a too-light approach to the serious business at hand. Lumet allowed the humour to be overdone and the film's problems were not helped when the distributors insisted upon a new ending.

Originally Connery's escape from the building was in a van which was pursued by police helicopters into the Queen's Tunnel, taking them out of New York. Columbia objected and refused to release it until the climax was changed to one in which the villains were either arrested or killed, so that the future sale of the movie to television, where stricter moral codes were enforced, would not be jeopardised. Otherwise, it had been brought in on a tight budget and completed in a breathless six weeks. It showed. Though moderately successful, it was an odd sort of movie where everyone appeared to be rushing as if in a hurry to complete the task and get home. Connery spent most of the second half in a mask, and some of the bedroom scenes of gratuitous and roughly handled sex were unashamedly copied from the adventures of 007. Even so, he had high hopes that *The Anderson Tapes* would get him back into high profile again.

11

NEVER AGAIN (2)

Coinciding factors contributed to a decision that Sean Connery had vowed he would never even consider: that he should play James Bond again. The separation from Diane Cilento was not, as expected, entirely without animosity and there was a settlement to consider. There would be no public song and dance since they both abhorred any mention of personal matters in newspapers. Those able to observe the marriage at close quarters would have seen, as Connery later confessed, that it had been blighted by the demands of two very active careers. With one or other of them constantly involved throughout their time together with projects that took them traipsing off to various parts of the world, the difficulties of arranging their lives had merely exacerbated their problems during recent years.

Micheline Roquebrune's arrival in Connery's life had merely hastened the breakdown to its seemingly inevitable conclusion, even though Cilento apparently felt that reconciliation was not beyond the realm of possibility and she had no intention of rushing into a divorce. Above all, they both wanted to ensure that the split did not cause any problems for the children.

The upheaval in Connery's private life, and the eventual need to accommodate a financial settlement to ensure the future well-being of the family, came in the midst of a surprising contact from the Bond camp.

The first Bond film without him, *On Her Majesty's Secret Service* starring George Lazenby and Diana Rigg, had not done as badly as some of the prophets of doom had predicted. Audience reception had been reasonable. The critics had largely mourned the loss of Connery but recognised that the producers had done their best to compensate his absence with a film which showered largesse upon the audience, and had included some huge and spectacular climactic events as well as a tragic ending. In one sense it brought the first part of the story of James Bond to a logical conclusion, thus preparing the audience for a relaunch. In a curious way *OHMSS* stood apart from previous Bond films and – with the benefit of hindsight – from all future ones, too. It was as if a group of aliens had temporarily taken over but had not quite understood what they were actually trying to achieve. The box-office receipts, that ever-present judge of success, were expectedly lower than *You Only Live Twice* and substantially down on *Thunderball* and *Goldfinger*.

There was trouble in the Eon camp, however, with the ongoing divorce between Broccoli and Saltzman still in the realm of speculation. They were not particularly happy with Lazenby, considered by some to have ideas about his status beyond reality, and even before the film had been released the head of United Artists, David Picker, had been in touch with Eon to ask what they were doing about replacing Bond. He also enquired if there was any chance of persuading Connery to return.

Guy Hamilton had been approached in the autumn of 1970 to return to the Bond series and direct the next, *Diamonds Are Forever*. He was not told who the star would be, but understood, even then, that Lazenby would not be asked to do a second and other names were already being discussed. Burt Reynolds was one suggestion. Roger Moore was also back in the frame, though he was under contract to Lew Grade and currently filming the television series *The Persuaders* with Tony Curtis. United Artists executives were said to have suggested going for a big Hollywood star now that Bond had reached such an important point in the evolution of the series, but Broccoli still believed the character could carry whoever was cast, provided he had the right attributes. David Picker made it clear, however, that he believed that the next one was crucial to stop the impetus slipping away.

Writer Tom Mankiewicz had been hired to join Richard Maibaum for what he was specifically told was a revamp and updating job on Bond, to invigorate the character rather than the sets and the scientific department, and jazz up the story almost to the point of re-creation.

Hamilton joined Broccoli and Saltzman, designer Ken Adams and Mankiewicz in America for inspiration, consultation and the search for the star and his accompanying array of girls. Pre-production discussions were already well advanced. Jill St John was initially signed as Plenty O'Toole but was eventually upgraded to the larger part of Tiffany Case, which was more suited to her ability, and Lana Wood, Natalie's younger sister who had recently appeared in *Playboy*, was tested for the role of Plenty; she too was signed.

A relatively unknown actor named John Gavin (a friend of Ronald Reagan and later US Ambassador to Mexico) was tested for Bond. Though lacking in charisma, Broccoli gave him a holding contract.

By December still no star had been announced.

Increasingly the name Connery crossed the lips of the discussing parties. He was the definite choice of David Picker, who was still a major influence, though not a word of this was mentioned outside the conference room. Broccoli and Saltzman agreed it would be like a red flag to a bull if they approached Connery and so the faithful servant of Eon, Stanley Sopel, associate producer and writer of cheques which only Broccoli and

189

Saltzman could sign, was designated to contact him and sound out the possibility of a return. Connery's agent, Richard Hatton, arranged for them to meet at the Dorchester Hotel, and was empowered to mention 'a magnificent sum' as an inducement. Connery refused and the only business done at that meeting was by Connery, who sold Sopel a second-hand Mercedes from a garage in which he had acquired an interest.

By the end of January 1971 the script was completed, pre-production work was proceeding and a start date was already on the horizon. Picker decided to act. He flew to London, arranged to meet Connery and made him an offer: $1.25 million to be paid over 18 weeks, plus a percentage of the gross profits. Connery fought a hard bargain. He sought a guarantee of payment if filming overran the 16-week schedule, and they agreed upon a penalty payment of $145,000 a week. Picker also agreed that United Artists would finance two other films outside *Diamonds Are Forever*, of a subject of Connery's own choosing and in conjunction with his own production company.

Little by little, Connery extracted the ultimate deal: the highest fee with the most watertight guarantees concerning overtime, and a percentage that would produce substantial dividends later. It was a financial package which probably could not have been bettered by any male actor around at the time. John Gavin, the earlier hopeful, was paid $50,000 compensation and quietly exited stage left, his moment having passed.

In March the announcement was made. Connery, who had said never again, was coming back – but what was not made clear was that the whole of the advance fee of $1.25 million was to be made over to the Scottish International Educational Trust. The organisation had become a registered charity with Sir Samuel Curran, vice chancellor of Strathclyde University, as its chairman, and racing driver Jackie Stewart and the former shipbuilder Sir Iain Stewart among its co-founders with Connery. In fact, there was a good deal of newspaper discussion as to why he had returned to Bond after so vehemently stating the opposite a year earlier. John Coleman, writing in the *New Statesman*, made the same suggestion as many others – 'that it is reasonable to suppose that money had something to do with it'. Two weeks later the *New Statesman* carried a letter from John Nobbs of Coatbridge, Lanarks, angrily reaffirming Connery's intention to donate a million dollars or more to the Scottish trust fund and added that 'this is one credit which is not, I suspect, being shown at the start of the film'.

Connery had already financed the organisation of Scottish golf tournaments from which the fund had benefited by about £17,000 and had extracted a promise from Columbia executives in Hollywood that there would be a special premiere of his film, *The Anderson Tapes*, in Glasgow in the summer which he intended to turn into a major charity event for the trust fund.

Having said that, John Coleman's view in the *New Statesman* had been basically correct. Money *was* at the root of him signing the new Bond deal, because it actually aided him on three fronts which were important at this time in his life and career. It provided him with the opportunity of giving something back to Scotland with the donation; there was a residual value in the contract in the way of his percentage of the profits, which would help with whatever financial settlement he had to make with Cilento on their divorce; and finally, and perhaps from his point of view most importantly of all, there was the agreement of United Artists to back any two films of his choice, the deciding and most important factor. That is why friends and colleagues who were not totally aware of his intentions or of the extent of the deal he made with Picker were surprised and amazed by his decision. Without the benefit of the full facts it was easy to say, as the *New Statesman* columnist had done, that he was doing it just for the money.

And so he signed on the dotted line, and Broccoli and Saltzman were glad because they knew it would restore Bond to health and ensure a resumption of business. They kept out of the way and gave him a clear field of operation so there were no rows; anyway, they were probably smarting over remarks he made in an interview with David Lewin for the *Daily Mail* about his hopes of producing his own movies at some point in the future because he was tired of 'fat slob producers living off the backs of lean actors'.

He reckoned that for the first time in his life his future was wide open because he only had himself to worry about. It was perhaps because of this attitude, struck and mellowed almost with fatalistic appraisal of this crop of current events, that he arrived to begin work on *Diamonds Are Forever* with a relaxed and amenable view of life in general, apparently unperturbed by the revival of the press gang following him around.

The producers chose Las Vegas as a location for the sixth Bond film believing it would provide the most extensive and consistent press coverage. Even Connery seemed happy, this time, to go along with the demands of the publicity department. There was a self-imposed discipline, however, as director Guy Hamilton had been told that on no account must he overrun the production schedule because of the extra money they would have to pay Connery, so press interviews were not allowed to get in the way.

To watch Connery in action this time provided a snapshot of what it could have been like from the beginning. It was surely no coincidence that he was now talking up the movie as 'the best Bond yet … the best script … the best action': his income, after all, was directly affected by the picture's success. It was eventually apparent to all, however, that *Diamonds Are Forever* finally and positively buried the character of Bond as originally perceived, presenting a new, bleached-white version. It was, it must be said, disappointing in many respects.

Connery, though, was very relaxed and clear about his acting future. 'The press was filled with dark rumour,' said Jill St John. 'With Diane Cilento gone, they were trying to find an off-screen romance between Sean and myself. It would not have been difficult, I can assure you, but it didn't happen. He was as professional and straight as ever.'

While they were filming in Las Vegas a preview copy of *The Anderson Tapes* was sent to Connery and he arranged a special viewing for the crew of *Diamonds Are Forever*. One can't help feeling that he was disappointed with the final version of *The Anderson Tapes*, although he gave no hint of it. Quite the reverse. He was full of hope for the movie, believing that anything with Sidney Lumet's name on it would be a success, and Connery seemed fairly confident of the fact otherwise it's unlikely he would have arranged the special showing for friends and crew. There was applause at the end, but certain defects – especially the weak story which today would barely be good enough for an hour on television – might not have been so obvious.

Connery had faced the challenge of some American dialogue, in which he was expected to say alien slang words like 'dough', and some of the time talked as if he was sliding into Americanese but trying to stop himself. The result was that on some flashes of dialogue he talked as if he had a mouthful of lettuce leaves. Judgement of Connery's performance, therefore, rested upon whether or not the viewer was convinced by the film. *The Anderson Tapes* received good notices in America, quickly edging into profitability and becoming the 15th most popular film of the year, but it did not do especially well in Britain partly because the story of bugging was American-orientated and partly because its autumn release was distracted by the preliminary hype on *Diamonds Are Forever*.

It made an interesting interlude to the filming of *Diamonds* in Las Vegas, though, and added to the publicity build-up. Other interludes were rarely permissible for Connery in this hectic shooting schedule, although he insisted on being able to sample the local golf courses and a helicopter was laid on to deliver him promptly to the first tee whenever the opportunity presented itself.

After nine weeks in Las Vegas they moved back to Pinewood for the last of the studio work, completed on time at the end of August for release by the end of the year. It proved to be another smash hit, breaking box-office records around the world. And, as Connery pointed out with a glint in his eye, he was on a percentage of the last four Bond films: between *Diamonds* and the reissue of the earlier films his immediate financial position looked fairly invincible. He had invested considerably in various business – he was even a director of a bank – which gave him a certain amount of freedom, if not the basis for artistic licence, for his future employment. This could be the only reason, surely, behind some of the films he became involved with after leaving Bond for the second time.

Connery had the satisfactory glow of double exposure, with two films out almost simultaneously from which he had an interest in the box-office receipts. At home it was also doubly beneficial to his Scottish International Educational Trust. His insistence that the European premiere of *The Anderson Tapes* should be in Glasgow had contributed £5,000 to the trust, aided by a group of Connery's friends flying north for the occasion, including Stanley Baker, Jimmy Tarbuck, Ronnie Corbett and others, who braved the flight even after a bomb scare. The trust was already being used to help young people in need and other projects were under discussion, including another of Sir Iain Stewart's experiments on labour relations. The trust also part-funded a training college for trade unionists in the town of Glenrothes, Fife, and the basic idea of creating discussion and seminars on finding solutions to the problems of industrial unrest attracted a good deal of interest among politicians, not merely in Scotland but in London, too.

Connery, as vice chairman of the trust, said he wanted to extend its work for the benefit of Scotland as a whole and it would not, he said, be restricted by any political affiliations or ties. It was basically about helping the young people of Scotland, though the trust could not hope to do it alone; ultimately he wanted to see Scotland's nationalism rise and the country pull away from the influence of England to whom it had played second fiddle for years and this, in a small way, could be helped by strengthening industrial ties, solving industrial problems and stemming the flow of Scots emigrating in search of employment abroad. His comments, like some of his recent films, received a mixed reaction.

If the Scottish educational project had become a channel through which he could eradicate some of the guilt at earning as much in a week as his father had earned in an entire lifetime, then the first film he chose to make under the United Artists agreement provided no better excuse than self-indulgence. Even above his desire to put as much distance as he could between himself and James Bond, Connery knew the record of the play he had chosen and that it would get a virtual zero rating in popular appeal – as did United Artists when he told them what he intended to do. He also knew that it was such a difficult work, emotionally and psychologically, that its success or failure balanced on a razor's edge.

And yet he went ahead anyway, obviously with some personal motive beyond the comprehension of the cautious executives at UA. But a deal was a deal; Picker had promised him a million dollars and they stuck by it. The project he selected was a screen version of John Hopkins' psychological drama *This Story Of Yours*, which had been staged at the Royal Court Theatre in 1968. It closed after only three weeks despite rave notices, and the *Financial Times* commented 'the English do not deserve to have great men'.

Connery had toyed with the idea of reviving it for the stage and now took the bull by the horns to make a film under the auspices of his own newly formed production company, Tantallon Films, with UA backing. The formation of such companies by well-to-do stars was nothing new. It had been happening in Hollywood since the studio system ended, but very few actors in Britain had made the move.

He said at the time that he had no ambition to become a major producer and admitted his ignorance about the higher economics of business, but he had seen Taylor and Burton – whom he named specifically – drawing considerable benefit in terms of finance and artistic freedom, and he sought a similar avenue for his own development. He contacted Sidney Lumet and sent the director the Hopkins script by courier. He said from the outset that he realised it was a dicey subject and that they could well be shot down in flames.

It was a harrowing story, eventually appearing under the rather unattractive title of *The Offence*, in which a police sergeant, a failure in both his private life and in his work, interrogates a man suspected of child molesting. He uses such brutal methods that the suspect dies under the sergeant's questioning, and then the scenario is reversed, with the policeman facing a charge of manslaughter. Lumet made his feelings known, that the demands the John Hopkins script would make on the actors would be 'devastating', but agreed with Connery that it could be made into a strong psycho-drama for the big screen.

Three co-stars were signed, all friends or past work colleagues of Connery's – Trevor Howard, Ian Bannen as the molester and Vivien Merchant, the wife of playwright Harold Pinter who was renowned for her stage presence and especially for her brilliant portrayals of her husband's work. She and Connery had appeared together nine years earlier in the West End production of *Judith*, and he cast her as his slatternly wife in the film.

It was a strong cast. They enjoyed the play because it was an 'actor's play' and stretched their abilities to the limit like a superb and extensive exercise in dramatic improvement – which was all very well but there was an audience out there, somewhere. 'It was incredibly demanding and I didn't take easily to film acting,' said Merchant. 'I came to it late, and I used to hear these stories about how much film actors were paid and I would think that was a great deal of money for little work. After I'd finished it, I thought it should have been ten times as much.' They worked ten-hour days and completed shooting in little more than a month on a tiny set at Twickenham, $80,000 short of budget.

Connery was pleased with the result and satisfied with the amount of creative control he had been able to exercise from beginning to end. Critically, some went as far as to say it was his best work yet and John Huston later told him that the last 40 minutes of the film, in which the audience saw the police sergeant slowly disintegrating before their eyes, was among the best he had ever seen on film. That at least gave Connery an insight into the power a strong actor might have in influencing a particular project. But what else? Sadly, not a lot. No one expected it to make a fortune although Connery did expect to make a profit – it was hard not to, he said at the time, on a film made for under a million dollars. But even that optimism was misplaced.

The Offence was not given a blazing send-off by United Artists and the huge Odeon in Leicester Square, where Connery as Bond had them queueing around the block, sadly proved to be a graveyard. *The Offence* quickly died and was not even available in some countries, including the major market of France. Connery was naturally angered by this lack of confidence by the distributors who, in the end, were able to exercise the final control of exposure, and in this instance they erred on the side of caution. Connery's own assessment, that the film might have been more suited to the smaller arty cinemas, was correct. It was almost nine years before *The Offence* went into the black. Not that that mattered by then, because the movie had garnered considerable respect amongst film buffs and is still rated today as one of his best.

It is possible that, at the time, the fulfilment of his ambitions outweighed the disappointment that *The Offence* did not do well financially. Nor did the second production available to Connery under the Bond deal with UA ever come to fruition. By then, with inflation raging, it was difficult to find *any* project of sufficient status that could be filmed for under a million dollars. He commissioned Hopkins to write a screenplay based upon the life of explorer Sir Richard Burton, but it was such a complicated story involving exotic locations in far-off places that UA's million dollars would have disappeared within about four minutes of finished photography. He talked Germaine Greer into writing an outline for a screenplay and she turned in a worthy idea about the decimation of the Aborigines, a good social issue but ultimately expensive and devoid of popular appeal.

It was difficult then, and equally so now, to discover a rationale in his selection of material, given that he had a constant supply of scripts and offers from which to choose. He took a briefcase full of them to his house in Spain to relax after completing *The Offence*. Though short in actual work time, the film had drained him and his father, Joe, had died from cancer while he was making it. Joe had been ill for some time and the best Connery could do was to ensure his comfort in his last days. Mr and Mrs Connery Senior had finally moved out of the tenement block four years ago when Joe retired and, apart from travel and the provision of certain modern aids, the new home was the only concession Joe Connery had made to his son's fame and fortune.

Micheline Roquebrune was by now Connery's regular and soothing companion, and they spent the remainder of 1972 and early 1973 mostly playing golf. Behind the scenes, moves toward his divorce were proceeding with protracted negotiations between his lawyers and Cilento's. Jason stayed mostly with her until he reached boarding school age, and amicable access rights had already been negotiated.

Bond was out of his system again and the new Bond, Connery's pal Roger Moore, was preparing to go into harness after Eon's 'Situations Vacant' farce in which advertisements for potential Bonds had been placed in Army journals under the heading: ARE YOU 007? The British actors' union Equity called a halt. Bond was gone, and Connery was intent on burying the image. He told everyone that, but what was his ideal? What were his goals? Nothing outside of Bond seemed to be panning out exactly as planned and he headed straight down the path of more misadventure on his next two films, *Zardoz* and *Ransom*, both completed in 1973 with high hopes and, ultimately, low returns.

He took on *Zardoz* almost at a moment's notice. Burt Reynolds had dropped out because of a back injury and director John Boorman – fresh from his Oscar-nominated *Deliverance* with Reynolds – needed a star in double-quick time. It was entirely Boorman's project: he was producer, director and writer. He located Connery on a golf course near Marbella, flew out a script and received an enthusiastically affirmative answer four days later. *Zardoz* was a weirdly wonderful science-fiction film filled with all kinds of high-blown futuristic fantasy, theorising on life in the year 2293. It was not a film to be tackled on a shoestring budget, but that was what Boorman faced as a condition of his backers, 20th Century Fox, after two other major studios had turned him down because of his insistence on artistic control.

Connery admired him for that, and threw in his total commitment. The adversity of pressures, Boorman assessed, brought out the best in everyone, especially the star. 'It was sad, really,' said Boorman's film editor John Merritt, 'because *Zardoz* was an expansive picture which needed the luxury of a big budget to achieve its aims.' Filmed entirely in Ireland, the budget was so stretched that Irish extras in distant shots had to have red boots painted on to save money.

Connery once again achieved the applause of his fellows and of the technical staff of the picture. 'He is a very intelligent actor,' said Boorman. 'He understood it from the very beginning and his performance was a revelation ... there was something mystical about him which was just waiting to be brought to the surface. He is very instinctive in everything he does and one of his strong points as an actor is that he had a very direct approach to every scene.'

There would be no point in attempting to explain the plot or the meanings or even the reasons for making *Zardoz*. It was artistic and outrageous, the most baroque of all Boorman films, and contained much experimentation with colours, reflections, projections and curious images created by broken glass. It allowed critics from publications that circulated among the intelligentsia to be snobbishly pompous in their reviews, pretending to understand all that was going on and talking in terms of distinguishing physical and moral forces and, as one said, 'does much to dispel one's doubts about the apparent loose ends in the philosophical tapestry'.

Others in the more plain-speaking sections of the media tended towards the view that it was pretentious nonsense. Even the artistically tolerant *New Yorker* considered *Zardoz* to be a 'glittering cultured trash pile', and a number of disappointed fans at the London premiere, once again in the vast Odeon of Leicester Square, left before the end. Connery, in spite of everything, said he enjoyed the experience and thought the film was good but before its time – which sounded more like an apology than an excuse. Like Boorman, he had taken a lowish fee and a larger share of the profits to keep costs down. *Zardoz* collapsed at the box office and left them all out of pocket. It will only be remembered, but not by many, for its originality and verve, and for the fact that Connery spent most of the film half naked.

No such remembrances stir for his next, *Ransom*, a topical thriller based on a hijacking and the kidnapping of the British Ambassador to Scandinavia. It was filmed entirely in Norway under the direction of Finn Casper Wrede, who had just received accolades for his *One Day In The Life Of Ivan Denisovich* which is no doubt one of the factors which attracted Connery. *Ransom* was a controversial film, the producers facing accusations of cashing in on the spate of terrorism acts involving airliners.

The Norwegian Pilots Association protested that Oslo Airport was used as a setting and Connery gave interviews explaining that *Ransom* was intended to demonstrate how to prevent a hijacking, not perform one. It was a modest movie with a modest budget, and in the end achieved a less than modest reaction. In America, especially, where even the new title *The Terrorist* failed to revive its fortunes, it immediately sank into a black hole.

It was one of the most eminently forgettable films that Connery made, raising questions once again as to why he became involved in curiously off-beat – or off-beam – projects which were constructed from such a modest base with less than a 50-50 chance of success. Outwardly Connery seemed unperturbed by the run of box-office failures, but one person who worked with him around that period believed he covered his tracks by appearing strong and confident – stances which at times could again be mistaken for superior self-satisfaction verging on arrogance. Amongst his peers, however, he was inclined towards a straightforward display of professionalism. The word kept cropping up in every interview or recollection, especially when Connery was working with directors he liked and with whom he was also friendly. Sidney Lumet was one of these. At the end of 1973, the director was in contact again, suggesting Connery might like to appear in the all-star production of *Murder On The Orient Express*. Lumet said he had decided to pack the film with stars to keep the audience interested in what was a fairly static situation because the action occurred entirely on a train which for most of the time was snowbound near Yugoslavia.

It had virtually no potential for visual excitement and thus Lumet concluded the cast would compensate for the lack of scenery. Already signed were Ingrid Bergman, Sir John Gielgud, Anthony Perkins, Albert Finney, Lauren Bacall, Wendy Hiller, Vanessa Redgrave, Michael York, Richard Widmark and a host of others. Connery agreed without hesitation. He turned in one of his most conventional and pleasing performances for some time as Colonel Arbuthnot, one of the murder suspects in the killing of Richard Widmark, being investigated by Albert Finney's overplayed Poirot.

For the desperately declining British film industry, *Murder On The Orient Express* was a shot in the arm. It was a good film, marred slightly by a looseness of direction. In spite of the cast of major stars, Lumet completed on time and within the budget. It received six American Academy nominations, and Ingrid Bergman converted hers to an Oscar for Best Supporting Actress. Agatha Christie, then 84, turned up for the royal premiere.

In October 1973 Connery was granted his decree nisi from Diane Cilento on the grounds that their marriage had irretrievably broken down after living apart for the statutory two years. Connery went to court and his counsel, Jeremy Tatham, gave a hint of the behind-the-scenes discussions over finances when he informed the judge, 'The husband and wife not only wish for a civilised end to the marriage but wish to end the financial litigation between them for ever. After 15 months of negotiation, I think we have achieved this by capital sums which they would prefer not to mention in open court. The first is a sum payable to Miss Cilento in the full and final settlement of all her claims against Mr Connery. The second is a sum setting up a trust fund for the two children of the family. Further, custody of the children remains by agreement with Miss Cilento with suitable and amicable access.'

It was clear that Connery had divested a substantial sum on ending his marriage to Cilento and it was noticeable that he did not exclude Cilento's daughter, Gigi, then 16, from the settlement. He considered her his family. The exact terms of the settlement never filtered out into the public domain. On leaving court Connery made it plain to reporters where he stood with the statement, detailed earlier, about his intention to keep 'private matters private', and would reveal nothing of the agreement between himself and his former wife.

By and large, he has stuck to his word in succeeding years.

12

NEW BEGINNING

From 1974 to 1975 Sean Connery was in a state of absolute and complete change. He needed to alter course, desperately, as a surge of superstars began to emerge in one film after another, all coming out of Hollywood with leading men formerly in his shadow. Once he had been described as the highest-paid actor in the world; true or false, it did not matter because people believed it and believed that he was in the top drawer. The approach of middle age confronted him precisely as he was wrestling with the most difficult time of his career and personal life, when Hollywood itself was undergoing yet another new era led by the packaging of old and new stars in big budget productions aimed at both ends of the cinema audience age spectrum.

There was an inspired new 'new wave' of writers, directors and actors in Hollywood. Roman Polanski and Jack were making *Chinatown*, the quintessential movie of the 1970s embodying some of the decade's major themes such as corruption and conspiracy, commenting metaphorically on Watergate. Nicholson followed it with another huge statement in *One Flew Over The Cuckoo's Nest*.

There was Robert Redford and Paul Newman (after *Butch Cassidy And The Sundance Kid*) together again in *The Sting*; there was Dustin Hoffman in *The Graduate* and *Midnight Cowboy* with John Voight; Al Pacino and Marlon Brando in *The Godfather*; Sidney Lumet kept all eyes on Pacino with *Serpico* while James Bond lived again in the shape of Roger Moore. But Bond really did not matter anymore; the movies were comic strips set against some of the brilliant material coming out of Hollywood in the 1970s.

Connery had not been part of it, not even on the periphery. On the face of it, he still seemed relatively unperturbed about the direction of his career and yet barely one single aspect of his life would remain unaltered following a purge on work, business and his domestic arrangements in the period immediately after his divorce.

Until 1974 he was officially resident in Britain, although of late he had been spending more and more time in Spain. Then he acquired a property in Monaco where he registered himself for tax purposes. It was carefully worked out by lawyers and accountants and within a year he had severed his ties with Britain, except for the Scottish trust fund. He sold or otherwise extricated himself from various business enterprises which had been demanding more and more of his time and diverting his attention from the main earning potential. He put his apartment in Chelsea on the market and bought a new villa near Marbella into which he moved with Micheline and her youngest son, Stefan.

The move was prompted by the finalisation of his divorce from Diane Cilento and the arrival of Harold Wilson's second Labour government in which the new Chancellor, Denis Healey, was promising to squeeze the rich until the pips squeaked. Connery, who had various companies registered abroad in overseas tax havens, could not, ultimately, escape the simple fact of paying tax. He wasn't alone, of course. Back in the 1950s Noel Coward had been called every kind of traitor for becoming a tax exile when he discovered that after all his earnings over three decades he still had an overdraft of £20,000. Richard Burton had told Connery long ago how he was confronted with a statement from his business manager in 1958 which showed that if he earned £100,000 in a year £93,000 would be donated to the Inland Revenue. Burton resolved it by basing himself in Switzerland. 'You will never be a millionaire living in London,' he had advised his fellow star. 'It is simply an impossibility.'

Not much had changed since and Connery's own business affairs indicated a similar predicament. The tax was only slightly less crippling than when Burton left. Like everyone else in the supertax band, Connery had been paying 83p in the pound on his earnings and, as he admitted, any true Scot would have baulked at this attack on his wealth. In fact, he had discovered he was not as financially strong as he thought he might be, especially after his commitment to pay Cilento a lump sum and set up a trust for the children, and he publicly denied that he was worth three or even two million pounds. He ought to have been, but there were other reasons which would only become clear at a later date, when he discovered that his money had been ill managed by a man who ranked as one of his most trusted advisers.

Some daring columnists called him unpleasant names, but he resolved to depart British shores come what may and was later followed by a few singers, a couple of racing drivers and some speculators who thrived on capital gains. Michael Caine made headlines when he said, 'I want to live in England and sod it I will stay here. But I can understand people who do leave.' He said for every film he made he had to make two more for the taxman. Two years later, with Denis Healey's prophecy of squeezing the rich in full swing but having failed to resolve the nation's financial problems, Caine himself took his family to Beverly Hills where he remained until the tax situation had eased under Margaret Thatcher. Connery, when he moved in 1974, was also prompted into a new beginning by the permanency of his relationship with Micheline Roquebrune. She was a European in the strictest sense and her life was more attuned to the continent than to Britain; Connery's ties in the home country were also diminishing after the dual effects of his divorce and the changing patterns of work.

He and Micheline were married in May 1975 in Gibraltar, although the news did not leak out for months afterwards. By then he had already placed himself in exile. Changing circumstances mean changing faces, and it was a curious fact that when friends and colleagues in Britain were being asked to recall personal reminiscences, many related back to the early 1970s. Sir John Gielgud remembered dining with him 'when he was married to Diane Cilento' and Joss Ackland's memories were from the same time.

These contacts were replaced by other people in a different setting. Donald Pleasence met him socially; they became good friends when he had a house in Spain near to Connery's. Racing driver James Hunt, another escapee from the British tax system, became a near neighbour in Spain and they exchanged dinner dates. He called on Connery to be a virtual referee when Richard Burton, by then with Hunt's ex-wife Suzy, came to stay at Lew Hoad's house and James invited them over for dinner. Connery was in the middle, fit and tanned from his long strolls on golf courses. Next to him Burton, only four years his senior, looked an old man, his face ravaged by hard living – a face which director Eddie Dmytryk said could alter dramatically during the course of a day's shooting and especially after lunch. But perhaps that was part of the Burton appeal.

Connery's friendships, according to the testimony of several, seldom died but were often put on hold. If a man can be judged by the range of his associates, then his was epitomised by diversity. Contact could become minimal and closeness was not enjoyed by many, Eric Sykes explaining that the golfers who joined him on pro-celebrity tournaments for charity became his most regular crowd as he reached mid-life.

'We saw a lot of him,' Eric said, 'but usually our meetings were in some way related with golf because he was crazy about it and became disgruntled if more than a few days passed without a round. Mind you, he could become equally disgruntled once on the course, for different reasons. Later, as he become busier and more international, we began to see less of him. But Sean's friendship is enduring. I might not see him for a year, and then it would be as if it were yesterday that we last met.'

So, yes, friends were invariably friends for life, Sykes said, but the opportunities for seeing them, of meeting them for lunch and repartee, were taking second place to work and sport so that dinners with contemporaries –Michael Caine, for instance – tended to be arranged at fleeting moments whenever he was where they were, or vice versa.

Connery began to concentrate on Hollywood. It was a necessity imposed not merely by the exodus from Britain. Fewer and fewer American film producers were travelling to Europe, because the economic benefits were no longer available; the US Congress closed the last loopholes for tax-haven productions in the mid-1970s, although not before shrewd accountants and professionals had pumped $150 million into film projects with the bulk of the cost being borne by the American treasury. Major films like Connery's forthcoming *The Man Who Would Be King* (1975), *The Front* (1976) with Woody Allen and Zero Mostel, and *The Missouri Breaks* (1976), starring Jack Nicholson and Marlon Brando, all involved some complicated tax-shelter financing arrangement. They were among the last.

No such assistance was available in the UK, where the British film industry, such as it was, had to find its own finance within the British Isles. Banks and industry had just come through the worst property crash in living memory and some spectacular failures sent everyone withdrawing into their financial shells. Risk businesses were out, and the film industry was always a risk.

In Britain it was sinking, yet again, into the mire of low-budget pictures and mundane scripts. In that era of raging inflation investors were few, and producers found backing increasingly hard to come by. Even Harry Saltzman had pulled out, having sold his interest in Bond films to United Artists for a reported $17.5 million, which made Connery cough and splutter for a week or two.

But by the end of 1974 three films were already on the horizon that would also signal the beginning of a new phase in Connery's working life. They also virtually ended his working connections in Britain, subsequently limited in any event by the restrictions of the tax laws which allowed him just 90 days in the country each year. Those three films, *The Wind And The Lion*, *The Man Who Would Be King* and *Robin And Marian*, saw Connery enjoying creating new characterisations in some classic adventure stories which, ultimately, would help shape the rest of his career and prove there was a greater depth to his abilities, which some were venturing to doubt.

Even this was only a beginning, the coming to terms with the new Connery. The transition from the cool, catlike movements of a slim, well-groomed and smart young man into an actor who could be any character, with a bushy white-tinged beard and mellowing voice, thicker and with more resonance, seemed infinitely more difficult to perceive by the beholder than by himself.

Though his work in *The Molly Maguires*, *The Offence* and *The Red Tent* had been praised, and there were some remarkable moments in them, he needed to get back into the high-profile area of film-making. He had severely tested the loyalty of his staunchly faithful followers and some conjectured that he faced the imminent danger of descending from stardom to famous personality. The chance to show his abilities more expansively and in other popular areas came first when writer-turned-director John Milius offered him his best payday since Bond to star in *The Wind And The Lion* opposite Candice Bergen. There was, even so, some wonderment again when he accepted since it would cast him as a nomadic Arab chieftain who prayed to Allah several times a day, and, as critics were prompt to point out, Allah might well have been anxious to discover who was addressing him in the middle of the desert in those dulcet Scottish tones. Connery accepted with alacrity and Milius knew full well that everyone would be expecting a rather more Arabic-sounding actor in the role. It was interesting casting which would give the critics something to angle their reviews upon.

This was a colourful historical adventure story loosely based upon an incident soon after the turn of the century, when an American businessman named Pedecaris was kidnapped by a nomadic Arab, El Raisuli. It caused something of a diplomatic flurry which was quickly resolved without bloodshed. In the hands of a Hollywood scriptwriter, however, a small incident in the desert was a major story. The businessman became a woman (Bergen) who was kidnapped along with her two children and taken away by the Berber tribe led by Connery, alias El Raisuli, a superbly charismatic figure and certainly no villain – as Theodore Roosevelt, who finally directs operations personally in an election year, discovers. It was all a touch far-fetched, but compulsive stuff with some topical messages for those who cared to look.

So Milius wrote his screenplay and began touting it around Hollywood, though for seven years no one showed more than a flicker of interest. In the meantime, he became famous. He wrote *Jeremiah Johnson*, which starred Robert Redford, in 1972, *The Life And Times Of Judge Roy Beam* starring Paul Newman (1973), and made his debut as writer-director in *Dillinger* (1973), starring Warren Oates. Nothing breeds success like success and a producer with whom Milius was chatting one day granted him a rather grand sum of $4 million for a 13-week shooting schedule at various locations in Spain, which fell neatly into Connery's new lifestyle.

A magnificent musical score by Jerry Goldsmith received an Academy nomination. Bergen came in place of Faye Dunaway who was working with Nicholson and Polanski on *Chinatown*, and was excellent. Though the location work was tiring as they moved from one Spanish city to the next using backdrops like the Madrid Palace Hotel, which might be taken for the White House, and the Alcazar in Seville which became an Arabian palace, Bergen found

Connery a joy to work with. 'He was a gentleman and then a friend,' she said. 'And to me he will always be the Great Raisuli, Lord of the Riff and the only Scottish Berber.' Of course, the critics did not like Scottish Berbers and Connery was the butt of some jokes, but generally the film was well received in America.

The influential *Time* magazine insisted that Connery had become a superb screen actor, and his performance as Raisuli was both dashing and funny. The UK was less impressed and smarting because he had departed its shores for tax-free climes, which was not easily forgiven regardless of the reasons. Internationally, he had regained some of his fading popularity, as shown when the world premiere was staged at New York's Radio City Music Hall in May 1975. *The Wind And The Lion* was a reasonable success financially, which gave Connery new heart for his forthcoming adventure story – *The Man Who Would Be King*, for which he and Michael Caine had been holding themselves in readiness for almost two years.

The Man Who Would Be King was, and remains, one of Connery's best films and came to him only through a series of mishaps and coincidences. The saga began back in 1952 when John Huston, who from childhood had been an avid reader of Rudyard Kipling, had discussed the possibility of making a film of the short story Kipling wrote while working as a young journalist in India. In 1955, when he had finished directing *Moby Dick*, Huston secured assurances from backers and took off for India to survey the locations and write a screenplay. He intended to offer the roles eventually played by Connery and Caine to Humphrey Bogart and Clark Gable. A draft screenplay was completed in 1957. Bogart died that year and Huston put the whole project to one side to begin work on *The Misfits* with Gable, Montgomery Clift and Marilyn Monroe. He planned to return to the Kipling story later, as Gable was still keen on doing it. Sadly, Gable collapsed from a massive heart attack and died soon after completing *The Misfits* and Huston put the screenplay back in his pending file.

But he took it out occasionally, and then wrote a second version. There was talk of offering it to Brando and in 1967 Huston tried to build it around Peter O'Toole and Richard Burton, but once again the project never got off the ground. In 1973, after completing *The Mackintosh Man*, an unsuccessful spy thriller produced in Britain with Paul Newman heading an otherwise British cast, Huston re-revised the Kipling script, adding a good deal of invention and creative thought to the original story. Newman had expressed interest in the idea of teaming up with Robert Redford again.

'I sent Paul the script,' Huston recalled, 'because in our mutual guilt over *The Mackintosh Man* we were anxious to do something we could hold our heads up about.'

Newman read the script and telephoned Huston.

'I think this is one of the best plays I have ever read,' he said. 'But honestly, I don't think it is for me. I reckon the two roles should be played by Englishmen. For Chrissakes, John, get Connery and Caine.'

Producer John Foreman, who had also been working with Huston on the Kipling script, immediately sent cables to Connery and Caine while the scripts went by courier. Within a week both men had talked it over and agreed to sign – subject to the monetary arrangements. Therein lay a tale that just about summed up the complicated and devious nature of getting financial support for any movie by the mid-1970s, and one that ultimately ended in considerable anguish for the two stars.

Foreman had worked out a budget of $5 million which, as Huston noted in his autobiography *An Open Book*, would not have been a problem in the old days when the studio system was in place. He would simply have sought backing from a studio and gone into production. But the studios were economising and few were laying out all the finance. 'Packaging' was the new way of getting a film into production. A producer had to put together the script, the creative staff, the stars and the director and then seek an amalgam of backers who would each come in for a percentage of the cost and take the same percentage of the profit.

Columbia took a percentage in return for the European distribution rights. Another company, Allied Artists, which had no production facilities and was involved merely in distributing the picture, put up a percentage for the North American rights, and they brought in a third party with what Huston described as some Canadian tax-shelter money. This was to become the set procedure for movie financing.

The variations could be infinite and the people controlling the purse strings were accountants, tax experts, financial wizards and lawyers. 'They are hardly a creative breed,' said Huston. 'For the most part they are illiterate when it comes to making pictures. The whole hierarchy with a few exceptions is made up of people who imagine that because they can wheel and deal and shuffle investment money around (seldom, if ever, their own) they have presumptive rights to opinions and dictums.'

The words were spoken with hindsight, and tinged with Huston's apparent anger over the way the film progressed into pre-production. Foreman had already begun travelling the world to find suitable locations and Huston was working on the script in London when a lawyer whose name was Peter turned up with an executive from Allied Artists, a Mr Wolf, and produced a list of changes they wanted made to the script. They also wished to discuss casting. Huston said he listened politely and with great patience, and they eventually departed apparently assuming that he would do everything they wished. Of course he did not, and Peter and the Wolf threatened to pull out.

The arguments dragged on, as did difficulties in getting various governments to approve the locational shooting, and were not resolved until the beginning of 1975. Connery and Caine were kept informed of progress and agreed to go ahead at the fee originally negotiated in 1973, of $250,000 each. 'They were also to receive 5 per cent of the film grosses,' said Huston. 'I, unfortunately, was on the net.' If, as was expected, the film took $10 million, Connery and Caine would have received a further $500,000 apiece – in theory. In practice it was rather different.

The actual making of the film was a happy, cheerful family affair filled with incident and delight against a backdrop of rough country and odd customs which provided some difficult moments of negotiation. Only an initial sortie by newspapers who had just discovered that Connery had remarried broke the calm.

Caine and Connery had long wanted to work together. They spent hours going over their scripts, perfecting their lines like a comic double act with impeccable timing and a repartee that seemed almost spontaneously ad-libbed in their roles as the two former British soldiers who journey to the distant province of Kafiristan to set themselves up as kings and become enormously rich. 'It was like watching a polished vaudeville act,' said Huston. 'Everything on cue – all I had to do was decide how best to shoot it.'

Filming was on location in Spain and Morocco. Wives were present and the whole shoot turned into a party. Huston discovered that Micheline was born in Morocco and suggested that she might be able to arrange for John Foreman to get an audience with the King of Morocco, who might then personally persuade customs men not to open cans of undeveloped film as they were being brought in; several thousand feet had already been wasted. Micheline succeeded and it was arranged that the King's jeweller should take Foreman to the entry point 400 miles away to clear everything. On the way the producer asked the jeweller about the possibility of striking three gold medallions similar to the one Connery wore around his neck for the film. He wanted to present one each to Connery, Caine and Huston as a memento.

A few days later the jeweller arrived at the film location with the medallions and presented him with a bill for US $15,000, a tidy sum in Moroccan money. Foreman said he was sorry, but he would have to think it over. The jeweller pointed out that to refuse the King's gift might cause a diplomatic incident. Mystified, Foreman enquired why, if the medallions were a gift from the King, was there a bill for $15,000? The jeweller explained that was his own personal fee, and Foreman had to pay up.

Money was a worry for Foreman; the payroll was always late arriving from Allied Artists and he often had to dip into his own funds to pay bills. There were also the simple logistics of selecting 500 extras each day from the pool of 2,000, not one of whom spoke English and who all needed fresh, clean costumes almost daily. The locals watched in amazement as 200 Moroccans and 12 British technicians built the ancient palace of Sikandergul on a 2-acre site at the top of a hill near Marrakesh at a cost of £500,000 and then pulled it down again 13 weeks later when the filming was complete.

Huston had his own problems. Tessa Dahl, daughter of Roald Dahl, had been signed for the role of Roxanne, the bride-to-be of Connery's Danny Dravot but, fair-haired and fair-skinned, she looked quite out of place among the 2,000 Berbers who poured out of the foothills of the Atlas Mountains to sign on as extras.

Huston had joined Connery and Caine and their wives for dinner one night and explained the problem.

'She just won't do,' he said. 'Won't do at all.'

And then his eyes fixed upon Caine's wife, Shakira. She is Indian, and exactly what Huston was seeking.

'Oh, no,' said Shakira. 'Oh, no, John. I can't do that. I've never acted in my life.'

Caine was also somewhat reluctant and repeated what his wife had said. Connery was slightly unsure of acting opposite his best friend's wife who was to become his own wife in the film.

Huston got his way. He explained that Shakira's role hardly required any acting ability, except in the final scene where she bit Danny Dravot and made him bleed, revealing to the elders who were to crown him king that he was not immortal. In the end Shakira agreed, and made both her debut and farewell performance on screen in one go, just as it was for the 100-year-old Berber from the Atlas Mountains who had never seen a camera nor even a film in his life and played the High Priest of Danny Dravot's village.

It was a remarkable film in many ways, and especially in Huston's handling of it. The reviews were the best Connery had

Two very different
looks for Connery –
Outland in 1981 (*top*)
and in *Name of the
Rose* in 1986.

Top: As his career
developed, Sean
continued to vary
his roles. From
immortal mentor
in *Highlander* …

Right: … to father of an
action hero played by
Harrison Ford, in
*Indiana Jones and the
Last Crusade*.

Top: In 1990 Sean Connery starred in *The Hunt for Red October*, a film based on the Tom Clancy novel.

Bottom: Starring alongside Catherine Zeta Jones in *Entrapment*, Sean's high profile gave a helping hand to Catherine's growing career.

Playing King Arthur, Sean Connery headed another star studded cast list, working alongside Richard Gere and Julia Ormond.

Connery starred alongside Nicholas Cage and Ed Harris in the 1996 blockbuster *The Rock.*

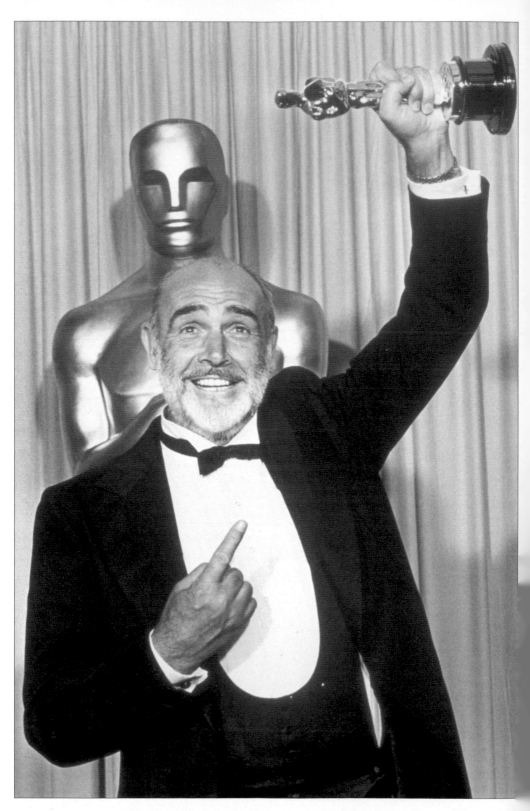

Would you look at that! As a highly acclaimed actor, Sean won his long-overdue Oscar in 1987. Since then he has continued to receive much recognition for his work…

.. including the moment he heard the words, 'Arise Sir Sean': in the summer of
2000, Connery received a knighthood, another long-overdue tribute to his amazing
life and career.

Second wife Micheline Roquebrune attends all of his events with him and her love for her husband became the inspiration for some of the paintings in her own exhibition shown here.

received in years. 'Everything works,' said Dilys Powell in the *Sunday Times*. 'The victory of the British adventurers, their acceptance by the people, the gradual assumption by the more ambitious of the pair of the status of God. Sean Connery gives him power, a fine display of hubris … and Huston has caught the essential of the original story and the feeling of enterprise and bravado which the author saw in the British soldier in India.'

The film was given a royal premiere at the Odeon, Leicester Square, in December 1975, though Connery was not present. In America Huston's film was acclaimed with considerable vigour, and one critic was convinced it was his best work since *The African Queen*. *Time* magazine listed *The Man Who Would Be King* – and Connery's previous film, *The Wind And The Lion* – in their top ten best films of the decade, and with this kind of largesse Connery and Caine sat back smiling and waiting for the grosses to tick away with their 5 per cent each.

Two years passed …

Something was wrong with the figures. Connery looked at the total gross receipts and totted up the cheques he had received and reckoned he was quite a bit short. He telephoned Caine who said he thought it was on the low side, too. It seemed quite obvious to the pair of them that they had not been paid the full amount due under their contracts. Such happenings were nothing new in Hollywood, and became an ever-increasing problem from the early 1970s onwards when the practice of packaging films opened up new and complicated areas of financing a film. Actors and independent producers became party to often long and complicated contracts, some running to 150 pages or more which – it soon became clear – were open to a mind-boggling variation of interpretations. It stemmed from the rise in the practice of actors and directors demanding an up-front fee plus a share of the profits. In the early days, the term used was net profits but many actors soon discovered that the accountants weighted their production costs with all kinds of extras which in the end meant there were no 'net' profits.

There were ways of 'loading' the profits in favour of the backing studio. Connery had already complained about the revenue from his film *The Anderson Tapes*, which highlighted another way in which actors felt they were being unfairly treated. He claimed that Columbia, as distributor for *The Anderson Tapes*, sent it out on the circuits with what Connery described as 'a Mickey Mouse' second feature to which Columbia allocated 50 per cent of the revenues every time the two films were played together. And so, according to Connery, his film received equal income to a piece of junk that would otherwise have been a disaster.

There were also other areas where policing the financial well-being of any film had developed almost into an impossibility. With the distribution rights often divided into territories, the final accounting was subject to varying tax and licensing laws, which again made the interpretation of contracts openly debatable.

Often the markets were subdivided, with separate deals being struck for North America, Europe, Japan and the Far East, and Australia. An added complication was that film funding sometimes came through private offshore companies whose owners' identity was not necessarily revealed and whose books were virtually impossible to inspect. American studios involved in overseas sales could also have their cake and eat it where taxes were concerned. When a film was sold abroad the studio charged all foreign taxes against the profit on foreign revenues, but in doing so reduced its own tax commitment by an equivalent amount. The seemingly legal practices were vast and various, and any accountant trying to get to the bottom line of such a film would have to send teams around the world who still might not return with a complete story.

Another minefield of possible profit diversion was television rights. A studio could, for example, sell the right to half a dozen of its films to television, using one good film and five cheap movies in which there was no profit participation. The six would get an equal share of the package price, thus reducing the liability of the one film where they had to split the profits.

As these rows over money became more common, the most powerful and popular actors began to demand that their percentage of the revenue should come from the gross takings, from the very first dollar earned. Some, like Elizabeth Taylor, had rowed with successive studios about their creative accounting, but at the end of the day very few cases actually came to court. Lesser actors and actresses were advised by agents and managers that they would be branded troublemakers and would never work in Hollywood again.

Those who did stand up to the studios and production overlords were invariably hit with substantial counter-claims and writs against the actors or producers, alleging mismanagement, bad performance of contracts or other maladies which had, at the end of the day, affected the profitability of their film. Scared of losing an expensive litigation, the actors invariably settled for a figure below that which they felt was rightly theirs, or even none at all.

Sean Connery changed all that, and set a standard for his colleagues to follow.

He and Michael Caine decided to go for Allied Artists, even though the amount they were owed was a fleabite compared with what they might end up paying if they lost. It was the principle involved, the Scot said. As of 30 September 1977, *The Man Who Would Be King* had yielded gross receipts of $8,207,998, of which the two actors claimed they were entitled to $410,400 each as their 5 per cent share in addition to the $250,000 they had been paid in advance. They had received $301,254 and felt that Allied Artists had defrauded them out of $109,146 each.

Allied Artists immediately issued a counter-claim charging that Caine and Connery had deliberately conspired to damage the company through the publication of false and defamatory statements. In the ensuing battle of words Connery was quoted on his views about corruption in Hollywood in the *New York Times*, and was immediately handed a writ by Allied claiming $21 million damages for libel and a second claiming $10 million punitive damages from each actor.

JOHN PARKER

At this point lesser men might well have retreated behind their lawyers' skirts, seeking an amicable out-of-court settlement or backing down completely. There was no question that had Connery and Caine lost they would have been wiped out financially. Caine said Connery would not be bullied and added that 'the wankers at Allied Artists' should have been with them the night he and Connery went to a comedy club in Los Angeles where a new and nervous comic was being heckled by a group of English tourists sitting behind them. Connery turned round and whispered to the leader, 'One more word out of you and I'll smack you through that fucking wall! Now give the kid a chance.' The hecklers did as he requested. He has this thing about fighting for the underdog, and being against social and moral injustice.

Defiantly, Connery went further than any previous actor in dispute with a production company. 'I've never cheated anyone in my life,' he said, 'and I don't see why people like myself who really work hard should be stolen from, cheated and defrauded.' He refused to back down, as did Allied Artists. The case went to court and a New York judge ruled in the actors' favour. Costs were awarded against Allied Artists which, on the face of it, looked a sound company having just scored another financial windfall with a film called *The Betsy*, starring Laurence Olivier and Robert Duvall, which had apparently grossed $9,162,486 in its opening three weeks.

Regardless of the $18 million or more that Allied had taken on Connery's and Olivier's two films alone they tumbled into bankruptcy.

Connery and Caine showed Hollywood that the actor could win and some spectacular litigation began pouring into the courts, giving rise to a whole new industry which exists today on a grand scale in Hollywood with accountancy experts, financial wizards and lawyers specialising in policing the grosses and the contracts. Stars who followed Connery into court in the succeeding five years included Blake Edwards, Mary Steenburgen, James Garner, Dustin Hoffman, Richard Harris, Tony Curtis and Joan Collins.

Nor had Connery finished with litigation. It had become something of an unwanted necessity, and his life for the six years after his first action against Allied Artists became dominated by successive legal cases in which he sued studios, his old sparring partner Cubby Broccoli and his personal business manager in multi-million-dollar suits.

Yet, the actor continued to work at a breathtaking pace during the second half of the 1970s. The third of his trio of mould-breaking films, *Robin And Marian*, was begun the day after he completed his commitment to John Huston. By then a number of other projects were on the stocks and he had discarded many others. Even so, quality and good fortune were not ever-present among the ones he selected. With few exceptions, there were basic flaws in most of the next half a dozen films that he agreed to take on. Even *Robin And Marian*, which consolidated his position as the new hero of adventure tales and received accolades all round, especially from his peers, was glum and unspectacular, although the Southern California Motion Picture Council gave it an award of merit for excellence as family entertainment.

Its most fundamental trouble was that the most familiar of all adventure classics was used as a vehicle for a Richard Lester exercise in psychoanalysis, putting Robin Hood, the myth and the legend, on the couch. It was Robin Hood 20 years beyond the familiar version when, after years with King Richard suffering the cruelty of the Crusades, he returns to Nottingham to pick up where he left off, battling with the Sheriff and courting Maid Marian who by then had become the Abbess of Kirkly. It seemed a reasonable prospect at the time, and the black-and-white words of the script were appealing.

The picture had the significance of marking the return to the screen of Audrey Hepburn, which attracted Connery to the part and, naturally, the focus of the media turned, wrongly, towards the romance and especially the 'love-making in a field of corn'. The in-vogue director Richard Lester had been offered a choice of projects by Columbia, and chose what he described as a beautifully honed screenplay by John Goldman which provided a totally new slant to the Robin Hood story – as indicated by the working title of *The Death Of Robin Hood*, changed by the producers at the last minute to one they considered more commercial.

There were some good colleagues in the cast, old friends like the excellent Robert Shaw (Sheriff of Nottingham), Richard Harris (King Richard), Kenneth Haigh, Ronnie Barker and Denholm Elliott, and there was much bonhomie in the off-duty hours in sunny Spain where the film was shot over a rapid six-week schedule. It fared reasonably well at the box offices of Europe but never left the zone of disappointment in America, in spite of some decent notices for the star. There were unforeseen elements which affected its success. The concept of an ageing and dying Robin Hood damaged the myth, and many did not enjoy seeing that happen.

With Robin's small band of followers slaughtered by the Sheriff, he continued to talk of great days and battles ahead. In spite of the permissiveness of the age, to have Marian living in sin, killing Hood and poisoning herself to save her beloved from the vain illusion that there was no place for him in the new age, did not go down well. The script took the burden of the critics' displeasure. With such a decent cast they were clearly expecting better.

Connery's authority was stamped all over the film and – regardless of the success or otherwise of the movie – he was re-established as a far stronger force than he had looked a year earlier. 'He was hot,' said Lester, 'superbly confident to work with especially in his instant analysis of the script, and I told him I wanted to work with him again as soon as possible.' Hot or not, the inexplicable happened – Connery plummeted head first back into mediocrity with an expensive film, *The Next Man*, that was so bad no one would pick up the British distribution rights and it was eventually sold direct to ITV in a package deal six years later.

The Next Man was a sadly dull and disjointed thriller about a female assassin hired to kill a Saudi Arabian Minister of State at the United Nations. While telling his story director Richard Sarafian, previously acclaimed for *Vanishing Point* in 1971, stopped to look at the location scenery in various parts of the world, and the narrative became blurred en route. There were some exceedingly hostile press comments, once again largely aimed at those around Connery rather than at him.

13

RECESSION

Dickie Attenborough was very keen to secure Sean Connery's signature for his new project. The initial support of a big name star was always important to the launch of any movie, of course, and almost the first question any backer would ask in the interview for money was 'Who's your star?' In the case of the WWII epic *A Bridge Too Far*, being packaged by veteran producer Joe Levine with the support of United Artists, it was a question of a number of major stars to help ensure that the huge budget required for the film would be recouped at the box office. The biggest names on both sides of the Atlantic were being mentioned.

Levine's selection of a director surprised some, in view of the size of the project. In Hollywood terms, Attenborough was more or less considered a rookie, and English, which meant that people were hardly falling over themselves to be in his film. His previous credits, *Oh! What A Lovely War* (1969) and *Young Winston* (1972) had received mixed reviews, but he was admired by many and clearly by Levine, who was sufficiently in favour of Attenborough

223

to entrust him with a $24 million budget, big money in anybody's language in 1976.

It represented a huge recognition of confidence in any director to bring to the screen an all-star version of Cornelius Ryan's harrowing account of the Allied defeat at Arnhem in 1944, although there were still those in Los Angeles who picked up their copy of *Variety* on the day Levine made his announcement and said, 'Richard who?' Casting was modelled on Darryl F Zanuck's *The Longest Day* – also based on a Ryan book – with a selection of Britain's finest set alongside a similar number of Hollywood. Levine and Attenborough both took a risk attempting to bring such a tragic event in Allied war history to the screen. Even 30 years later it was a topic fraught with controversy over the military planning and the strategic effectiveness of committing the First Allied Airborne Army and the British First Airborne Division to a disastrous attack on Nazi strongholds at Arnhem in September 1944. Of the 10,000 men who parachuted in only 2,163 returned, and a phrase from Winston Churchill's speech a few days later in the House of Commons became their epitaph: Not In Vain.

Connery was an early target of Levine and Attenborough and was sent a script while still working on *Robin And Marian* in the late summer of 1975. He was the number-one choice for the role of Major General Roy Urquart, a real-life Army officer and dour Scot who led the first push into Arnhem and who was still around to advise and criticise. He had never heard of Connery but his wife and daughter had, and the daughter especially was thrilled that James Bond was going to play her dad. Connery was not initially eager to do the film. He twice turned it down because he found the story of the events at Arnhem quite disturbing and the idea of filming them troubled him, but eventually he agreed. Then he had second thoughts and withdrew. More discussions followed with the director and producer in Hollywood and, finally, he became one of the first to sign. The large British contingent included Laurence Olivier, Dirk Bogarde, Anthony

Hopkins, James Fox and Denholm Elliott, to which was added an all-star American line up of James Caan, Robert Redford, Elliott Gould, Gene Hackman and Ryan O'Neal. A late addition was Michael Caine, who complained bitterly that 'everybody else is in this fucking film except me' when he met Connery and Attenborough in Hollywood.

Joe Levine employed Hollywood hype to announce what he considered to be a dream cast list, unveiled simultaneously in New York, London, Tokyo and Amsterdam. They were already well advanced with the massive pre-production work which entailed a cast of more than 100 actors and 300 technicians, not to mention 3,000 extras to be recruited from the Dutch army and universities and colleges. There was also the logistical problem of arranging the acquisition of aircraft, tanks, guns and assorted armoury from around the world and moving it to the location zone 30 miles from Arnhem ready for the first skirmishes to begin in June 1976.

A last-minute hitch even threatened to jeopardise Connery's appearance. Micheline had read in a newspaper report that Redford had negotiated a fee of $2 million for his role in *A Bridge Too Far*, whereas Connery had signed for $350,000.

He telephoned Joe Levine. 'Is this just newspaper crap or what?'

'No,' said Levine, 'that's what we had to pay to get Redford. His agent wouldn't budge. We wanted him in the picture, so we paid.'

Connery swore and complained. He was fed up with the media hype that surrounded the American actors, especially because his was damn near the largest part in the picture. Redford's was small by comparison, though admittedly he was exactly the kind of blue-eyed, all-American hero required to launch an almost single-handed attack on a Nazi-held bridge where he is shot and rescued by James Caan in true clichéd fashion. Levine blamed Connery's agent for accepting the fee, but agreed to increase it by 50 per cent. Connery stayed on the picture and did not allow the upset to affect his work.

He led the British to acquit themselves in far greater style than the normal stereotype perception by Hollywood of British Army officers and their dim-witted troops, compared with the swashbuckling, handsome and sexy Yanks. It was an old-fashioned perception largely attacked and transformed by Attenborough whose direction of a massively complicated and long story can only be applauded, in spite of American critics who seemed incapable of accepting that the sheer scale of the project and the emotional aspects of revisiting this disaster might account for some of the flaws. It was a spectacular, grandiose film. Connery's contribution, along with sterling performances by Dirk Bogarde, Anthony Hopkins and Edward Fox, was among the highlights.

Attenborough to this day reckons it ranks as one of Connery's finest performances and 15 years later, when the director had reached his own pinnacle and had worked with some of the finest actors in the business, he added a further remarkable accolade when he spoke at a special British Academy tribute to Connery in 1990. He described him as 'the most professional actor I have ever worked with in my life ... clever in terms of characterisation ... brilliant in performance ... and king in the eyes of the technicians.'

The difference in the reception between British and American peers and critics was quite marked. There were eight nominations at the British Academy Awards, including one for best film. Edward Fox won Best Supporting Actor, and the film also lifted the Best Cinematography, Sound and Music awards. Some of the British press came close to raving, whereas the Americans nitpicked about the length and did not honour it with a single Oscar nomination. Commercially it did well, taking $21 million in the US and doubling that figure with European earnings.

Again Connery did not attend the premiere in Leicester Square, where the real Major General Urquart joined Earl Mountbatten to recall the actual events on which it was based. Mountbatten thought Connery had done Urquart proud which, if anything, rather justified Connery's misgivings about the project in the first place.

However, Connery did get time at the end of it to bring his wife, son Jason, now aged 14, and stepson Stefan, to Britain for a brief visit to Fountainbridge. It was Micheline and Stefan's first trip to see Connery's birthplace. They went to his mother's house and then back to the tenement for a look around. They arrived there in the nick of time: the bulldozers were scheduled to move in and flatten the old place shortly afterwards. Jason, Connery revealed later, thought it was 'interesting'. Micheline and Stefan agreed it was awful while his mother still had an overwhelming affection for the tenement in which she had spent almost 50 years of her life. It was to be his last trip down that particular memory lane.

Already bubbling below the surface were two aspects of Connery's life which were to loom large and consume an excessive amount of his time and energy, while causing him a good deal of anguish, during the coming five years. The first involved a discovery by Micheline that his financial affairs might not be as secure as he thought. In the aftermath of the move out of England and during the preparations for litigation against Allied Artists for the underpayment of his profit share on *The Man Who Would Be King*, Micheline had gone to the Swiss offices of his business manager, Kenneth Richards, a former Army major and now a film accountant who had acted for Connery since 1972.

He was hired at a salary of £4,000 a year plus a commission of 1 per cent of Connery's earnings, later increased to £12,000 a year and 2 per cent of earnings as a measure of the actor's faith and confidence in him.

Micheline first became involved over a mundane matter concerning a washing machine from Connery's Chelsea apartment, which was unaccounted for; Richards, who had taken charge of the disposal of Connery's property, offered an explanation which Micheline accepted. Connery, permanently busy, always admitted he had been unable to concern himself sufficiently with his business affairs. It was Richards' role to deal with payments in and out, check the film company statements, handle some of his investments and generally manage his tax affairs.

After the washing-machine incident Micheline asked to see all the books concerning her husband's income and investments. The two men were, by then, heading for a spectacular fall-out which came with the discovery by Connery that a large amount of his money had been invested with a French property development company which was now in trouble. Connery found that the total money which had been lent from his private funds amounted to $3.25 million. He said he had never authorised the loan – although Richards claimed he had – and the chances of getting it back seemed grim. Work stopped on the development site, which included apartments, a country club and a hotel, and the only security Connery had for his money was a seemingly bankrupt scheme.

He demanded that Richards hand over all documents and information relating to his business affairs. He insisted upon a complete breakdown of expenditure and investments. In December 1977 he formally dismissed Richards as his business manager and they were destined to end up in court.

Other litigation, though not concerning him directly, was in the offing for a development that, ultimately, would produce the biggest surprise in filmland: the return of Connery as James Bond 20 years after his first appearance. The initial approach had come a year or so earlier when Connery flew to America for post-production work on *The Wind And The Lion*. Kevin McClory called him and said he was thinking of trying to reactivate the rights to *Thunderball*, ownership of which he shared with the estate of Ian Fleming. Under the original agreement hammered out in the court battle with Ian Fleming a decade earlier, the rights to the *Thunderball* script reverted to McClory in 1975.

The idea was to write a new script based loosely upon the first and produce a remake of what was the most financially successful of all the Bond movies.

Connery shook his head and said McClory must be joking.

McClory said he was not, and why didn't Connery hear him out? Perhaps as a ploy to get him on the hook, he suggested Connery might like to become involved in the ground work, possibly joining forces producing the script, but certainly contributing his knowledge and experience from the Bond films. Connery became more interested when McClory revealed that novelist Len Deighton, also a tax exile and living not far from McClory's own home in Eire, had agreed to become involved in writing the new screenplay, and the three of them would, he was sure, have a great collaboration. Connery, intrigued, took a flight to Ireland and joined Deighton in County Louth, where they worked on a new screenplay.

By then word was out that Connery might be planning to return as Bond, although there was no official confirmation of that when McClory took a large advertisement in *Variety* to announce that his company, Paradise Films, had commenced production preparations for a new film about James Bond of the Secret Service, adding that Mr Irving Lazar, otherwise known as Swifty and the hottest agent in Hollywood, had read the script and declared it to be one of the most exciting screenplays he had ever read.

Down at the offices of Eon Films Cubby Broccoli chomped on his cigar, reached for the telephone and said, 'Get me my lawyer ...'

Suddenly, all went quiet on McClory's Bond. It was the lull before the storm.

Troubles always seem to come in threes. It had happened on the litigation front, with writs over *The Man Who Would Be King*, Kenneth Richards and now Broccoli over the Bond film. Connery's next three pictures were trouble, too: *Meteor*, *The First Great Train Robbery* and *Cuba* – three financial flops which did nothing for either his confidence or reputation. Only the middle film of the trio was satisfactory on a personal level in that it was a decent film which he enjoyed making. Again, external circumstances torpedoed expectations of success. Before completing *A Bridge Too Far*, he had made the mistake – only visible with hindsight – of signing for the starring role in *Meteor* alongside Natalie Wood and Karl Malden. Even if it was a mistake, the money was an improvement on his recent fees and was especially useful at a time when he realised his net worth was nothing like what he had imagined it was, although he was by no means broke.

At the beginning the *Meteor* project looked impressive. It was being hyped as the disaster movie to end all disaster movies – which it was, but for the wrong reasons. In lesser roles were Henry Fonda, Brian Keith, Richard Dysart and his old friend Trevor Howard. MGM was lashing out money hoping that director Ronald Neame would bring in a repeat performance of *The Poseidon Adventure*, and had guaranteed a budget figure that exuded confidence. What could go wrong?

Well, just about everything, and on a disaster movie of these proportions there was considerable scope. The story sounded good: a team of international scientists joins forces to try to stop a five-mile-wide meteor from crashing into the earth and ending civilisation in one bang. It was highly dramatic stuff co-written by Edmund H North, who wrote the early science-fiction classic *The Day The World Stood Still*. Connery and Wood were the principal leaders of the action who eventually succeed in their task of hitting the meteor with a nuclear bomb, although by then it was so close that chunks of it fell to earth causing Switzerland to be covered by an avalanche, Hong Kong to be deluged by floods and the Hudson River to burst its banks as large holes are punched in New York City.

At the time of the latter catastrophe, the Connery and Wood characters are in a subterranean workstation and the actors had to wade through (specially heated) mud and slime for hour upon hour for the ten days it took to film the sequence. Apparently there was trouble getting the consistency of the mud right. Much rested on the special effects, which eventually took the picture well past its original budget. The actors were kept hanging around for months waiting for the picture to start, and when their work had finished the producers had the task of filming the special effects for which they did not have sufficient money. Makeshift constructions were built which, to an experienced model-maker, could be identified as containing a high content of plywood and glue. The whole thing was rather farcical and there were moments, said the critic for *Boxoffice*, which made Godzilla look like a masterpiece. It wasn't all bad, of course. There were some good scenes of tension but *Meteor* fell to earth like a stone and offered no resistance to the murdering critics.

Connery wasn't surprised. He and Wood had both scented failure halfway through but pressed on. The film was finally released in 1979 after several postponements while frantic efforts were made to improve the special effects, and Connery vainly tried to give it a boost with interviews. But *Meteor* quickly entered the *Boxoffice* list costly flops.

The First Great Train Robbery was a better film. It was well acted, nicely constructed and entertaining, and directed by Michael Crichton who also wrote the script (based upon his own novel), about an elegant, ruthless criminal who gathers together a small but expert gang to help him rob the Folkestone express of gold bullion destined for the Crimea in 1855. 'My dream,' said Crichton, 'was that the historical world was going to be lovingly re-created and then I was going to shoot *The French Connection* inside it.'

It was not a cheap movie, and Connery's little concert party for the robbery was an interesting group consisting of Donald Sutherland, Lesley-Anne Down, Wayne Sleep and Michael Elphick. Crichton's perception of the importance of signing Connery to lead them was shown when the location for filming was moved in its entirety from London to Ireland. Because of his tax position Connery could not work in the country where the robbery was supposed to have taken place, and when he first explained why he could not do the film Crichton pulled out of Pinewood and hired Ireland's National Studios for the two-month shoot, which began in the early summer of 1978.

Sutherland reported that they had good fun making the film. Crichton complimented Connery for his style and agreed that his suggestions on tightening up the script were a definite improvement. There were moments of true tension during shooting when Connery insisted upon performing the stunts on top of the moving train himself. It was an antique engine and carriages borrowed from the Irish Railway Preservation Society and Connery had been assured that it could not go faster than 35 mph. But as the sequence progressed Connery began to get worried; the train was rattling along at an estimated 60 mph, as later confirmed by the helicopter flying overhead with the cameramen. When finally it stopped, he questioned the driver and discovered that the engine had no speedometer.

'How do you know what speed you are doing, then?' Connery enquired.

'Oh, that's easy,' said the driver. 'I just count the trees.'

Crichton's film should have done better. The title struck a chord in Britain where it was readily identified with the real-life events of 1963, when Ronnie Biggs and Co. carried out their own Great Train Robbery. Reasonable business was recorded. In America, however, it made absolutely no impact on the cinema-going public. Connery blamed the lack of publicity, though it was certainly true that the Americans simply did not relate to the title – which in the US was just *The Great Train Robbery* – as they had in Britain.

The third financial failure in a row was equally surprising since the script had been written especially for Connery. In 1977 Richard Lester decided that his work with Connery on *Robin And Marian* had been so worthwhile that he would construct his next film around him. He sat down to write the outline and then commissioned dramatist Charlie Wood, famed for other Lester films such as *Help* and *The Knack*, to write a screenplay. Lester had never written a film for a specific actor before and, as things panned out, nor would he again. It proved to be an excruciatingly difficult task and the script was unfinished when he showed it to Connery.

Cuba told the story of a former British Army officer (Connery) hired by General Batista to defeat guerrilla forces in the period leading up to Castro's coup. There was a love interest in a local Cuban woman who was to have been played by Diana Ross, but she pulled out and Brooke Adams took her place – and regretted it. In spite of the unfinished script, producer Denis O'Dell had prised his production budget from a consortium of backers and all was set fair.

The regions of southern Spain, well known to Connery, provided ideal locations, and with a little help from the set designers could easily be transformed into the Cuba of the late-1950s. Adobe buildings with peeling whitewashed facades, political graffiti declaring *'Libertad Por Los Obreros'*; the seedy Hotel Roma, which was the location of the tryst between Connery and Adams, had been found in a cobblestoned backstreet of Cadiz, and not only did it have the same name it was so run down and authentic looking that nothing was changed or added. Even the Plaza de Espagna in Cadiz was quickly converted into the Havana square where Castro was hailed by thousands when he came out of the hills. Hundreds of extras had been recruited from the nearby Rota military base and all was in place, except for a finished script. Lester admits that he had not then decided how to end the film, but Connery placed a good deal of trust in the director to work it out.

In an interview during filming, entirely on location in Spain, he told syndicated columnist Marilyn Beck, who had flown in from Hollywood, 'When they brought me the *Cuba* script, it wasn't completely worked out and was too long. But I was convinced that it was a fascinating story with political intrigue, adventure, a clash of cultures and a love story.' When he arrived to begin shooting there were delays over the script, and Connery himself helped with the rewriting. It was not unusual for him to do so. 'I've had a hand in writing or rewriting virtually every film I've done,' he told Beck.

Connery had been pressing for a September 1978 start because

Cuban-style weather was beginning to fade away with the European winter. He knew that the shorter days and the rainy season would set in by the end of November. By January they were still in the thick of it and the rains came in abundance, along with other serious distractions.

They were set up near Cadiz, on one of the 78 sites where filming would take place. The day before Madrid's military governor, Constantino Ortin Gil, had been assassinated. Roadblocks and armed soldiers were everywhere. Connery remained in his hotel room as grips and production personnel waited in the pouring rain while a special mass for Gil was said in one of the sites reserved for filming.

Lester, covered in waterproofs, called out to a Spanish member of the film unit to discover what was going on. 'How long will the mass last?' he enquired.

The Spaniard replied in broken English, 'I don't know. I've never been to one.'

'Well, can you find out?' said Lester miserably. 'We can't hang around here all day. Look at this lot!' He gestured to the camera equipment that was being bogged down in pools of mud, and gazed upwards at the heavens where the dark skies showed no signs of producing Caribbean sunshine. Finally he called a halt for the day.

Worse was to come.

A B-52 bomber hired for a major action sequence at the end of the film crashed on the last day of rehearsals, and the only film of it was what Lester could rescue from the run-through. The train that was also supposed to be part of the same scene blew its boiler on the first take and was out of action for the duration, and then the massive selection of hardware needed for a battle between guerrillas and Batista's army failed to turn up. The entire Army division promised by the Spanish government was cancelled at the last minute because of the assassination of the governor. Lester had to make do with two Land Rovers and some cardboard cut-outs of tanks.

Connery, at this point, was ready to pack his bags and go home. He would have done had it not been for Lester, for whom he felt rather sorry. Minor changes were still being made as production resumed and were sufficient to cause Brooke Adams some consternation. 'You think you have learned your lines and that you know your character,' she moaned, 'and you read and re-read the story. But by the time you come to do the scene, it's changed and you don't know where the hell you are.'

A party of British journalists flown to Cadiz for some pre-launch publicity found Connery fractious and elusive. After a day's shooting he did not wish to get involved with the arrangements for an informal drink and interviews. 'Give me a break,' he said. 'I've done my bit.' And he got into his Mercedes and drove off in the direction of Marbella and home. Producer O'Dell shrugged his shoulders apologetically to the waiting press people. 'He's got a lot on his mind at the moment.'

That was certainly true. He knew by then that *Cuba* was not going to be terrific. The film was more dramatic in the making than in the final product. Connery said it was the worst mistake of his life, going into a film with an unfinished script. Lester had confused the issue by rolling up into one package elements of drama, documentary and Hollywood romance as he tried to emulate *Casablanca*.

The film died an instant death, running for just two weeks in London with only a limited run in the provinces. America was not interested, either, because anyone who was anywhere near abreast of political thought and public opinion would know that Cuba was not a place to inspire US audiences. Connery was good, in spite of the troubles, and only as the historical event fades into the distance does *Cuba* as a film became more agreeable.

At the time, though, Connery was left smarting once more. It merely added to the problems confronting him on a range of issues. He had dropped his London agent and signed on with Harry Ovitz in Los Angeles, though he had signified to his new man his intention to be personally involved at every stage of negotiations. From now on he wanted to know everything about his professional and business life.

He had geared himself financially closer to America than Britain, having bought a condominium in Los Angeles and a 600-acre pig farm in Iowa which ran under management. Eric Sykes, who saw a lot of Connery on the golf courses during the late-1970s, said he believed he was replanning his life to shut out any more risk.

'He had quite obviously suffered a few hard-felt lessons,' said Sykes, 'and made no secret of the fact that he had been taken for a few rides by some very clever international people. He had now decided to be his own man and run everything himself; no managers or hangers on, just him and Micheline. He's as straight as a dye and won't take any funny business and people certainly know where they stand with him. God help anyone who tried it on ...'

Connery had disposed of the action against Allied Artists. He had fought off the mound of writs over his alleged libel against AA executives. He had won his claim for payments owed on *The Man Who Would Be King* but the likelihood of getting his money or the £20,000 costs of the lawsuit seemed remote as Allied Artists headed for bankruptcy.

Action had already commenced on another front. Kenneth Richards had filed writs claiming 2 per cent of Connery's earnings for his last 4 films as well as those up to the time he was sacked as business manager, 13 films in all. Connery had responded by issuing counter-claims for damages of $3 million, alleging negligent handling of his affairs. The exchange of writs were the opening shots in a legal battle which would drag on for years and present Connery and his wife with what he later described as an 'ongoing nightmare'.

By then Cubby Broccoli, United Artists and the estate of Ian Fleming were variously involved with writs to stop Kevin McClory bringing a revised version of *Thunderball* to the screen, and they were especially keen to halt any attempt to get Connery into a rival Bond movie. There appeared to be a concerted wave of anti-McClory press material around, claiming that he was financially unsound and that there was never any possibility of him going ahead.

Connery was guardedly supportive of McClory. United Artists were, after all, also the distributors of three of Connery's films currently on release, *A Bridge Too Far*, *The First Great Train Robbery* and *Meteor*. He had already made his feelings known about UA's apparent lack of commitment to publicity on *The Great Train Robbery*, and if the view was abroad in Hollywood that Sean Connery was becoming a nuisance then it might have paid him to tread carefully. Caution and canniness were supposedly inbuilt mechanisms to the Celtic psyche, although he seemed more concerned about stopping reporters asking him about playing Bond again. 'Plenty of people were wanting to contribute to the picture financially,' he said in a press statement at the time. 'There were no problems on that score. But I was under the impression that it was totally clean. Free from any litigational problems. When we started to talk quite seriously about the possibility it became so complex. The lawyers came out of the woodwork by the hundred. Then the publicity started to work on it and I said, "That's enough!" and walked away.'

So McClory was fighting moves on several fronts to stop him getting anywhere near a production studio with a new Bond script, regardless of Connery's alleged disenchantment. Broccoli and UA had already been exchanging heavy correspondence insisting that, while the rights to *Thunderball* reverted to McClory after ten years, under the original deal hammered out in the British courts in 1965 only a verbatim remake of *Thunderball* was permissible and any new script would constitute a breach of copyright.

McClory countered that when he collaborated with Ian Fleming in 1959 – before Broccoli and Saltzman had come on the scene – *Thunderball* was not the only Bond they wrote together; there were at least two other screenplays and as far as he was concerned he was entitled to use them as the basis for a Bond film to be produced by himself.

Broccoli and UA now brought up the heavy artillery to suppress the rival Bond. The effect was to stall and delay McClory, who faced the threat of hefty legal bills. A few hours of research and a calculator quickly demonstrated why it was so imperative that McClory should be stopped, whatever the cost.

Up to the end of 1977 the complete series of Bond films had taken $1.2 billion dollars in box-office receipts. Total production costs came to $66.5 million, and after adding in all other costs such as the distribution of 1,500 or more prints of each film, promotions, publicity, parties, advertising and so on, James Bond had yielded a total $400 million in net profits – and this excluded television, cable and video rights and the merchandising, which were subject to separate licensing arrangements and attracted many more millions. The 1978 Bond production, *Moonraker*, was expected to turn in the highest figure of all, around $125 million – $45 million in America and $80 million overseas, and actually matched those figures admirably.

For distributing the picture United Artists took 33.5 per cent off the top before any expenses were deducted. They also took half the total net profit which they shared with Broccoli, having purchased Harry Saltzman's 50 per cent holding in Danjaq, the Swiss finance company that Broccoli and Saltzman set up in partnership back in 1961. All of which meant that the one single Bond film represented *40 per cent* of UA's total film revenue for the whole of 1978.

If there was salt to be rubbed into sore wounds, it might have been no consolation to Connery to discover – as he did that year – that Roger Moore had been paid $500,000 up front for *The Spy Who Loved Me* (in 1977) and ended up clearing $3 million after his share of the profits. He was expected to pick up around $5 million for *Moonraker*.

McClory was said to have offered Connery the same figure, $5 million plus a share, to make another Bond and that was the stage it had reached when the writs rained down and Connery pulled back. It was quite clear to him then that UA had decided to settle the issue once and for all and establish that McClory would be infringing their copyright. McClory decided to take them on, knowing full well that he would be ruined if he lost the protracted legal arguments that lay ahead.

And, for the time being, it rested …

14

NEVER SAY NEVER

So, the start of the 1980s found Sean Connery enveloped by worrying litigation and disappointments. He tackled them with dogged determination but no man could avoid being laid low by the weight of pressures; the letters, the meetings, the telephone calls which even time on the golf course could not eradicate. He had also been under pressure physically. *Cuba* had been his 15th film in 10 years and he had barely taken a break, apart from a few weeks here and there. If fate had been kind, past projects as productive as they had promised and everyone as straightforward as he had expected, then he would have had fewer problems than were confronting him. But life is full of what-ifs and buts.

He had pursued a somewhat tortuous path through the maze that he had set before himself. He might well have been contemplating at this moment that he could have taken the straight road to absolute fame and huge fortune by remaining in Bondage. But he chose the country route, with detours and diversions and uphill struggles. He was pushing a boulder up the mountain, and every so often he couldn't hold it and it slipped back. At the turn of the year he was in Hollywood, with some reluctance, promoting the release of *Meteor*, with *Cuba* following a month or so later. Neither provided him with any great cause for celebration. He dined with Michael Caine and Roger Moore and moaned long and hard. Caine said he was deeply 'pissed off' with life in general.

After that Connery retired for a rest and a lie down among the scented shrubs and citrus trees in his beautiful gardens tended by Micheline at San Pedro de Alcantara, the former fishing village not far from Marbella. This is where he went to get away from the world, behind the security gates surrounding his long stucco villa, the Casa Malibu, from which he could repel all boarders except a few well-chosen friends and golfers who would join him on any one of the dozen local courses.

He returned to the bosom of family life, playing golf with Micheline and his friends, although family life had hardly suffered from his work. Of his last four films, three had been shot close at hand. He had made sure that the children were protected from the star-gazers who followed him, and he believed in every other respect he had been a good father. Jason had not been brought up as the classic film star's child, lavished with money or cars to compensate for an absentee parent. Connery had chosen Gordonstoun for him, the rigorous and spartan educational establishment in Scotland dubiously renowned for its policy of character-building toughness. Jason left school and did not go to university, having decided to follow in his father's footsteps and become an actor. He received no help, other than the benefit of the family name, and went into repertory; nor did he call upon the facilities of the trust fund his father had set up for the children when he and Diane divorced. Connery once explained his motives to James Fox during filming a few years later.

'I found it interesting,' Fox told me, 'that he advised Jason to get a job in rep rather than hang around drama school, to get practical experience and to earn money. He made Jason find out if he could stand on his own two feet. He could, and the young man succeeded and gained his self-respect.' This was when Connery gave Jason a copy of his textbook by Yat Malmgeren, the Swedish ballet dancer, on the discovery of inner control and movement by which he himself had set so much store years earlier.

There were other family matters arising. As Connery weighed up his position at the start of the decade, there were examples all around which confirmed the advantages of having chosen the life in exile. But there were disadvantages, too, such as when his mother Effie suffered a stroke and paralysis, and he hired a plane to fly to Edinburgh to be at her bedside in a year when he had not used up all of the 90 days he was allowed in the country. He also kept in close touch with the Scottish International Educational Trust which benefited substantially from his contributions and now had an established record of assisting the underprivileged in art and education.

By the end of 1980 he had not appeared in front of a camera for almost 18 months when he finally responded to the cajoling efforts of directors and producers to bring him out of his self-imposed seclusion. Again he chose off-beat projects that none of his counterparts in the higher echelons of the profession might have accepted. First, Terry Gilliam contacted him. Connery had long been a fan of the Monty Python's Flying Circus team and Gilliam's new project was much in that vein, a surreal fantasy entitled *Time Bandits* which George Harrison's HandMade Films had agreed to back with £2.5 million.

Michael Palin had joined Gilliam in the writing and the story of a dreaming schoolboy named Kevin, whose imaginings run riot and provide a plethora of adventures as he is kidnapped by a gang of dwarfs and taken on a journey through time. All kinds of characters dart in and out of the action. John Cleese was Robin Hood, Ian Holm Napoleon, Sir Ralph Richardson the Supreme Being. But they needed a hero – and a big name – for one of the extended cameo parts, the role of King Agamemnon.

'It was vitally important to Terry Gilliam and myself,' Michael
Palin recalled, 'to have Agamemnon played by a strong and
charismatic actor but, most important of all, by an actor with a
sense of humour. Connery was our ideal casting for the role and
although ideal casting rarely works out in practice, in return for a
few golf courses Connery was persuaded to play and with a
mixture of heroics and humour created exactly the right feeling of
adventure, reality and fantasy which was the whole spirit of the
film. There are very few actors who could convey the strength and
seriousness of a legendary historical figure while being struck on
the head by a boy from the 20th century called Kevin.'

True enough. Connery agreed to do it, and because Gilliam and
Palin were going to be stretched for money he agreed to take a
small fee up front and a percentage, in spite of recent experiences
where the percentage became a fairly meaningless attribute. It was
an enjoyable succession of typical Pythonesque jokes. Connery's
contribution was filmed over a few days in Morocco close to the
Aloha Golf Club, where he and Micheline spent all their off-duty
hours and met up with James Hunt. Connery's association with
this somewhat modest picture, in terms of outlay, paid off
handsomely. *Time Bandits* fared moderately well in Britain, where
it opened in July 1981, but really took off in America after the
distributors Avco spent more on the promotion than the film had
cost to make. Consequently, it zoomed to the top of the US film
chart and stayed there for a month, a superb achievement for the
all-British outfit. It marked the beginning of what was to be a
return to favour in the early to mid-1980s of UK films abroad.

Time Bandits was the second film, incidentally, that Ian Holm
had appeared in with Connery, but as so often happens his
segments were at a different time and in another place, as they
were on the last occasion when he was King John in *Robin And
Marian*. It was an odd fact that points up exactly what living in
foreign parts had meant to Connery and demonstrates what little
contact he had with other members of his profession. Holm, who
was one of the country's busiest actors, said of Connery in a letter

to the author in 1992, 'I think he's a fine actor and I admire him greatly, but do you know? I've never met the man!'

Time Bandits was a warm-up to another fantasy, *Outland*, a sci-fi thriller which producer Peter Hyams was planning to bring to the screen on the back of the sudden popularity of space films, the current gold seam in Hollywood. Steven Spielberg's *Close Encounters of the Third Kind* (1977) with Richard Dreyfuss, *Star Wars* (1977) with Harrison Ford and Carrie Fisher and its sequel *The Empire Strikes Back* (1980), and *Alien* (1979) were among the box-office leaders luring audiences into cinemas faster than any new fashion since James Bond himself 20 years earlier.

Writer-director Peter Hyams himself had scored a 1978 hit with *Capricorn One*, a smart space thriller with Elliott Gould, and now had another such film ready to go into production. *Outland* was an adult movie that relied on the story rather than the hardware and special effects for its appeal, and perhaps that was a mistake. Hyams admitted that it was a rather blatant reworking of the classic Gary Cooper Western *High Noon*, set on a Jupiter moon. The potential for character development is what struck Connery when he read the script and, though he was also probably swayed by Hyams' insistence that anything set in space these days made money, he chose it as a film that could steer him back into the mainstream again after his skirmishes on the edge of the wilderness.

There were rumours that his confidence was badly dented and he was unsure of himself. If he was it did not show, and he went into the project with a full weight of commitment.

Connery's role was as a Federal Security Officer sent to mining base Con-Amalgamate 27, a sort of frontier town in space where, like the sheriff in a Western, he had been posted to supervise law and order.

As soon as Connery accepted and reached agreement on fees and percentages, he became involved in all aspects of production. He worked with Hyams on the script, giving his opinions on set design and even on the casting, which had become his style. He also persuaded Hyams to shoot the film at Pinewood, which he knew had some of the best special effects technicians anywhere in the world, a fact which some of the recent producers of space films had already discovered. This piece of advice also brought problems for himself.

It meant that because he was on screen for much of the picture the whole production had to stick rigidly to the 10-week shooting schedule so he kept within the 90-day rule. As he drew close to the deadline nerves became frayed and tempers short; he had to fly out of the country at weekends and return on Monday mornings. The tax laws riled him.

Michael Caine, firmly ensconced in Hollywood and turning out pictures like a mechanic on a car production line – three in 1978, two in 1979, two in 1980 and two in 1981, 'Some bloody good, some pretty average and some lousy,' in own his words – did a double act with Connery in berating the 90-day law on every occasion they talked about the British film business, struggling once again to get off the ground, and how they and others could bring major productions into British studios if only the tax situation was more amenable.

Not many people listened, and some of those who did were more likely to dismiss them as the selfish moans of a pair of tax-exiled millionaires interested only in money and not especially their art, which was obviously not true. The fact was that the number of British actors who were in that position could still be counted on one hand; they were Burton, Sellers, Connery and Caine, hardly the most mercenary, artistically uncaring of men.

Once they had reached a particular level, which they had to fight to maintain, there was simply nothing available for them in the home country, anyway. Apart from the occasional fits and starts, usually centred around Richard Attenborough who won an Oscar for his direction of *Gandhi* in 1982, or one-off flashes of brilliance like *Chariots Of Fire* (1981), there was little else to offer, even though the technicians and the technology available in Britain were renowned for their excellence.

Other benefits were lost, too. As part of his deal in *Outland*, Connery insisted that the film should have a Scottish premiere. It was set for Edinburgh in August 1981 and was then shown at the Edinburgh Film Festival. A number of major stars, including Jack Lemmon, supported Connery's charity efforts and all proceeds went to his trust, which was the beneficiary of more than £8,000.

Bringing *Outland* to Edinburgh signified Connery's faith in the picture, because he knew he would be putting himself in the direct line of fire for press and public observations. *Time* magazine had given him encouragement when the film opened in America two months earlier, concluding that Connery was perhaps the one true 'romantic hero in the movies now', a rather pleasant accolade to receive. Reviewers were mixed in their opinions of *Outland*. Whereas the *Sunday Telegraph* rated it the best thriller of the year and lively, intelligent entertainment, *Monthly Film Bulletin* wearily dismissed it as 'the same old dreary electronic gadgetry and the same old hollowly echoing metalwork sets'. To analyse the problems more deeply, it is possible to see that Connery had repeatedly achieved some truly superb characterisations. Both his heroes and his villains were played with an excellence rarely matched among his contemporaries in each of the fads through which he passed – the current one being the *Star Wars* era – and yet he seemed destined to be lured into films that never quite hit the mark. Trawling through the reviews of successive films in the 1970s, the theme continued throughout … that Connery's performances were generously praised. Time and again, as friends and colleagues were interviewed for this book, the view was repeated over and over that his work had maintained an applaudable consistency.

Some good films he had made had not been fully exploited, and the bad films were bad in spite, rather than because, of his presence. He had also had the misfortune, on occasions, to work with world-famous and brilliant directors on pictures that were considered not among their best works. A suitable analogy would be Connery trying to ring the bell at a fairground and only managing it four times out of ten, not because he wasn't strong enough but because the mallet kept breaking.

And it was still breaking.

As he completed *Outland*, he was already negotiating with two renowned directors seeking his services. Both were talking about potentially highly successful movies, and one supposes it is often necessary to take such famous and successful men at their word.

In terms of directors they do not come much more renowned than Richard Brooks and Fred Zinnemann. Brooks, a double Oscar winner, had been involved in some classic films including *Cat On A Hot Tin Roof, Blackboard Jungle, Elmer Gantry, Sweet Bird Of Youth* and Truman Capote's *In Cold Blood*. He was a man the stars do not normally question when he calls and says, 'I want you for my next picture.' Likewise the genial Fred Zinnemann, who won an Academy Award nomination for *High Noon* and an Oscar for his brilliant direction of *A Man For All Seasons* starring Paul Scofield (who also won an Oscar, as did the picture, the writer Robert Bolt and the cinematographer Ted Moore). Zinnemann's long list of credits and some superb films would give any actor a feeling of confidence.

Brooks had known Connery for some years, and when he offered him the lead in a film called *Wrong Is Right* Connery first had to prise the script loose for a reading. Brooks was known for his reluctance to give actors this facility and his usual technique, used wherever possible, was to give them a daily portion of the script. He would work on his films as if they were top secret, which meant the whole of the characterisation was not visible in one sitting. That's the way he worked and that's the way he had achieved some of his major successes. On this occasion, as on all others, Connery would not even consider the job until he had seen the words and was the only member of the cast to be so honoured. The screenplay was a weighty 280 pages, and much too long in Connery's view. It was perhaps something of a compliment that Brooks invited Connery to join him in reworking it, especially since he had written the play himself.

It was a vast and long statement, vilifying the American nation with Brooks's view on contemporary society, told through the eyes of Connery's character, a global television reporter who had become the first major international deliverer of news via the satellite technology that became commonplace a decade later. It was intended as a sharp and cynical overview of a world manipulated by the CIA, and Brooks had taken a potshot at pretty well every major political institution. It was a controversial film that stirred up opposing reviews. Some found it merely boring, others were angered by the assault on American values, while the reviewer from the *Hollywood Reporter* was electrified and compared it to *Dr Strangelove*.

In London the distributors did not quite know what to make of it. They changed the title to *The Man With The Deadly Lens* and plastered the hoardings with Bondlike posters of Connery holding a video camera in the same way that he might have held a gun. Critics were singularly unimpressed, though Connery again gleaned personal accolades; but it barely lasted a couple of weeks in the capital's prime cinemas. So much for the encounter with Richard Brooks.

Fred Zinnemann should have been better, and as soon as Connery had finished the rapid shoot in New York he was due in Switzerland to begin a two-week intensive course in mountaineering before beginning work on *Five Days One Summer*. He lingered en route long enough to read legal reports and issue instructions on matters proceeding against his former business manager, Kenneth Richards, and to find out if there was a conclusion to Kevin McClory's ongoing battle in the law courts to get approval to bring his reworked version of *Thunderball* to the screen. The case was close to settlement and McClory, whacked by almost seven years of intense legal tussle, was hopeful of achieving a result favourable to himself.

Meanwhile, Connery learned that Kenneth Richards was continuing to press for a commission on all Connery's income since he was fired in 1978, and he was still unable to effect the return of the money invested in the property development in France. It seemed now that the case would have to go to the High Court, and Micheline was locked in consultation with lawyers trying to trace the whereabouts of the lost millions. The row was coming to a head and Richards had already effectively told Connery, 'See you in court.'

The actor was also beginning to toy with the idea of new legal action against Broccoli and United Artists. At present it was the germ of an idea, but before long he would unleash it sensationally in the American courts.

On to Switzerland where Fred Zinnemann, a charming man whose tenacity and directorial skills were legendary, loved by Grace Kelly for *High Noon*, disliked by Burton for reasons unknown and who angered Taylor because *A Man For All Seasons* beat *Who's Afraid Of Virginia Woolf?* in the Oscars, was waiting for him on the high snow slopes of the Alps. It was to be Connery's base for the next four months, and Micheline came in and out, dealing with his business matters and social affairs and keeping him company. He also found a golf course.

Zinnemann had wanted Connery for *Five Days One Summer* after seeing him in *Robin And Marian*. He did not especially like the film, but he liked Connery's performance. Alan Ladd Jr and Jay Kanter, who were producing for Warner's, were also happy, although their support was surprising because Zinnemann's film was like nothing at all in the current fashion.

For Zinnemann, this was more than just another movie. He explained to Connery that it was the realisation of his own dream, and his enthusiasm was infectious enough to make Ladd and Kanter part with approximately $15 million of someone else's money so the director could take a large number of people up a mountain and shoot some stunning photographs.

Someone had once asked Zinnemann to describe his personal idea of happiness and he had said, 'To sit on top of the Matterhorn, wondering how the hell I would ever get down.'

As a teenager he had managed to climb a few of the snow-covered peaks in Austria but the magic stopped when he left Vienna for Paris before the war. For a long, long time he dreamed of making a movie about the mountains of his youth, a movie in which they were not just scenery but actors with characters of their own. There was elation in being a tiny speck lost in the brooding, mysterious landscape, but the greatest thing by far, he said, was the total silence.

He began searching for a suitable story and after a few false starts he came across a short story written by Kay Boyle in the 1930s called *Maiden Maiden*, about a Scottish doctor and his young mistress on a holiday in the Alps. She falls in love with the guide and is faced with a difficult choice until one day the doctor and his guide are overdue from a difficult climb. The girl is waiting in a mountain hut below; only one man can be seen far in the distance, painfully moving down the glacier. The girl rushes to meet him. Clearly there has been a fatal accident but until the last moment she – and the audience – have no idea which man has survived.

Connery was offered an exceedingly attractive package to play the lead as the doctor. It was explained in advance that he would have to work most of his own stunts as the photography was so often in close-up that doubles would be spotted. He did not mind, even though he found himself some days hanging upside down on a climbing rope with the perspiration of fear freezing on his brow.

A group of climbers was hired to provide safety for everyone working in dangerous spots. Hamish MacInnes, head of the Mountain Rescue Service in Glencoe, brought his group on a busman's holiday and, with Connery present, they soon became known as the Scottish Mafia. All were world-class climbers, 'hard-drinking lusty eccentrics' according to Zinnemann, and they had more fun and more laughs than any group of men he had ever known.

'Besides being a genial, delightful gent,' said Zinnemann, 'Sean Connery was an excellent actor and a good sport. His physical courage and his gruff, sarcastic sense of humour made him enormously popular with the crew. He would much rather have played golf than muck about in mountains but he didn't grumble when asked to drop, suspended on a rope, into a 200-foot-deep crevasse. He projected an air of complete authority.'

The mountain drama was filmed against a backdrop of breathtaking scenery. It was true and real, with dangerous climbs and spectacular landscape, one peak being so inaccessible that it could only be reached by helicopter and everyone had to be ferried in separately over a period of hours.

Anna Massey, who was among the well-matched supporting cast, seemed to find the whole experience invigorating and joined the long list of actors and actresses who became Connery fans after working with him. 'I found Sean completely charming,' she said, 'and wonderful to work with, and that is not just actor's speak. His sense of humour is delightful. I am also a great admirer of his work. He seems to have on screen an effortless energy.' Reviewers were certainly not unkind, one ranking it among Zinnemann's best and most mysterious works, though most could not disagree that the story was rather thin.

In November, during a break from the Alps, Mr and Mrs Sean Connery, he in smart dark overcoat, white shirt and tie, and she in high-collared, light-coloured blouse under a navy-blue jacket, looking like a pair of lawyers, were walking up Fleet Street, London, towards the High Court where the first of his long drawn-out legal battles was to be concluded before a judge. Kenneth Richards had maintained to the last that he was due the 2 per cent commission from Connery's earnings, because of what he maintained were contractual obligations and a promise that 'as I grow, you grow'.

Connery continued to assert that he had sacked Richards for mishandling his affairs and as such he was due no further payment. Richards gave evidence that, from 1972, 70 per cent of his time was devoted to Sean Connery's business affairs for which there was first a verbal contract and later a written one.

Connery's QC attacked the accountant for writing a letter to

Connery which, he said, was tantamount to blackmail, alleging that Connery would go to prison if 'certain matters' were brought to the attention of the Inland Revenue. Connery was clearly affected by the case, and at one stage as the questioning of his former adviser went on he asked for a glass of water. A measure of how closely Richards was involved with Connery's affairs was shown by the fact that Richards had apparently been able to remove private documents from Connery's desk in the study at his home, have them photocopied and then return them.

The judge, Mr Justice Talbot, said that never had he witnessed a party's case to be so destroyed by cross-examination, and furthermore he was satisfied that Connery had accounted properly and adequately to the Inland Revenue over his financial affairs. Richards' claim for damages was dismissed and as they left court Connery said to waiting reporters, 'When people read that I was near to tears at the announcement of the verdict they don't realise the significance of my counter-claim against Mr Richards. His claim was for a trivial sum compared to what he owes me, and now it is up to the court to decide the amount.'

At another hearing Connery was awarded an interim judgement of a million pounds damages against his former manager until a further court hearing, to be set at a later date, when the full amount was to be assessed. In the meantime, he was able to top up his bank balance with a swift fee for a supporting role in the British-made Canon Films' *The Sword Of The Valiant*, a picture of Middle Ages mythology which was neither here nor there and for which he was required for six days' work. He probably never saw it. The film, though made with British actors, failed to find a British distributor and was not seen until bought for television six years later. By then Connery was in need of some high-profile sustenance, and he got it from Bond.

In the summer of 1980 Kevin McClory won his battle with Broccoli, United Artists and the estate of Ian Fleming. An Appeal Court decision in America cleared the way for McClory to move ahead with the production of his film, based upon his rights to *Thunderball*. But McClory was tired and fed up. It had been a long battle. United Artists had a bank of lawyers able to pursue every legal tactic available to them. He had no backing and everything had come from personal resources because the studio originally putting up the finance for his film had pulled out when the situation turned nasty.

He began casting his net for production money, knowing he needed 15 or 20 million, minimum. He talked about getting Connery to play James Bond again, but nothing moved for months until Jack Schwartzman, a wealthy Los Angeles lawyer associated with Lorimar Pictures, decided to launch his first full-scale bid at producing a picture and made an offer for the whole project.

Long discussions followed before an agreement was reached in the late summer of 1981. In exchange for an undisclosed sum of considerable proportions, McClory handed over two folders of A4 paper containing the script he had written with Ian Fleming for *Thunderball* along with the one Sean Connery had written with Len Deighton five years earlier entitled *Warhead*.

They signed what became known as the Warhead Contract and Schwartzman gave the whole job lot to screenwriter Lorenzo Semple Jr, formerly of *Batman*, for a 'treatment'. Schwartzman had already decided long ago there was only one actor who could turn this dusty, yellowing batch of paper into money, and that was Sean Connery. He telephoned. Connery did not say no, though it became clear to Schwartzman that he would have to make him an offer he could not refuse. The competition was setting the pace. There had been much press talk early in the New Year of 1982 that Roger Moore was seeking $5 million plus a percentage for the next Bond, *Octopussy*, with which the rival Bond would be competing. Broccoli had adopted his usual negotiating stance, that anyone could play Bond, and there was talk that he was offering it to an unknown actor who was friendly with his daughter. Moore settled. Four million was the reported figure and that became the one to beat. Connery, on a shot to nothing, reportedly sought to beat that figure and a fee of $5 million was mentioned.

Micheline said it would be fun and even suggested the title, *Never Say Never Again*, which had absolutely nothing to do with the story; it was a joke because he had said he would never do Bond again. He had called Bond 'Frankenstein's monster' and a lot of other rude names besides. But why, at the age of 52, had he decided to go back in? Was it the fear of a recessive career? Did he see it as a chance of revitalising his image and checking in with the younger generation? Or was it the money, straight and simple?

The question was put to him many times, but he gave different answers to different interviewers and there was never a satisfactory ring to his replies. He told one interviewer he was 'curious' to revisit, another 'for the fun of it', and a third 'I thought it might be interesting'. So that was that. Schwartzman got his man and Connery agreed to don the toupee once more and become James Bond for the seventh and 'positively last time'.

The negotiations ended and the heartaches began – but then $5 million plus a percentage of the gross never came easy. The two competing Bond films were both due out the following summer of 1983. Even then the attempts by United Artists to block the movie were still going ahead, and continued to the last. But Broccoli was the least of Connery's problems now.

15

BOND REVISITED

The 1960s were history. The Beatles would never be seen on the stage again, but Sean Connery was back, fit and healthy, tussling with the alter-ego he once hated, ready to re-create the image of those far-off days when he could draw as big a crowd as the Fab Four. Twenty years after he first appeared as James Bond he was preparing to wage the final battle with Blofeld. Regardless of the reasons, there was a degree of courage in the decision, as his friends recognised, for it could have been a disastrous move. True, Roger Moore was actually a year older and already reaching the point of considering retiring himself from the role. Connery had a craggy look to him. His face, always giving the impression of being older than his years anyway, had that certain lived-in appearance. He was thicker bodily, though still very fit from years of golf, tennis and swimming. He actually looked how James Bond, 20 years on, would have looked in reality.

Even so, he would need to get into trim by a heavy schedule of workouts in the gym. He had also been so intent on burying his association with Bond that audiences had become more familiar with a man of many faces and moods. How would they react? His true fans would remember him as smart and handsome, glinting eyes flickering with mischievous humour, the master of the double entendre and, above all, as a mover, gliding catlike across the screen exuding body language.

Could he get it back? Or was it too late? There was far more than money riding on the outcome. His reputation, no less, was at stake and there were some who would have enjoyed seeing him fall flat. It was because of these considerations that, initially, he insisted upon a high level of involvement all the way through script, casting and director approval. What he had failed to account for was what he later described as ineptitude among the producers, which would cause some considerable anguish as work progressed. None of the familiar aspects of a Broccoli production would be visible, such as the opening shots, the music and a few regular faces. Connery had to compensate for that and was adamant on going for a quality production and at least the producer, Schwartzman, who was funding the picture from his own resources, did not stint on the $25 million-plus budget. The director was Irvin Kershner, who had hired Connery for *A Fine Madness* and recently scored a hit with *The Empire Strikes Back*.

Kershner, a witty and meticulous man of professorial style and one of Hollywood's last remaining gentlemen, had long been in a backwater because, if anything, his integrity did not find him many supporters. He became the exception to the rule and it was eventually rewarded. Connery admired him and it was largely his doing that found Kershner now directing a James Bond movie.

He had much in common with the star, and to listen to him talk was like hearing Connery in a different voice. 'Obsession and stupidity,' he said, 'have kept me going. Stupidity because this greedy, narcissistic, appalling, dishonest business with its crazy insecurity isn't where anyone should live a life.' Kershner worked with Connery in selecting the actors who were, in the event, to add considerable class to the production, Edward Fox, a health-freak

258

'M', Alec McCowen as 'Q', the very fine Klaus Maria Brandauer as Bond's arch-enemy Largo, and Max Von Sydow as Blofeld.

They were all strong actors for whom the roles were entirely suited, and a great deal of thought had gone into matching faces and styles to the character to be portrayed. The same applied to the female roles, with Kim Basinger as Domino and Barbara Carrera as the awesome Fatima Blush. The black actor Bernie Casey became Felix Leiter of the CIA, a modern, if token, thought. Connery was none too happy about the final screenplay which Schwartzman had commissioned from Lorenzo Semple. He, being American, had missed some of the nuances so vital to Connery's Bond. Connery and Kershner, who was also new to Bond and was deliberately treating this picture as if it were the first one, decided they could not deal with the problems themselves and so Sean brought in the British comedy writers Dick Clement and Ian La Frenais to help bolster the humour. Though the British writers did 'a magnificent job on it' the Writers Guild of America would not allow credits for them on the movie. Connery begged them to change their minds but the administrators were adamant. And so the contribution of Clement and La Frenais went unrecorded.

Delays on rewriting the script and other production matters meant that filming did not begin until September 1982. Connery had said he did not wish to enter a race with Broccoli's *Octopussy*, based upon a Fleming novelette though with a mere nod towards the original plot, and anyway it was clear he was going to lose. Press reports kept a check on both to provide fans with a running commentary and a press release, issued by Warner's publicity department and deposited in the Los Angeles film archives, could have been written 17 years earlier when Connery did *Thunderball*:

> *Sean Connery checked his diving equipment for the last time, adjusted his mask and slipped under the coolly inviting waters of the Bahamas. Fifty feet below him on the sea bed waited an army of highly skilled underwater film technicians. Blazing lights lit up the murky depths and were reflected back in tiny*

sparkles off the iridescent shoals of fish that swam with regularity past the cameras ... as did an all-too-real 12-foot killer shark. The underwater director had been working for weeks with his team and a number of tiger sharks; they are all experienced men but sharks are unpredictable. Connery insisted on doing his own stunts. The scene had to be shot and he was willing to do whatever he thought necessary for the success of the film ...

All of that was true. The sharks were real, and three particularly menacing ones were aggravated sufficiently to attack. Any one of the 300 teeth shared between them could shave a man's chin and a mouthful could snap a man's leg as if it were plywood. Fifteen divers were paid $2,000 for the duration, and it was their job to drive the sharks into position and ward them off the star if they got too close. There were other spectacular scenes which Connery did personally, and one later in the South of France, when he had to plunge with the heroine into the Med on a horse, attracted some vilification from the RSPCA when the film was released.

To the casual observer it all looked good, but, without the established 'machinery' of the Broccoli Bonds, production did not run smoothly. 'All kinds of shit was flying,' Connery admitted in an interview afterwards. 'Quite frankly, I could have just taken an enormous amount of money and walked away from the whole thing and the picture would never have been finished. I could have let it bury itself but once I was in there, I found myself in the middle of every decision. Myself and the assistant director produced that picture.'

Roger Moore's Bond was, meantime, darting through the streets of a crowded city in north-western India in his dinner jacket to escape his nemesis, the decadent Kamal played by Louis Jourdan, and the usual Eon crowd were around for support. When they finished the scene Moore returned to the hotel, hot but unflustered, strolled through the hotel courtyard and into the swimming pool, fully clothed and without breaking his stride, and up and out again into the arms of his wife Lusia. He was clearly ambivalent about Bond and suitably self-deprecating about himself. A *Time* magazine reporter sent to track down this pair of competing Bonds asked Moore in all seriousness how he brought his acting gifts to bear on the subtle character changes demanded of James Bond. 'Sometimes I wear a white dinner jacket and sometimes a black one,' Moore replied.

The Connery Bond locations moved around the world, to the South of France and the Monte Carlo casino, northern Africa and Nassau, before final completion at Elstree Studios in London. Connery was working 12, 14 hours a day, often starting at 6.30am.

By then Broccoli and Moore had completed filming *Octopussy* and rushed their film out for premieres that summer, creaming off the best business in the USA. Connery, however, got the better of the reviews. Some critics were scathing about *Octopussy*, saying that it was a sterile succession of stunts linked by an implausible plot.

Connery, perhaps with the benefit of sentiment, was welcomed back with open arms, and that was apparently important to him. Many were pleased to record the exemplary return of the *real* James Bond. Richard Schikel in *Time* magazine was typical: 'It is good to see Connery's grave stylishness in this role again. It makes Bond's cynicism and opportunism seem the product of genuine worldliness (and world weariness) as opposed to Roger Moore's mere twerpishness.'

It was just like old times, too, in the cinemas. Although American business was less than that recorded for *Octopussy*, worldwide it was attracting huge attention. The movie broke records in the Far East, opened in London's West End in seven cinemas and coincided with retrospective festivals of Connery's work at the National Film Theatre in London and in Europe.

A special premiere was staged in Glasgow for charity and Neil Connery read out a speech from his brother. *Never Say Never Again* rapidly went to number one in the British film chart, reached six in the American list and was voted the second most successful picture of the year behind the man who had taken on the adventure mantle for the 1980s, Harrison Ford in *Indiana Jones And The Temple Of Doom*.

Bond had undoubtedly given Connery another massive boost, and vice versa. He was back at the top of the tree and could have named his own price for another Bond film, and other projects began arriving daily for his consideration.

The success of *Never Say Never Again* masked his anger over the production difficulties, which almost matched some of his rages of the past. This time he was not complaining about his alter-ego taking over his life. The kind of silly adulatory pressures that were heaped upon him in the past were no longer a problem. It was the damned business of making the film. He was tired and disillusioned. It was as if he was cursed, and this time it was another set of people and for different reasons. He mostly blamed the producer who, he said, took a place in the Bahamas halfway through the production, had an unlisted telephone number and could not be reached.

It was, he moaned, like working in a toilet.

Whatever problems there were, Connery shielded most from the rest of the crew and not unexpectedly the actors and technicians were full of praise, as usual. It becomes almost monotonous to record it, but the views of the workers remain steadfastly similar from picture to picture and had not changed from the time when the *Marnie* crew bought him a thousand-dollar watch. Edward Fox reported, 'Suffice to say he was highly professional, very skilful and a real star; as a man, he was generous to a fault to fellow actors and always considerate and helpful.'

They were largely unaware of the rearguard action he was fighting. At the end of it he walked away in a fury and did not make another film for more than two years.

Three months after the release of *Never Say Never Again*, Connery went to London to obtain, finally, the long-awaited adjudication of his claim for damages against his former business manager,

Kenneth Richards. The case had now dragged on for almost six years and this was the final scene following the previous award of a million pounds interim damages.

On 17 February 1984 Connery's lawyer Keith Schilling repeated in the High Court that Richards had loaned several million dollars of the actor's money to Jean Canela, a French property developer, and it was doubtful that the money would ever be recovered. The judge awarded Connery £2.8 million damages against Richards which, because of the very substantial fall in the value of the pound against the dollar compared with when he last appeared, was considerably less than original expectations. However, it was all rather academic. Though Connery said he was delighted at the outcome, he doubted then whether he would ever recover his money. Richards claimed to have no personal assets of any value, and a year later was declared bankrupt. The Richards case, and the money involved, was important to him as a matter of principle. It was a mere fleabite when compared with the next litigation Connery launched, a claim which stunned both the showbusiness and legal professions in general and the money-conscious film community of Los Angeles in particular. It was considered audacious and courageous, depending which side of the fence you were on, once again striking at the very heart of the Hollywood system that employed him, but on a grander scale than any actor had previously undertaken. Brando had recently sued Warner's for a slice of *Superman* profits and there had been a succession of claims since Connery's case against Allied Artists in 1978, usually in arguments about the assessment of profits.

This dwarfed all of them.

At the heart of the action, it seemed, was Connery's continuing feelings about the exploitation of actors, and the actions he took only went to confirm what many had believed was gnawing away inside: that Cubby Broccoli's extraordinary wealth had been inexorably linked to his own career as Bond and that he had not received a fair share.

He had talked recently of having retained an 'exceptional' Los

Angeles lawyer and on 20 June 1984 he entered a claim for $225 million against Cubby Broccoli and United Artists (who had recently merged with MGM). The suit, filed in the Los Angeles District Court, was a long and complicated statement that Connery and his advisers must have worked on for months. The District Court documents relating to the case showed the extent of Connery's escalating influence over the Bond projects in the early days, and the web of interlocking companies he set up to handle his affairs. They demonstrated, too, the highly complex pattern of studio financial channels through which income from each film is pumped as it is played around the world, with cash diving in and out of tax havens.

Connery's claim threw caution to the wind and seemed to pay no heed to the prospect that he might never work in Hollywood again – the same possibility that existed, but did not materialise, when he sued Allied Artists for unpaid revenue on *The Man Who Would Be King*. He was, it seemed, intent on having a final mother of all battles with United Artists and Cubby Broccoli in an attempt to secure a retrospective portion of the fortunes they had made out of Bond, whose films by 1984 – for the complete series – had topped $1.5 billion in gross business, excluding merchandising.

His suit accused UA/MGM, Cubby Broccoli and two of his companies of deceit, breach of contract and the infliction of emotional distress upon himself. Lawyers for both firmly denied the claims and from Broccoli there came the plaintiff reply to any who asked questions about Connery, 'My only crime was to make him rich.'

Connery's main contentions were that: UA and the producers had not paid him all that was due under profit-sharing deals; and his profit participation in the Bond films constituted a stock participation in the company.

On the latter point Connery was testing the water in many respects, for as one Hollywood legal specialist was quoted as saying at the time, 'They're pushing new ground here. Truthfully, the definition of a security is a fuzzy area and they are correct to challenge it. Once they establish that he got his profit participation in exchange for services, you can try and establish that was the sale of a security in the company. But I've never heard of profit participation being successfully classified as a security.'

To prove his point, Connery's lawyers filed a complete statement of his business affairs into court which reveal his company structure since he first signed for *Dr No*. The overhead company, in whose name he had filed the lawsuit, was Inforex Corp, NV, a Netherlands Antilles corporation which was concerned with the profits of *From Russia With Love, Goldfinger, Thunderball, You Only Live Twice* and *Diamonds Are Forever*.

In common with all major performers, writers and directors, Connery used 'loan-out' companies often incorporated in tax havens such as the Netherlands Antilles or Switzerland and ostensibly those companies supply services – i.e. an actor – to a specific production. Elizabeth Taylor and Richard Burton were among the earliest to establish a pattern to protect their money from the taxmen of the various countries in which they worked, or where their work was shown. Although no salaries were specified, the court documents showed that after the success of *Dr No* Connery negotiated a profit-sharing deal for the next Bond film, *From Russia With Love*, which guaranteed him one per cent of all gross money received in excess of $4 million in America. In 1964, he renegotiated his deal again, and Broccoli and Saltzman agreed to pay him, in addition to the up-front fee, 5 per cent of profits from *Goldfinger*. It was a standard Hollywood net-profits deal, the profits being the amount of money left after all certified production costs had been set against the total income – and the cause of severe contention between many an artist and studio in the past.

In 1966, when Bondmania was at its height and *You Only Live Twice* was in production, Connery again renegotiated his position, to receive 5 per cent of profits for his services to the producers' British-based company, Eon, and an additional 5 per cent of profits from sales outside Britain and the US as recognition of his international drawing power, especially in places like Japan where Bondmania was the most demonstrative. This represented a substantial improvement on his previous deal.

The extent to which United Artists and the producers were prepared to go to keep him in the Bond series is best demonstrated by the figures lodged for his last film for Broccoli, *Diamonds Are Forever*. In addition to the $1.25 million fee which he donated to his education trust in Edinburgh, he negotiated terms which provided him with 10 per cent of the *gross* receipts from the first dollar the movie took, rather than a share of the profits, so that if it took $50 million in America he would receive $5 million. The court documents showed that there was a separate agreement covering the United Kingdom, giving him an additional 2.5 per cent of the gross receipts, increasing his total share to 12.5 per cent of every pound the film took in the UK.

He had also, in the middle of the renegotiations on profit sharing, pulled off something of a coup in the film business when he won agreement to be paid 25 per cent of all profits from the merchandising of James Bond and the 007 trademark, set up between his own companies and Danjaq, the Swiss-based finance company then owned jointly by Broccoli and Saltzman.

This was unheard of, and it was a deal that set the pace for future generations of performers seeking a share of the merchandising. The most notable of them was *Batman* in which Jack Nicholson, as the Joker, secured exceedingly beneficial merchandising terms which earned him millions of dollars.

One last but important point, not just for Connery but again for all actors and performers involved in these complicated service contracts: he won very strict accounting procedures which were to be followed on the calculation of his profits, and the facility to audit the UA books at any time if he felt he was being underpaid.

It was the latter point that had, in part, given rise to the lawsuit. His lawyers claimed that UA had not properly followed the payment procedures, and they had only discovered the discrepancies within the last two years, which was why he had not lodged an action earlier. This again was vehemently denied by UA and Broccoli. The major thrust of Connery's case was that neither he nor his companies had received profits due on the film *From Russia With Love* and he had received no percentages from the merchandising of the James Bond character, in which he had been used as the model.

The suit claimed that from March 1979 to November 1983 UA withheld at least $300,000 due in profits from *Goldfinger* and other Bond films, plus a further $975,000 withheld previously. Connery also charged that Broccoli and his companies made improper deductions of expenses from Connery's profits from several Bond movies.

There was going to be no quick solution, and the case rumbled on for months. A preliminary report of its initiation appeared in the newspapers but nothing further was heard. No announcements were made and behind the scenes lawyers were writing to each other in voluminous quantities. So what happened to the largest claim of its kind brought by a single actor in the history of Hollywood?

In June 1992, Maurice Segal, an aide of Cubby Broccoli's told me, 'Connery's lawsuit against UA and Broccoli, launched in 1984, has been settled out of court. Terms were kept confidential by agreement of all parties. Cubby Broccoli and Connery see each other only rarely and the relationship while not close is always civil.'

Connery did not appear in front of a camera after completing Bond in the winter of 1982 until the summer of 1985, and that only occupied his time for a mere seven days. He played golf in various parts of the world. He and Micheline spent time at their homes in the Bahamas and in Europe, they visited the farm in Iowa and did all the things that time does not permit when working. They caught up with family life, which included observing Jason's growing skill as an actor. He had dedicated himself to making his own way in life, and had secured himself the television role of Robin of Sherwood in which he had to face the difficulty of being compared to his father in the same role. In June 1985 his mother, Diane Cilento, married again. She had more or less dropped out of acting and turned to writing after the moderate success of her novel, *The Manipulators*. She married her new husband, playwright Anthony Shaffer, at her ranch in Queensland. He had an address in Trump Tower, New York.

Sean Connery's meetings with colleagues in the profession and longstanding friends had for years been spasmodic. Time slipped past, and Micheline said he had become more relaxed, attempting to keep one part of himself remote from his career. After *Never Say Never Again*, scripts were being rejected almost out of hand at a time when he could have been cashing in most heftily, and then quite out of the blue he agreed to take on a non-starring role in another off-beat film of uncertain potential, which confounded friends and critics alike. 'What is Connery up to now?' the industry pundits were asking. They still hadn't got it. His career was like a busy dual carriageway, which for part of the time he drove in the fast lane, and every so often slipped back to a slower pace: the former for his mainstream movie selection and the latter for the arthouse and off-the-wall material that he had pursued even before he became famous.

This time, in the latter category, it was *Highlander*, hardly the vehicle of a superstar. The story of fantasy and mythology roamed variably and in rather muddled form from the 16th-century glens of Scotland to New York City in modern times. It was written by student Gregory Widen as part of his thesis at UCLA, and his tutor suggested he hand it to an agent who in turn passed it to producers Bill Panzer and Peter Davis.

Connery accepted the role of Ramirez, an immortal Egyptian warrior who has been floating about the earth for nigh on 2,500 years and becomes the mentor of a Scottish clansman (Christopher Lambert) struck down in his prime in 1536, who discovers he is also immortal. The whole business ends up in a battle royal among immortal heroes and immortal enemies in modern New York. Connery's sparse contribution to the film was nonetheless among its highlights and star billing demonstrated his importance to the movie's success. His scenes had him riding horses in a reckless manner through the glens, without a double, sword fighting till the sweat was dripping from the end of his nose, again without a double, or rowing a 110-year-old heavy timber boat across a loch.

Christopher Lambert found him initially a man so imposing, who so dominated the proceedings by his mere presence, that there was something almost foreboding about him. He considered him barely approachable until they were better acquainted. He also discovered Connery's penchant for involving himself in every area. It was not unusual to see him talking quietly, almost secretively, to director Russell Mulcahy before they filmed a particular shot; he would be discussing the best possible angles, the way his sword should be handled or a fall made.

More especially, Connery was introducing Mulcahy to his personal whims and fancies, since this was the first time he had worked with him, such was his desire to inject a personal humour into his role. 'The dramatics take care of themselves,' he said. 'The humour you have to find.'

There was the added bonus for Connery that much of his action was filmed in Scotland, around Glencoe, Loch Shiel and Glen Nevis. Local newspaper advertisements for extras were reminiscent of his own introduction to acting when Anna Neagle came to town 30 years before. He flew in and out by helicopter, and for once he was happy to sign autographs and mingle with the crowds.

Highlander was produced at a time when the major Hollywood studios were in another temporary vacuum, warily pursuing the transition from the glistening hardware of *Star Wars* to adventure stories, ancient and modern, for which Steven Spielberg had set the pattern with *ET* then *Indiana Jones* and finally with Michael J Fox in *Back To The Future*. Arnold Schwarzenegger had just scored an unexpectedly huge hit with *The Terminator*, a nasty but compelling story of a man from the future sent back to cause mayhem and murder.

Guesswork ruled and no one was quite sure what would be the next big hit. Thus *Highlander* was given a very reasonable budget of $16 million and it was quirky enough to take off, geared as it was to the great new youth market being attracted into cinemas and video shops around the world in a surge of interest which gratified film-makers no end. The added attraction of *Highlander* was the music by Queen, high in the charts with *It's A Kind Of Magic*. But, as always, there's no accounting for taste. America did not much care for *Highlander*, and only $2.8 million was taken in box-office receipts after a classic exercise in how not to market a picture. Reviews were not encouraging, either.

Highlander was a natural for that year's Edinburgh Festival, where it was given its UK premiere, and after a shaky start British and European audiences, attracted by Connery's star billing and music from Queen, soon warmed to it. In spite of mixed critical reception and some attacks on muddled direction by Mulcahy, it picked up encouraging business, later becoming a cult video with sufficient continuing interest to revive the theme for *Highlander II: The Quickening* in 1990.

As so often in the past, Connery stood out in everyone's memory of the film. He was marching on regardless of commercialism and picking up scripts whose underlying appeal was the art and the challenge rather than the money and the profile. It remained the case that some worked and some did not. This had been a continuing pattern in Connery's approach to his work, which would continue on into the late-1980s when unconventionalism and adherence to what might be seen as his rule of thumb throughout his acting life – that of simply not conforming to rules by which Hollywood and the rest of his profession operated – were recognised and understood.

There was, perhaps, no better example of his approach to his work than an event which occurred soon after he had completed *Highlander*. The BBC, which he loved as an institution and, as he would never forget, had given him the first 'big break' in Alvin Rakoff's *Requiem For A Heavyweight*, contacted him to sound him out for a radio play. It was a small production, of course, but Donald Pleasence and John Hurt had also agreed to appear in a black comedy by Peter Barnes entitled *After The Fire*, the story of three pimps who meet at the funeral of a beloved whore. Connery agreed instantly, though it would entail him flying over from Spain at his own expense for a job lasting about 15 minutes on Radio Three, whose audience would be as modest as the fee. Donald Pleasence recalled,

'It was a very funny play. The three pimps meet in a pub after the funeral and reminisce. The thing was that Sean had never done radio drama before, and I don't think John Hurt had either. So we all enjoyed the experience; we had a brief rehearsal and then did it and went home again. Anyway, it cost us more than we got paid. The BBC budget for this sort of thing is very small. Sean had come from Spain and there were no cars provided so we had to get our own taxis and ended up well out of pocket. But that did not matter; the point of the story is that Sean Connery, world movie star, had travelled all that way to appear in a 15-minute radio play just for the sheer pleasure of it. The play was at the BBC Maida Vale studio and when we had finished we asked if there was a car available and they said no, sorry, and pointed to a taxi rank down the road. Sean went off first, heading back to the airport, and John Hurt and I followed. Sean took the only cab on the rank, and we waited for the next one to come along. He recognised us and said, "Cor, wait till I tell my missus." To which John Hurt replied, "You should have been here five minutes ago."'

Like all fees for engagements of this nature in the UK, Connery had the cheque for his radio appearance sent to the trust, so all in all the small play to a small audience on BBC radio cost him dear demonstrating, as Pleasence said, that the point of it was the craft, the acting. Others, apart from the trust, were to benefit. Soon after appearing on Radio Three Connery read in the *Sunday Times* that the future of the National Youth Theatre was in jeopardy following a stark warning from the Arts Council that the theatre could expect no cash injection from the government. It needed

£100,000 to ensure its survival for another year. The NYT had long been a proven success story, with names like Helen Mirren, Derek Jacobi, Ben Kingsley and Michael York among its past scholars. Connery reached for his chequebook and sent a donation of £50,000 and expressed the hope that other donations would follow to ensure that this 'great source of British talent' continued to provide some of the finest budding actors, writers and directors in the world. It should not have to go cap in hand for money.

Meanwhile, his own continuing approach to work was again evident in his next choice, *The Name Of The Rose*, shot in the winter of 1985 and in many ways the film that set a course for his inevitable confrontation with advancing years. It ranks among his best performances, though again he had selected a movie almost deliberately going against the grain of current trends and challenging audiences to go and see it, which they did in very large numbers. As with three other major Connery films in the second half of the decade, *The Name Of The Rose* was based upon an international bestselling novel by Umberto Eco, a semiotics professor at Bologna University. It was a weighty mixture of religious philosophy and murder mystery while also a discourse on monastic life in the 1300s, which might sound utterly impossible to turn into a movie.

Connery is a Franciscan monk who travels to a monastery with a young novice (Christian Slater) and finds himself investigating a series of murders thought to be the work of the devil. It was a total change of pace from the sort of material on offer in the mid-1980s when films like *Beverly Hills Cop*, *Rocky IV* and *Police Academy* ensured that Eddie Murphy, Sylvester Stallone and Steve Guttenberg were hiring security vans to take home their wages. Director Jean-Jacques Annaud had worked for three years, almost obsessionally, on the draft script striving not to trivialise the book, yet attempting to give popular appeal; he had made ten attempts at the screenplay and had sweated blood getting together the $16 million he needed to make the film from sources in Italy, Germany and France.

This was one occasion when Connery did not involve himself in anything other than his acting. Filming took place in a specially built and very cold monastery, and it took more than nine months after filming ended to bring the completed work to premiere. Connery must have been pretty pleased, for he did something he had never done before and went on the chat-show circuit in Britain and attended a special press reception in London. The American critics weren't kind, and the distributors, 20th Century Fox, angered Connery by their complete lack of understanding of what it was about. They failed to do their homework or mount an adequate marketing campaign, and *Variety* rubbed some vitriol in sore wounds: 'A plodding misfire, sorrowfully mediocre.' Roger Ebert, 'America's most influential film critic' of the *New York Daily News*, said, 'What this movie needed was a clear, logical screenplay … there are so many good things, the performances, the reconstruction of the period, the overall feeling of medieval times that if the story had been able to involve us, there would have been quite a movie here.'

So the American audiences did not take to it in any demonstrative way. In Europe it was a contrasting story, so different as to put credence to Connery's complaint about the way it had been handled in America. It was hugely successful, outpacing such films as *Out Of Africa* and *Top Gun*, and broke all house records at the Haymarket Cinema, London. It went immediately to the top of the chart in Rome, deposing Connery's other European hit, *Highlander*, and *Crocodile Dundee*. It was a runaway success, with takings reaching $100 million in Europe and, for Sean Connery, was a substantial and well-rewarded achievement.

16

TURNING POINT

T*he Name Of The Rose* assisted Connery through the barrier of
middle age and recast him, in the words of Eric Sykes, as an
elder statesman of the movie industry, although at the same time
he was careful not to bury the sexual magnetism and chemistry
that perennially enthralled his female fans. It was a crucial time,
said Sykes, and *The Name Of The Rose* did more than any
previous film to reposition Connery. This was particularly
important to Hollywood producers and directors who, with one
eye firmly fixed on the video market, needed stars with solid
pulling power now more than ever. With fees scaling unheard of
heights for top-billed performers, and production costs, prints,
publicity and promotions all doubling, if not trebling, every year,
movie producers were staring at soaring budgets to get a film
into the market.

It did not necessarily mean that the movies were any better,
however. Quite the reverse, and some outrageous figures were
being bandied around for what turned out to be fairly average
movies. Many of those that fell into the blockbuster category

should have carried a corporate health warning, and studio after studio fell victim to hype as swan after swan turned into loss-making dodos. Throughout the 1980s mergers and takeovers, and the arrival in force of Japanese money, left a couple of dozen actors, directors and producers seemingly very rich, but it almost killed off the underbelly of the film business following a period of careless extravagance

As major studios and production companies changed hands, some twice or even three times, finances became even more critical. In 1991 it cost $100 million a year to open the gates of the 20th Century Fox studios before they even started to make movies. The money men were insisting on bankable names, though even those would not guarantee success, and the term 'packaging' took on a new significance as producers struggled to mix and match old and new movie stars, attempting to crash the hugely rich youth market while retaining the interest of the older audiences.

Connery now came into his own, although he was doing nothing different. He was the same actor doing the same professional job he had been for the past couple of decades. He had aged, mellowed and grown wiser and totally secure, but he did not suddenly become a different person or a greater actor. It was just that there was a general realisation, almost a dawning, that he was there and available for some big projects that needed underpinning with strong characterisation and his kind of audience attraction.

He was at last recognised as one of the most significant and popular character actors of modern times. His strengths were obvious, as was his ability – the greatest test of all, perhaps – to shrug off indifferent movies. The bonanza in the video market had become an increasingly dominant factor in all calculations of the film business and the growth in rental potential certainly had an effect on the range of movies being produced. Well-known names and faces on the covers of rows of cassette boxes became vitally important as the supermarket factor hit the economics of movie-making in a big way. Less than a dozen names were among the key sellers and Connery's was one of them. He was set to reap generous rewards as accolades and multi-million-dollar deals came forth in abundance.

British film producer Trevor Wallace, who had long since relocated to Hollywood and carried out a watching brief on Connery purely out of personal interest, said 1985 onwards represented another new beginning:

'You know, in Hollywood he had never quite got rid of the James Bond tag. Connery? Oh, James Bond. It was silly. Then he finally buried it almost overnight and became Sean Connery, and he's a terrific actor with huge versatility. As Mike Caine would say, not many people knew this because for a long while he was a bit of a mystery man here in Los Angeles. Few people really knew him well and certainly in this place there were few who ever got close to him, unless they played golf. He never joined the club or the party circuit, and shunned the Hollywood nights. He also had this unfortunate reputation among the administrators of Hollywood of being a bit of a troublemaker with his writs, and by staying in Europe he had remained an outsider. Then, as often happens here, actors become fashionable for a specific reason. It was at that point people began to see Connery as this huge character, with a face that could be anything – cruel or gentle, cynical or innocent. He could be somebody's lover, somebody's dad or some tough, imposing figure suited to a role for which – when you look around – there are not that many good actors to fill.'

Wallace also identified *The Name Of The Rose* as one of Connery's finest because he had been stretched by a difficult script. It was also a turning point at which his characterisations more suited his advancing years and began to show a greater depth. He quickly consolidated his position with another demanding role, as Jimmy Malone, the grizzled Irish-American cop in *The Untouchables*. The director was Brian De Palma, whose own career was ready for revitalisation after some controversial films set in funky counter-culture, a string of duds and then his bloody but sometimes poetic thrillers like *Carrie, Dressed To Kill, The Fury* and the chainsaw bloodbath of *Scarface*.

The Untouchables told the story of how treasury agent Eliot Ness (played by Kevin Costner) brought Al Capone (Robert De Niro) to justice in the corrupt, frontier atmosphere of 1930s Chicago, when the mob ruled and shot each other with Tommy guns fired from the back windows of big, black cars. For Connery the production had some intriguingly impressive talent. The script was by David Mamet, a recent Pulitzer Prize winner for his Broadway play *Glengary Glen Ross*. Connery believed that getting Mamet was a master stroke, in that he was born in the Windy City and knew the history backwards. He was very knowledgeable about the ethnic problems as well as police corruption. He was able to go back to basics and made the story almost biblical. Most impressive of all he made the characters clean cut and direct, and this aided De Palma in his direction, given as he was in past movies to showy self-indulgence.

Connery's Malone was a streetwise Chicago cop who knew the dangers from the underworld and just concentrated on staying alive. His interpretation was typical of many Connery roles, contrasting the tough outer casing of a character with the person underneath who was capable of feelings and having real relationships. Mamet's screenplay had taken artistic licence with the facts of the Capone-Ness battle. The two men never actually met, as in the film, and Connery's Malone, the ageing police veteran unpromoted because of his refusal to join the corruption, was an invented character.

Malone was at the centre of the film as the man who tutored the treasury agent Ness in the ruthless ways of Prohibition-era Chicago gangs. In his final scene, the death scene, he crawls down a hallway leaving a trail of blood behind him after being machine-gunned and Eric Sykes summed up the feelings of many fans: 'For me, the film ended at that point. This is the difficulty with Connery. He is so imposing that he steals the picture.'

Kevin Costner enjoys telling a Connery story that while filming

The Untouchables on location, they were doing a street scene watched by a large crowd kept at bay by rope barriers. He and Connery were engaged in conversation when a young and beautiful blonde woman attracted his attention. Costner slid over to the ropes whereupon the woman handed him a book and said, 'Could you get me Sean Connery's autograph, please?'

The Untouchables, made for $25 million, was a showcase for the acting talents of the three stars and Connery was finally awarded an Oscar for Best Supporting Actor. He was low key about the award in interviews with reporters clamouring to get a conversation with one of the most elusive stars in the business. The best they could get out of him was that he considered the Oscar was not just for *The Untouchables* but for his body of work accumulated over the years.

He said he was proud of a lot of his films, and if he had to name one it would perhaps be *The Man Who Would Be King* which he thought deserved an Oscar. But he had no regrets about his past choices. Some had been wrong, he knew that; but he saw his work as a painter might judge his canvases, amassing a collection which was reassessed over the years. Bond had been a cross to bear, but he recognised that it had provided him with international acclaim.

Perhaps to prove something to Hollywood, and the whole of the film industry watching the Academy Awards at which he was given a three-minute standing ovation, he emerged from the mists with laser beams all around to present the award for the best visual effects and proclaimed, 'My name is *Connery*. SEAN CONNERY.'

Connery had taken a smaller fee than usual and a share of the profits in *The Untouchables*, which for once proved to be an excellent investment. The notices were exceptional, with words like 'masterpiece' being bandied around, and Connery was singled out by most. During the first weekend of its release in America the business recorded jointly by *The Untouchables* and *Beverly Hills Cop* accounted for 60 per cent of all box-office receipts. Worldwide it went on to take well in excess of the $100 million target which qualifies a movie as a blockbuster.

After he had finished filming *The Untouchables* and before its success was being registered in such generous proportions, Connery had signed for *The Presidio,* a story based upon the key US military establishment of the same name, a huge, sprawling base on the outskirts of San Francisco. It was billed as a thriller and a detective story and Connery's role was originally intended for Marlon Brando, who will be remembered for his last military posting with Elizabeth Taylor in *Reflections In A Golden Eye.*

Brando was not interested, and director Peter Hyams called Connery with whom he had last worked on *Outland.* Connery rapidly read the script and voiced a few reservations, which Hyams agreed they could work on. In theory, a $20 million budget should have given them scope for a rather more enticing film than was produced. Connery described it as a tough shoot, made more difficult by the fact that he was running perilously close to using up all the working days he was allowed in America each year and had to fly out of the country at weekends. Released in the wake of *The Untouchables, The Presidio* – whose title meant nothing to audiences outside America – did not fare well and it was perhaps fortunate Steven Spielberg already had plans which would allow Connery to resume at the highest profile currently available in the business.

Spielberg had seen a rough-cut version of *The Untouchables* before it was released and had decided then to approach Connery to play Jones's father in *Indiana Jones And The Last Crusade.* He had been searching for a senior British actor to take the role, which was portrayed in the original script as an elderly, absent-minded professor type. Various names were mentioned until Spielberg mused on the question of Connery. It was, after all, the James Bond series that had inspired Spielberg to do his *Indiana* series in the first place. *Raiders Of The Lost Ark* was the first true rival to Bond, and Harrison Ford was the new adventure hero of the screen. *Raiders* was a huge success, with record-breaking box-office takings approaching $250 million. Spielberg was not sure how Connery would take it, being asked to play the father of his successor – especially as the script called for a rather feeble, doddering old gent when in reality Connery was only 12 years senior to Ford.

Connery read the script and agreed on one condition – the one he always insisted upon – that he could have some input into the characterisation of Dr Henry Jones. Immediately he saw that he could be played in a more energetic fashion, rather like the Victorian explorer Sir Richard Burton whose life he had once considered turning into a film. Spielberg, one of the most powerful and influential men in Hollywood, had not been challenged about scripts for some considerable time. Connery's suggestions were to give Indiana's father the same kind of sexuality that the son himself possessed, the glint of the eye and the underhand humour which Connery could flick up without so much as the bat of an eyelid. Wasn't it possible for the old man to have had an affair with the leading lady before Indiana got there?

Eventually Spielberg came round to these ideas and extended Connery's part by four additional scenes. Connery had forced himself into a major role in what he knew would be a blockbuster movie, rather than playing the feeble character that was originally intended for him. It showed on his first encounter with Harrison Ford, where they sort of circled each other like gladiators until they began work. Spielberg said in an interview with *Time* magazine, 'They were like royalty ... everyone got quiet and respectful when they arrived on set.'

Location work took four months in faraway places around the world and the whole film was packed with action and stunts that Connery and Ford clearly enjoyed. They became the best of friends, always a sign of true compatibility on screen, and provided their own timing, rehearsing scenes much the way Connery had done with Michael Caine in *The Man Who Would Be King*. Spielberg recognised the chemistry and photographed most of their scenes together as two-shots, keeping both actors in the frame, a technique that takes advantage of good interplay between the leading characters. Ford repeated past assessments that Connery was very generous to fellow actors – 'Which is to say he just goes to work with no bullshit.'

Last Crusade was a huge success, of course, and many believed it was the best of the *Indiana* films. The critics enthused about the screen pairing, comparing it to Redford and Newman, and the box office tills began chiming away in every town and city where there was a cinema. Although competing against *Batman*, unbeatable that year in terms of money making, Paramount took $440 million worldwide and all concerned did very nicely indeed. Connery conducted a press conference by satellite from Spain as part of the publicity for *Indiana Jones And The Last Crusade*.

Inevitably James Bond was figured in the first question. He no longer warned his press aides to tell journalists not to even mention the name, for he was far more relaxed about that so long as Bond did not dominate the conversation. 'Aside from the fact that Indiana Jones is not as well dressed as James Bond, the main difference between them is sexual,' he said. 'Indiana deals with women shyly. In the first film, *Raiders Of The Lost Ark*, he's flustered when a student writes "Love you" on her eyelids. James Bond would have had all those young co-eds for breakfast.'

He was amused by the fact that after winning screen immortality as Agent 007 in the 1960s he was now cast as fathers and teachers. He was Christopher Lambert's spiritual guide in *Highlander*, an ageing priest and tutor to Christian Slater in *The Name Of The Rose*, Kevin Costner's mentor in *The Untouchables*, Meg Ryan's father and Mark Harmon's superior in *The Presidio*, and his depiction of paternal bewilderment was his last movie's greatest redeeming quality. He was also soon to be seen as Dustin Hoffman's father in *Family Business*. 'There's a new emphasis on father–son relationships in films,' Connery explained. 'Look at Kevin's baseball picture [*Field of Dreams*]. I think right now we're all looking for a guide, for a big daddy, because life just gets more and more difficult.' He added a personal note for topical comparison: that he was deeply affected by his own father's death because they had been so poor and so busy working that there had never been a moment when they had managed to talk about love of one another. Then suddenly it was too late.

Someone on the receiving end of his satellite broadcast wanted to know if he might consider playing the father of James Bond. 'Well, why not? If the part is as well-written as this one is I would. But it would cost them. It would definitely cost them.'

The cost remained important, as indeed it did in the quartet of almost back-to-back productions completed between the end of 1987 and the beginning of 1989 – including *Family Business* in which he played father to Dustin Hoffman (in reality only seven years younger) and grandfather to Matthew Broderick, which was under the directorial eye of his old friend Sidney Lumet.

The story had been chosen to *provide* such a circumstance, and if it did not then one would be written. The computerised business study centres, drawing their graphs of audience trends and age profiles, had carried out some careful research and reported in terms of the 'importance of maximising the potential for both box-office receipts and video rentals' which, translated, meant producing films that appealed to as wide a section of the market as possible.

With the video market soaring and bringing fabulous new dimensions to movie finances, the stakes were far higher than in the days when Steve McQueen was teamed up with Edward G Robinson in *The Cincinnati Kid* (1965) or Paul Newman with Jackie Gleason in *The Hustler* (1961). Multi-billions were at stake. It must have seemed viable, for example, to buy in three top talents like Connery, Hoffman and Broderick at a reported joint cost of $12 million for *Family Business*. Connery played the role of Jesse McMullen, a habitual criminal who leads his son (Hoffman) and grandson (Broderick) into a million-dollar crime. There was a slight altercation over the script. Connery wanted to make his character harder, to which Vincent Patrick, who adapted the screenplay from his own novel, retorted, 'I thought the grandfather was about as hard as they come – until I met Sean Connery.' Even Vincent was swayed. 'You suddenly realise he's the closest we have to Clark Gable, an old-time movie star. Everyone knows him and likes him; there's something very likable about him on a screen.'

There were other clashes which had to be overcome. Dustin Hoffman's style still has its roots in the Method which Connery shook off years ago and instilled in its place a strict discipline. Nonetheless Connery relaxed and, according to director Lumet, matched Hoffman improvisation for improvisation. Broderick, meantime, felt that Connery observed him in such a way that let him know he did not want 'some smart-ass kid in his face all the time'. Broderick was given to cheeky impersonations of his two senior partners behind their backs. Someone told Connery, and Connery said, 'Why doesn't he do it for me?'

'Because he's afraid,' came the reply.

'Good,' said Connery. 'He should be afraid.'

Family Business did not do as well as it might have done. Slack direction, a slender story and depressed times meant that the American grosses barely covered the fees of the three stars, let alone the production costs. It would be won back in the end, and was no different to other major movies on the circuits at the same time. A marketing study showed that *Batman*'s concurrent release on video had some impact, creating competition between going to the movies and staying at home to watch the VCR.

It was one of three major pictures released at the end of 1989, the other two being *We're No Angels*, starring Sean Penn and Robert De Niro, and *Blaze* with Paul Newman. Yet, surprisingly, in a year in which box-office records were being posted almost weekly, these three films took less than $6 million on 3,349 screens in America, compared with the same week a year previously when *Rain Man* alone took $7 million on just 1,248 screens, and May 1989 when *Indiana Jones And The Last Crusade* took $50 million in 7 days. In the same week, in America, the biggest market by far, there were 84.9 million video rentals, almost 20 million up on the previous year.

Cinemascore, which conducts audience research, provided

some remarkable statistics for the movie industry, among them the startling fact that the biggest purchasers of cinema seats or videos were in the 12–29 age group, who accounted for a huge 57 per cent of all sales in 1989. Narrowed down further, the under-25s accounted for 44 per cent of the market while the over-40s took a mere 23 per cent. This was probably why Paul Newman suffered his second major flop in a year with *Blaze*, giving rise to suggestions by audience researchers in Los Angeles that movie-makers should give serious thought to the bankability or otherwise of stars 15 or more years older than the prime movie-going audience.

The surveyors added, 'Names like Hoffman and De Niro don't mean a thing to a 16-year-old kid. He just wants to see *Batman* and doesn't care who is under the mask.' All of which must have been rather depressing for the over-40s in Hollywood and demonstrated once more how impossibly volatile and critical the financial considerations had become over artistic merit. Connery had done much better across the whole age spectrum. Old Bond movies were still iconic among the younger generation, and he had also kept his face in a number of movies that appealed specifically to young people, like *Highlander*. There was no question that he was still big box office, even when the likes of De Niro and Pacino went through some lean times. By the time *Family Business* appeared in the cinemas, he was already working on a new 'blockbuster' – a screen version of Tom Clancy's worldwide bestselling novel *The Hunt For Red October*, a story which had already sampled well across all age groups. An immediate start was required as his old pal Klaus Maria Brandauer, who had been earmarked for the part, dropped out because directing commitments in Europe had kept him longer than he had anticipated. Producer Mace Neufield and director John McTiernan decided they wanted Connery, although first had to convince Paramount executives, who had $40 million riding on the outcome.

It was another superb Connery showcase. Clancy's story, about a renegade Soviet submarine captain who plans to defect and surrender his ship to the Americans in the cause of peace, had caught the public's imagination. In the book, the Russians convince the US military that the captain is insane and intends to launch an attack on America: they want him found and destroyed. Ronald Reagan had, not unexpectedly, given his stamp of approval, calling Clancy's book a perfect yarn, and then the Russians revealed that such an event did actually happen. There had been a mutiny aboard a Soviet naval vessel in 1975 and the perpetrators had been arrested and court-martialled.

Typically, Connery became deeply involved in *Red October* from the moment he agreed to do it. 'Coming to the part so late would have scared other actors,' said Neufield. 'But he brought with him his size, presence and the absolute authority that the role called for. He also helped other actors, because no one wanted to screw up around Sean Connery.'

Connery's first move was to call in John Milius, with whom he had worked on *The Wind And The Lion*, to go through his lines as the Russian submarine skipper, Marko Ramius. The characterisation he visualised was a mixture, he said, of Stalin and Samuel Beckett. Clancy, he felt, was thin on characterisation and he waded in as usual with his own ideas. He was also a strict disciplinarian on set and worked with John McTiernan to bring some order into the logistics and complications of using a large number of Russian extras, most of whom could not speak English. The result was that everyone seemed to be talking at once and saying nothing. Connery, gruff and stern and occasionally angry, stood up and called them to order and through a translator insisted that they should remain completely silent at all times when actors were trying a run-through of their parts. McTiernan admitted to feeling intimidated by Connery, but said he 'knows his business, comes prepared and has those terrific qualities of strength, pride, obstinacy and virility'.

Though he had been rushed into it, Connery was in vigorous form. *Red October* was another remarkable peak in his career and, with a strong supporting cast including Joss Ackland and James Earl Jones, revelled in a mass of excellent reviews. It became a worldwide hit, proving with heartening figures to Hollywood that there *was* a demand for cracking adventure yarns that required a level of concentration and had a star over the age of 25. It wasn't just kids' pictures that could break the blockbusters barrier. *The Hunt For Red October* stayed in the US list of Top Ten films for four months and took $120 million.

The scene changes. It was still 1989 and *Red October* was some months away from its premiere (in March 1990) when Connery embarked on yet another project in this frenetic series of major productions. It was autumn and the skies were leaden. A biting cold breeze blew off the Moscow River as Sean Connery stepped from the gloomy Ukraina Hotel in Moscow to begin his second movie with a Russian theme while the last one was still being edited.

Connery was back in the Secret Service, but this time as a sleazy sneak rather than an upright Bondlike character. Now he was Barley Blair, a publisher recruited by the Secret Service to spy on Russians, a character created by John Le Carré in his bestseller *The Russia House*. The movie of the book was filmed during a ten-week location shoot in Moscow and Leningrad by director Fred Schepisi. It was 21 years since Connery was last in Moscow, filming *The Red Tent* with touchy KGB agents following the former James Bond, secret agent, everywhere. In the Gorbachev *perestroika* era, the Soviets are not the bad guys. The situation is reversed and Le Carré promotes the humanity of the Russians and denigrates the heartless manipulation of people's lives by the controllers of Western intelligence. The film started out in controversy, since the novel had been castigated in certain right-wing circles of America as being soft on Communism, there being no sign then of the total collapse of the Communist Party in the Soviet Union.

It was a laudably ambitious film of a labyrinthine novel, with Connery and his love interest Michelle Pfeiffer attempting to make the best of a screenplay by Tom Stoppard which had, sadly, failed to unravel the complications of the plot. It was at best a difficult story to film, and Schepisi admitted that without Connery's agreement to star they might have had difficulty in getting it made at all. It was, once again, down to box-office considerations, he said, and Connery was the first and last choice to play Le Carré's alcoholic central character, more interested in his next drink than world peace. His interest is aroused, however, by Katya (Pfeiffer), willing to risk life and limb to smuggle the vital notebooks of her scientist friend (Brandauer, now having completed his directorial task in Europe) out to the West. Blair is then exploited by British and American intelligence intent on keeping a chill air over the Cold War.

Fortunately for a film which sagged heavily in parts, Connery and Pfeiffer – adding to her own rating as one of Hollywood's subtly versatile actresses – were able to give it sufficient lift to remain interesting. James Fox, as the British spymaster, provided a keen performance and like his brother Edward before him (in *Never Say Never Again*) was impressed by Connery's approach: 'I was able to observe him as an actor, up close, for several weeks during our work on *Russia House* and I see Sean as a man who has fashioned himself into a fascinating film figure by the creative and disciplined use of all his powers. It's a measure of my respect for him that I very often think of his contribution to and influence on my own approach to acting today.'

Fox, no slouch in terms of his own capacity for work apart from a long break which he took for his own reasons, was obviously quite taken with Connery whom he saw as a motivator, analyst and teacher, whose advice he was happy to accept. And so, the decade was ending on a high note.

17

MORE ACCOLADES

In the five years since he returned to make *Highlander*, Connery's stock had gone skywards. The awards that followed told their own story. In addition to the Oscar for *The Untouchables*, Connery won the British critics award for Best Actor for the same film and he was nominated for Best Supporting Actor at both the Golden Globe Awards in Los Angeles and the British Academy Awards in London. He won the Variety Club of Great Britain's Best Actor award, and was named Best Supporting Actor by the US National Board of Review. He was voted ShoWest Male Star of the Year and in January 1990 the US National Association of Theater Owners created a new award category, Worldwide Star of the Year, and named Sean Connery its first winner.

This was followed by the American Cinematique Award for acting excellence whose director said, 'He was the unanimous choice of the board to be the seventh recipient – he is one of the world's most acclaimed and provocative actors.' The French weighed in with a citation for literary and dramatic merit. But the British contingent at the Cannes Film Festival were to be disappointed in May 1989 when he failed to turn up to receive an award for 'outstanding contribution to the British film industry', which had been presented the year before to director David Lean. Connery was working on *The Hunt For Red October* at the time.

He did, however, make it for another major accolade when the British Academy of Film and Television Arts presented him with a lifetime achievement award in 1990 in a two-hour show hosted by Michael Aspel, and later televised. There were clips from a selection of his films and a succession of sound-byte tributes from some of the stars he had worked with over the years and the golfers he had played against. Jimmy Tarbuck ribbed him about being bad at golf and said how difficult it was to get rid of the white fivers he paid out. Comedian Billy Connolly gave a typically satirical response to what he described as an evening of embarrassing sycophancy; he had decided to let the world in on a secret that his real name was not Connolly but Connery, that he was Sean's illegitimate son and now claimed his inheritance and, for good measure, added an in-joke about Scottish soccer to make Connery wince: 'Partick Thistle Nil.' The Princess Royal, president of BAFTA, summed up the evening's tributes:

'Professionalism is the word to describe Sean Connery. It shows consistently through his career and in everything he has ever done ... The things that he does for young people in this country off screen are tremendous. Maybe there is a feeling that we are short of heroes, but I know there is more than one generation that feels he is a real hero, and not just on the screen, and we thank him for that too.'

This year of attainment and professional recognition was topped off from an unexpected quarter – with the nomination of Connery by *People* magazine in America as the winner of their annual award as the world's sexiest man. The magazine said he had man's man appeal that KOd women without alienating men, reiterating the comment made by Pauline Kael, film critic of the *New Yorker*: 'Connery looks absolutely confident in himself as a man. Women want to meet him and men want to be him. I don't know any man since Cary Grant that men have wanted to be so much.' Connery, when approached by *People*, tried to divert the award to Mikhail Gorbachev because of his extraordinary combination of intelligence, baldness and Buddha-like serenity. To which *People* responded, Nice try, Connery – but you're it!

Meanwhile, back in tinsel town, the premiere of *The Russia House* was held in December 1990. David Cornwell (aka John Le Carré) reckoned it was just like 'old Hollywood' as a large cast of famous names turned out to support Connery and Pfeiffer at what was the first charity premiere in Los Angeles for more than 20 years to assist the Motion Picture and Television Fund for retired members of the industry.

Just like old Hollywood. There was a Russian-themed post-screening party under a vast 25,000-square-foot white marquee with pink drapes erected without poles in the parking lot opposite the Cineplex Odeon in Universal City. Thirty-five chandeliers hung from the tent's superstructure (which looked like the ribs of a huge whale) and 110 tables covered with gold linen added a touch of glitter, made complete by tapestries from the 1938 MGM film *Marie Antoinette* and a thousand pieces of antique furniture borrowed from Warner's props department. There was a small oasis of six full-grown trees in the centre of the parking lot which, for this occasion, were decorated with white lights. The asphalt of the lot was covered with blue vinyl, over which stepped 1,100 people from the current top drawer of movieland's rich and famous. 'To look at it,' said the film's producer, 'you'd never know we were in recession.'

No, you would not, except that the newspapers had been keeping everyone abreast of the financial troubles which had beset MGM/Pathe, the film's producers, and no set of statistics better summed up the parlous, precariously balanced state of Hollywood than the international array of representatives at *The Russia House*'s premiere. MGM/Pathe was owned by an Italian who bought it with money supplied by a French bank, was backing a Russian-themed picture being launched on a parking lot owned by MCA/Universal, just bought by the Japanese, based on a book by an English author, with a Scottish star and an American co-star. MGM/Pathe, regardless of its own troubles, donated $250,000 to the cause of the old retirees and the premiere made $575,000 for the charity.

Nor were the year's honours for Connery done with. In December 1990, Edinburgh city councillors voted to award him the scarcely given Freedom of the City of Edinburgh in recognition of his achievement in films and work for charities, notably his sponsorship of the Scottish International Educational Trust which he promoted 25 years earlier by donating his fee for *Diamonds Are Forever*. His continuing support, along with other personalities he encouraged to contribute, had helped the trust to support a large number of projects and individuals. Connery had continued donate funds over the years, most recently from his fee for *Robin Hood* and at that time, SIET was handing out in excess of £50,000 a year in grants.

Even so, the Freedom award in Edinburgh is not given lightly, and there were some objectors among the city council. The only previous member of the entertainment industry to be so honoured was Harry Lauder in 1927. Other recipients included Charles Dickens, Sir Walter Scott, Disraeli, Livingstone and Stanley, Alexander Graham Bell and Churchill. Those who opposed the resolution did so mostly on political grounds, given that Connery was an avowed supporter of the Scottish Nationalists. After all, Prince Charles had been rejected as a recipient of the Freedom of the City in 1975.

Connery's nomination was proposed by the Lord Provost, Eleanor McLaughlin, principally for the Scottish son's 'contribution to world cinema; to mark his largely unpublicised work in founding the Scottish International Education Trust and in particular to recognise the respect and high esteem in which he is held by the people of the City of Edinburgh'. The vote was 49-8 in favour, and in a poll conducted by the Edinburgh *Evening News* – a former Connery employer – 90 per cent of the thousands who took part were in favour.

If there was any doubt remaining, it was dispelled by the crowds who turned out to watch the celebrations. Thousands lined the streets, among them Alex Kitson, who had risen to Deputy General Secretary of the Transport and General Workers' Union. Kitson had met Connery two or three times over the years and was invited to the Freedom ceremony and to other receptions while Connery was in Edinburgh. 'He hadn't changed very much,' said Kitson, 'other than the fact that he had become a ScotNat. He made sure people from around his old district were invited, old schoolfriends, old workmates and a few remaining elderly people who were associated with his own mother and father. It was a nice gesture and he recognised pretty well everybody, and talked about the old times. I had said to my colleagues at the time, 'I'll wait until Big Tam sees me before I go up to him.' Anyway, he did and came right over and shook my hand and we had our pictures taken. It was a good night, and he was obviously very moved and proud.'

If anything marred the event for Connery it was an article in that morning's *Scotsman* newspaper which focused on the fact that the actor had long since lived abroad for tax purposes. Connery saw it as 'yet another inference that I don't pay taxes, which is equally untrue,' he thundered at a press conference later. 'When I moved out of Britain in 1974 I paid nothing but taxes on everything that was frozen in this country. You were not allowed to take money out. And I pay full tax in Britain and America whenever I work, with none of the benefits of living there.'

One further award was yet to come. Towards the end of 1991, he was informed by the French Ministry of Foreign Affairs that he was to be awarded the medal and title of *Chevalier de la Legion d'Honneur*, subsequently presented to him at a ceremony in Paris the following January. It would also have been a perfect time for Connery to have received major recognition under the twice-yearly hand-out of medals and honours from the Queen, given that in recent times the lists had been packed with names of personalities from the worlds of showbusiness and sport. But those charged with selecting the names for this increasingly politically biased honours system continued to ignore Connery as a candidate for a knighthood. He had undoubtedly stirred the rancour of both major political parties in the United Kingdom during his return to Scotland for the award ceremonies through his renewed support for the Scottish National Party, and indeed the whole idea of devolution for Scotland, Wales and Northern Ireland. His nationalistic views were well known and Connery now made a point of becoming a fully paid-up ScotNat at a time when the issues were thrust to the fore as Britain faced a general election. Both Labour and Conservative had so far refused to consider the devolution issue and the actor proved a powerful ally for the ScotNat cause, given his high profile and willingness to press the cause with talk of the urgent need for 'independence and freedom' before the old system became locked into the new European constitution.

Such comments continued to rankle with the senior elements of the British political system, not least the Labour Party who seriously needed the Scottish vote if they were to win a general election (which, in the immediate future, they failed to do). Equally, the Conservatives were also smarting over Connery's remarks, especially in the run-up to the 1993 General Election. 'There is only one party that is interested in Scottish independence and that's the Scottish Nationalists,' he was quoted as saying. 'At the moment, the country is run by the Conservatives and they have so few votes in Scotland that they ought to realise that there's something not right in this situation. The governing party doesn't really have a position in the country, so without bloodshed and bombs and whatever else, it should address it and the timing is perfect now.'

At the time of the Edinburgh celebrations he had just completed *Highlander II: The Quickening*, once again showing Christopher Lambert the ropes in a sequel to what had become a cult video. And then he kissed goodbye to Micheline to head off for the unwelcoming climes of what was supposed to be the Brazilian jungle – but was really Catemaco, Mexico, where he was to begin work on *Medicine Man*.

As someone coyly observed, 'Another day, another hundred grand,' because the money talk for this movie had been awesomely gross. With healthy competition for the screenplay, Tom Schulman (author of the recently hot *Dead Poet's Society*) was reported to have received $2.5 million. John McTiernan was hired as director in what the producers hoped would be a financial re-creation of the highly successful Connery–McTiernan partnership in *The Hunt For Red October*. Director and star were widely reported in Hollywood to have been guaranteed $6 million and $10 million respectively for their signatures, although McTiernan said it was much less and Connery had stopped talking about money in public. The total budget was over $40 million.

McTiernan's recent past had been in the arena of explosive violence and pyrotechnics (Bruce Willis in *Die Hard* and Arnold Schwarzenegger in *Predator*). *Medicine Man* was different. It had a tenderness that actors and crew alike struggled to maintain in the strained and tense atmosphere of filming in the mosquito-ridden, 100-degree humidity of a Mexican back of beyond where the only previous known visitors from external civilisation were a group of scientists working on medical experiments with baboons. Those failed and they left. The baboons stayed, and now along came Hollywood with its usual trailing soap opera of a crew, setting up camp and equipment to film the fictional story of an eccentric Scottish scientist, Connery, who has found the cure for cancer. But the rainforest that provides the only place on earth where secret extracts for his potion are to be found is being bulldozed and burned. There was a message hidden in here, too, and it eventually weighed heavily on the movie.

Opposite Connery was Lorraine Bracco, a tough-talking New Yorker and his Katharine Hepburn-type love interest. McTiernan pushed them to the limit in the steamiest, toughest location Connery had ever worked in, worse than the other extreme of Fred Zinnemann's snow mountain. The stars were dangled precariously on wires in mountain gorges, hung over cliffs, swung from trees, and rolled through waterfalls and mountain pools. There were clashes of temperament, especially between McTiernan and Bracco. Connery complained about the catering, and once had a stand-up 'discussion' with McTiernan on the way one particularly difficult scene was proceeding.

'Who wants to go home?' cried Bracco.

'We all do,' said McTiernan impatiently and angrily, and added under his breath, 'so shaddup!'

'No one more than me,' said Bracco, having the last word.

Connery was grumbling and grouchy. His preoccupations were, as ever, with the quality of his own performance and how the film would fare at the box office. Though he returned looking fit and vital, with a deep tan and flat belly, in conversations afterwards he was typically frank about the problems experienced in shooting the movie. One of the disappointments was that the script was constantly being rejigged, which went against his own well-known edict – established from past experiences – that filming should never begin until the script was right. There were casting problems, too. McTiernan wanted an African Queen-type love interest but did not have that script. Bracco had been selected after her role in *Goodfellas*: both Connery and the director liked her work and she got the job. As tempers frayed on location, however, a certain tenseness developed between her and McTiernan and Connery found himself in the middle of it. Raised voices could be heard echoing through the jungle.

McTiernan was said to be obsessed by the mechanics of what he was doing. True, there were the most complicated shooting set-ups to be worked out but Connery felt 'I had bent every actor's dictum and rule to accommodate what he wanted.' The heat of the jungle and 98 per cent humidity had everyone on a short fuse. There were other problems. According to Connery, the food was appalling and everybody became sick. There were no complementary elements to pacify the workers, like decent beaches or sports facilities. He was remarkably frank in a tell-all interview with *Premier* magazine: 'The tennis court was like a beach at Dunkirk and you couldn't swim in the water ... You couldn't eat in town; you wouldn't want to ... The noise of the insects and wildlife where I had this house was insanity, noises that were Neanderthal, primordial, noises that had never been heard anywhere ... the mosquitoes had me for lunch every day ... and the director kept changing the game plan everyday. I ordered the set to be cleared and told him in no uncertain way what I thought of him. I was boiling mad. Sure, I screamed and started ranting and told him I could not work in that hell hole. We managed to sort out our differences but it was hard.'

It was no surprise that movie, which premiered in May 1992, took some flak from the critics, and consequently the box-office figures were light against the high production costs. The negative reception did not reflect badly on his own performance and anyway, there was compensation aplenty. Through his new personal management structure under the heading of Fountainbridge Films, he had negotiated one of his largest single pay days plus a percentage of the gross, which meant that he matched the top rate for the major top-paid Hollywood male leads, although you could count them on one hand.

The Oscar for *The Untouchables* had enhanced this position, and by the time *Medicine Man* hit the cinemas, he was already deep in preparation for his next engagement, *Rising Sun*. Once again he was involved as an executive producer through Fountainbridge Films. The movie was based on the controversial and ethnically criticised Michael Crichton novel which had been strongly pilloried by Asians claiming racist insults. The book focused heavily on corporate warfare behind the Japanese techno-invasion of the US and Crichton immediately faced accusations of xenophobia, which he swept aside. This theme was toned down substantially in the movie, although not with Crichton's wholehearted approval. Eventually, he and his scriptwriting partner, Michael Backes, resigned their involvement in the movie when director Philip Kaufman (*The Right Stuff*, *The Unbearable*

Lightness Of Being), in consultation with Connery, asked for changes to their original screenplay so that it became more of a thriller, with less of the controversial theme of the novel, which in typical Crichton style followed the investigation of a murder in the heady world of big business. He and Backes told the media that they weren't fired. They simply decided to quit because 'it's not going in the direction we wanted it to go'. The truth, as one reviewer put it, was that Kaufman had sandpapered the original screenplay quite substantially to make it more politically correct, with the Japanese nicer and the Americans less victimised and more corrupt.

But, then, Kaufman could claim to have a fair knowledge of the underlying currents of the movie. Although of Jewish origin, and consequently well briefed on the obvious anti-Semitic issues of his own background, he took the subject of internment of the Japanese in America during the Second World War as his undergraduate thesis at the University of Chicago. He also instigated discussion with Japanese-American organisations to discuss the racial issues of Crichton's novel, and some may well have thought he was taking an over-cautious stance on an topic that was, after all, in the public domain. He also had the full backing of Connery, fresh from his difficulties with the script for *Medicine Man*, and it was also the Scot who suggested he might be given a partner played by a black actor, which was also at variance with the novel. Wesley Snipes was brought in and his character redefined during script polishing, which involved Connery, Kaufman and screenwriter David Mamet, brought in for the rewrites.

The story was set in 1990s Los Angeles, in the skyscraper offices of a Japanese corporation where a murder is committed during a social gathering in the building. A young woman in scant attire is found strangled to death on the table in the boardroom. A weary, old-fashioned and anti-Japanese LA detective (Harvey Keitel in brilliant form) arrives within minutes and is immediately immersed in the difficulties of dealing with the Japanese.

Fortunately for the LAPD, they have a special unit headed by an expert in the psyche of the Japanese mind, one John Connor, a character that Crichton said he created with Sean Connery in mind. Snipes, an LAPD officer assigned to the murder, is not happy when a mysterious phone call forces him to team up with Connery, whose contacts with the Japanese imply a conflict of interest because of their respect for him.

Snipes and Harvey Keitel embark on their interrogations in the way they were trained to do, but Connery, with his familiarity with Japanese customs, now begins a master class on the finer points of an investigation that requires a particular and subtle understanding of the way to handle those to be interviewed. He is required to make several long speeches, brilliant in their own way, in which he analyses the Japanese mind to predict their behaviour, tactics and responses. Connery is constantly telling Snipes to 'pay attention' which he does with a reverence that unfortunately creates its own suggestion of racism, unless of course Snipes was simply overawed by the sheer presence of Connery rather than being grasshopper to the master as is the intent of the script. These exchanges tended to become tedious and consequently had mixed reviews from the critics who were kept waiting for the appearance of this movie.

Originally, Kaufman was supposed to deliver the finished product for release in the spring of 1993 but he overran his editing schedules while his masters at Fox anxiously awaited a release date. Connery now adopted his role of executive producer and gave his full support to Kaufman, saying the director should not be pressed into releasing the film before he was ready. In fact at that time, the director's cut was still incomplete and eventually Fox – who needed the money – agreed an autumn release date. Naturally, a good deal of attention would be paid to this movie, first because of the Crichton controversy and second because of huge pre-production hype and headlines about the money, which is why Kaufman took his time on the final cut. He knew full well there would be excessive reaction from critical sources, some more eager than others to take a sideswipe. Not least was a scathing onslaught towards Connery himself from British writer Julie Burchill in the *Sunday Times*, posing the question, 'Does a surfeit of gold irretrievably spoil an actor's acting, make it in some way rather slow and indolent?'

Crichton and Backes were none too happy either, the latter quoted as saying, 'Cutting the politics out of it is like taking Z and turning it into *Zorba The Greek.*' Even so, there was still a body of opinion that believed the movie was Japan-bashing. Connery put his own spin on that: 'It's a dangerous precedent [to say that] ... because it's not. What it's really about is what's realistically happening in the United States. What the Crichton book was saying was that the Japanese and the Americans were in bed together whether they liked it or not. But there is a culture clash and there has to be a bridge to cross it.'

Now, the question – once again recalling the old adage about sending messages via Western Union – is whether Connery was better equipped than most to pull off those long speeches. Philip Kaufman was in no doubt that the maturing image and physical bearing of Connery on screen was an uncommon advantage for any movie-maker. 'Steve McQueen had it. Cagney had and so did Cary Grant,' said Kaufman. 'If an actor has it, it means he can take stuff out of a supermarket freezer and there's something special about it. The fact is people are very attracted to the way he behaves. They have an empathy with him ... and he has gravity under pressure.'

The proof is particularly evident when matched against the competition, bearing in mind that he was approaching normal retirement age of 65. The other half a dozen male stars with whom he was in direct head-to-head at the box office were much younger and with the exception of De Niro and Ford, their movies were, shall we say, less thought-provoking dramas. And Connery already had five others in development ...

18

A SECOND WIND

The transformation of Connery from a sex symbol of the Bond era had been a desperately slow process, but at last he had emerged as a kind of senior statesman of the silver screen while at the same time he was still fit, lithe, healthy and positively attractive to the opposite sex. He was the man who directors could rely on to bring strength, versatility or a steadying hand to big budget Hollywood projects or bolster the status of smaller productions. Even so the Bond connection was still hovering, and it was evident that even with the passing of the years he still harboured a hatred of the way 007 took over his life in the 1960s, blighting his entire career and causing him anguish in battles with Cubby Broccoli, Harry Saltzman and the film studios. But, at the same time, he now obviously appreciated that Bond had made him wealthy and famous beyond his wildest dreams, as is evident from the Bond images on Connery's official website. Over the years film critics had more or less forced themselves to remove references to Bond unless it was absolutely necessary, but few magazine and newspaper feature writers could resist the temptation more than 30 years after he had first stepped into the role.

That still rankled. The hackles went up if media interviews persisted on going back to that era and, even worse, failed to understand his quest to run a dual-purpose career by alternating strong commercial projects with art house material that he knew would attract minimal audiences. His anger was roused when he adjudged that an interviewer might not have appreciated that, or had wrongly adjudged some of his films to be failures simply because they did not make money. 'That's not the point, and never was,' he would retort, eyes flashing, mouth narrowing to a scowl. It has not been uncommon for him to inform interviewers and critics in no uncertain terms, 'I am a fully trained actor, you know.'

He had, however, effortlessly assumed the status in the mid 1990s where, like Cary Grant in his 70s, he did not look out of his depth with love interests half his age. Even if Connery's role selection remained varied fare it has to be said that some memorable performances came out of several of the 'little' movies, such as *The Offence* in 1973. One of his oldest friends in the movies, Sidney Lumet, who had directed him towards another great showing in *The Hill* in 1965, reckons it was quite late in the actor's career that a change in the public perception of him occurred and that they finally saw beyond the Connery they thought they knew.

'I don't think he's grown so much as an actor,' Lumet said. 'It's more that the estimation of him finally caught up with what he can do. I always knew his great ability. John Huston when he cast him in *The Man Who Would Be King*, he knew it too. Sean always had the capacity for giant acting but it's [in the 1980s and early 1990s] that people have started to see it, saying, "Oh! He can act!" He knew it would take a long time to break the Bond mould but the length of time it took disappointed him. Christopher Reeve went through much the same after *Superman*. In the Bond era, the general assumption was that Sean was this charming sex hulk. Non-professionals didn't realise what superb high-comedy acting that

Bond role was. What was overlooked was his enormous skill. They didn't realise they were watching acting.'

On the way through these barriers of public perception, Connery took quite deliberate diversions, as we have seen, into some curious choices of films. One that raised a few eyebrows was in development even as he completed *Rising Sun*, although to some extent this time he was probably more attracted by the literary quality of the work. It was also to be the first of five movies completed and released within a three-year period, which caused some overlapping in the end. The film title was *A Good Man In Africa*, based on William Boyd's prize-winning first novel of the same name, a biting satire on British colonialists. Connery was 'the good man', although his was not the lead role. That was in the hands of fellow Scot Colin Friels, a bumbling, heavy-drinking racist whose unpleasantness is rather tedious because he is the central figure, and on screen for much of the time. In a fictional African country riddled with corruption, Dr Alex Murray (Connery) appears to be the only one who doesn't take backhanders. He is stern and irascible, but intent only on helping those he encounters, Friel's character among them. The underlying movement of the story comes from Connery whose best line is somewhat aptly, 'Show me the man who is completely content, and I'll show you the lobotomy scar.' He is the imposing figure who guides Friel's Morgan Leafy into a more discerning lifestyle.

A strong supporting cast, including Dianna Rigg and Joanne Whalley-Kilmer, worked hard to keep this movie alive through a lot of plot, but director Bruce Beresford (*Driving Miss Daisy*) did not extract the best story from the novel. Critics were mixed in their reaction, as they often were when looking at some of Connery's less ambitious projects, but generally the reviews were favourable and saw him as the key to making it work. Nor did it attract much public interest, grossing just $2.3 million in the US against a budget ten times that figure.

His next, *Just Cause*, was back in the mainstream, as is the pattern of so many of Connery's back-to-back enterprises. It was a harsh modern story based on John Katzenbach's novel and, unlike *A Good Man In Africa*, Fountainbridge Films were listed as co-producers with Warner Bros, giving the actor a financial interest beyond his personal fee. According to the highly respected Internet Movie Database (IMDb) website, Connery persuaded art dealer Arne Glimacher to direct and produce *Just Cause* and thus had considerable input into the creation of the film. Glimacher, a close personal friend of Connery, was considered by many a curious choice, given that his CV consisted of only one previous movie, the low-budget *Mambo Kings* in 1992 (in 2001 he would also direct *Wild River Kid* with Bob Hoskins and Antonio Banderas). But IMDb states Connery 'insisted' that he should direct.

The movie itself was particularly noted for its brazen scenic similarities to past films. Reviewers managed to variously link this 'homage' to such films as *Jagged Edge*, *Silence Of The Lambs*, *Speed*, *Cape Fear* and Orson Welles's *Touch Of Evil*. Elements of all these were recognisable in *Just Cause*, a thriller with a touch of horror which finds Blair Underwood as Bobby Earl Ferguson, a young black man on death row for the rape and murder of a ten-year-old white girl after being beaten by police into confessing to the crime. This scenario has already been set up when the action switches to introduce Connery's character, Paul Armstrong, a liberal Harvard law professor voicing fierce opposition to the death penalty in a debate against a proponent of that issue (played by George Plimpton). As the debate ends, Armstrong is approached by Ferguson's grandmother.

He is now confronted with making the decision of whether or not to act on his principles and return to the professional side of his business for the first time in 25 years. He accepts the challenge and for the next 50 minutes the movie centres on Armstrong's detective work as he meticulously proceeds through his own investigation, blocked at every turn by the local police chief. Finally he stumbles on vital new evidence and Ferguson is freed. But all is not as it seems. Armstrong was targeted not simply because of his liberalism and brilliance, but also because his wife (Kate Capshaw) had previously been involved in Ferguson's prosecution and had treated the defendant badly. Furthermore, a fellow death row inmate, a chained psychopath portrayed brilliantly by an over-the-top Ed Harris, claims he committed the murder for which Ferguson was convicted. And so we are led to the crux of the matter, or as the movie blurb says, 'buried deep in the Florida Everglades is a secret that can save an innocent man or let a killer kill again.'

Although generally accepted as an entertaining thriller, the script was patchy and criticised for its lack of psychological depth, especially when compared with such movies as *Cape Fear* and *Touch Of Evil*. Once again, the reviewers' focus on Connery was favourable and, as renowned critic Roger Ebert wrote, 'When it comes to expressing quiet wrath, Connery is like few other actors ... overall this is an average film but it is one that is slickly enjoyable in the same way that many of the genre are – deeply flawed but energetic enough to more or less cover its plot holes. The strong cast all do well even if they are not given anything special to work with and some of them are no more than cameos. All told this isn't very good but it is quite fun anyway.'

Just Cause was released in the US in February 1995 to good business. After promising first weekend takings of $10 million it went on to gross over $40 million in America, showing a further decent return when the video rentals and sales were added in. British and European audiences were less enamoured with another movie on the theme of a nasty deep-south police chief beating confessions out of suspects, and returns in that quarter were disappointing.

Again, even as *Just Cause* went into the editing process, in which Connery was also involved as executive producer, he was also working on his next movie in the mid-1990s quintet of diverse fare, the big budget Arthurian tale *First Knight*, on which a spend of $70 million was riding. All the elements for a movie that matched the pre-launch hype appeared to be in place. Direction was in the hands of Jerry Zucker, best known in recent times for his 1990 tear-jerking drama *Ghost* which took a massive $500 million worldwide and another $100 million in video rentals to make it the fourth highest earner in the history of film – and all that on a budget of $22 million. This time he had $70 million to spend with Connery appearing in due majestic fashion as Arthur, with Richard Gere as Lancelot and Julia Ormond as Guinevere. Brad Pitt, Aidan Quinn and Anthony Hopkins helped round out the cast.

The story is yet another revamp of Camelot and it received immediate criticism over a fast and loose approach to the Arthurian legends, which may have been precipitated by the fact that the writers were told in advance who would be playing the leading roles and to prepare their script with those names in mind. And so we have Guinevere deciding to marry King Arthur because she believes she could love him, but more importantly because he will protect her lands from the evil Prince Malagant (Ben Cross). Lancelot's arrival on the scene changes everything when he saves her from the evil prince while on her way to the wedding. The enthralling triangle develops with Arthur's admiration of Lancelot, and vice versa.

The situation reminded a number of reviewers of the set-up in *Casablanca*, although the comparison jarred somewhat considering the rather carefree manner in which Gere played his love scenes. In any event, unlike Casablanca the scenario turns nasty when Guinevere finally decides to reject Lancelot in favour of Arthur. The latter observes the lovers' parting kiss and, in a rage, hauls them before a public tribunal for treason. All pretty banal stuff, made worse when Malagant arrives and shouts the immortal line, 'Nobody move, or Arthur dies!' James Cagney could not have said it better, and indeed the whole love interest scenes were written in the style of the Golden Age epics, which related to neither Athurian times nor the 1990s.

First Knight was entertaining enough with some wonderful sets by John Box and powerful action, especially the night-time battle scenes. Connery looked quite the king and was again the movie's bonding element, but it had the extreme misfortune to follow behind two others in the same genre that season, all arriving like London buses. The competition was strong, spectacular and rousing, first with Liam Neeson in a blood-red version of *Rob Roy* followed by Mel Gibson's spectacular *Braveheart*. The former, produced on a comparatively modest budget of $28 million – less than half that of the other two – was in many ways the better of the three, and certainly less pretentious. In the bottom-line figures that emerged as this season of medieval action was played out Braveheart was by far the winner financially, grossing $202 million worldwide. *First Knight* struggled to erase its $70 million budget.

Nor was Connery done with medieval plotlines. In Europe he had been engaged in the first of a series of intricate vocal recordings, initially at an audio studio near his home in the Bahamas for the first phase of taping voiceovers for a giant dragon, the star of Rob Cohen's farcical – but, as it turned out, profitable – movie *Dragonheart*, listed among the star attractions to open in the 1996 season. It was a remarkable, if sublimely silly, movie that had technical wizardry aplenty with an 18-foot-tall talking dragon called Draco as the centrepiece. For the first time in his career Connery had magnificent reviews for a role in which he was totally unseen. The booming power, depth and moral undertones of his voice simply held the whole daft business together and made it eminently watchable, although the critics took some convincing. *Dragonheart* was the brainchild of producer Raffaella de Laurentis and director Rob Cohen. Money was no object, especially in the perfection of Draco, a computer-generated horned monster that breathed fire and even had the facial expressions, mannerisms and even vulnerability of Connery – a feat achieved by some remarkable and lengthy research by Cohen. The director spent weeks trawling through Connery's movies, viewing scenes from as far back as *Darby O'Gill* right through to *Just Cause*, pulling out hundreds of clips covering the actor's every expression: 'We categorised every possible emotion – sardonic, amusing, sceptical, critical, charming, seductive, angry – and pretty much assembled his emotional life on film and analysed how he used his expressions and mannerisms, which we transferred to laser discs.'

The animation work was carried out at the George Lucas Industrial Light And Magic, at San Rafael, California. When this quite intimate study of Connery had been put together the character creators applied them to Draco so that Connery was not merely the voice of the dragon, but actually acting the part. The result was a remarkable creation, a brilliant milestone, the latest marker in the long line of screen monsters dating from King Kong and another feather in the cap of visual effects designer Phil Tippet (*Jurassic Park, Star Wars, Indiana Jones And The Temple Of Doom, RoboCop* to name but a few) and given life on the screen by a team supervised by Scott Squires at the Industrial Light And Magic studios. In the actual film, this compilation of creature computer graphics amounted to 182 individual shots of the dragon, accounting for exactly 24 minutes of screen time which cost $22 million out of a total spend of $57 million.

After all that the rest of the movie seemed subordinate to this central character, in spite of decent performances from a strong cast led by Dennis Quaid, supported by Julie Christie and Pete Postlethwaite. Quaid is 10th-century knight Bowen, who rides around a Celtic kingdom looking for dragons to slay for profit. Inevitably, the last dragon he has to confront is Draco, the unbeatable talking creature with a pile of knights' bones to prove his prowess to any other would-be dragon slayers. But the humour and pathos of Draco, the last dragon, is the star of the show as the computer-created monster merges seamlessly into the storybook reality. Close your eyes and it is Connery and, even with them open, the expressions and quirks of the real man are unnervingly evident. Although some of the dialogue was dense, few could fail to come away impressed.

More to the point in relation to the story of Connery, this movie added another dimension to this set of five he made in the mid-1990s as he approached and then passed the age of 65, demonstrating his continuing versatility. The final movie before he took a well-earned break merely confirmed the point. Finishing *Dragonheart* he headed straight for what *Premiere* magazine called a 'kind of Die Hard on Alcatraz', working with some of the finest young talent in Hollywood at that time.

The Rock came from the stable of Don Simpson and Jerry Bruckheimer, producers for Hollywood Pictures. The pair, who had roomed together at the University of Arizona, teamed up professionally in 1983 and became widely known in the trade as extravagant producers and starmakers, whose blockbusters – including *Flashdance* (1983), *Beverly Hills Cop* (1984) and *Top Gun* (1986) – helped define the pop culture of that era. In 1985 and 1988 they were named producers of the year by the National Association Of Theater Owners, and by the turn of the decade their films had generated more than $2 billion in box-office receipts, video sales and rentals and record albums. They were also nominated for 10 Oscars, 3 Golden Globes and 2 People's Choice best picture awards, while the soundtracks garnered 18 Grammy nominations. As it turned out, however, *The Rock* was to be their last picture together. Simpson died of a heart attack in 1996, although Bruckheimer went on to make numerous other major movies, including *Black Hawk Down* and *Pirates Of The Caribbean*.

For *The Rock* they hired a virtually unknown director, 32-year-old Michael Bay, a film prodigy from Wesleyan University whose only previous movie was another Simpson–Bruckheimer production, *Bad Boys*, the previous year. Before that Bay had worked on television commercials and music videos, notably some controversial promotional films for Tina Turner and Meat Loaf. They also picked a superstar in the making, Nicholas Cage, then 30 years old, who had just completed *Leaving Las Vegas*, although it was not yet on release. This scenario was totally new for Connery. Seldom in the past had he been matched with or directed by such young filmmakers, and media observers were watching for the possibility of conflict, with Connery well known for his personal preferences and directorial instincts in terms of the way *he* felt things should be done. He had, after all, worked with most of the finest people in the business for almost 40 years. Now he was confronted by a young director who had only one major movie to his credit, albeit a successful one grossing $150 million on a budget of just $23 million. Conflict would occur, especially as this was one of the most strenuous and demanding roles Connery had undertaken in years.

His on-screen colleagues in this picture included old friend Ed Harris, but his partner in the story was Cage whose long list of credits already demonstrated a versatility similar to Connery's own. For almost a decade, he had been one of Hollywood's busiest young actors, and although not the most physically attractive among his peers he secured a diversity of roles that had ranged through youth pictures, art house and blockbusters. Alongside Connery in *The Rock* he was about to move into a different league in a story that was right at the top of current thriller writers' agendas, and would become something of a precursor for events over the coming years. It also had a touch of Ian Fleming about it, modernised and updated of course, like the new and improved Bond movies which had just been relaunched with Pierce Brosnan as Bond in *Goldeneye*. Indeed, this was Connery back in the eye of the storm of a big action thriller which would do just as well as the latest Bond movie, released just a few months earlier. Like the new, modern Bond *The Rock* had style and plenty of scope for sly, dry humour, in which Connery was matched line for line by Cage. Clearly the two men, more than three decades apart in age, got on well, bounced off each other and enjoyed the experience. This kinship extended to out-of-hours conversations when Connery apparently gave Cage a few tips in what he should demand from film-makers in terms of percentages. 'Take extra care about who handles your money,' the older man advised Cage, 'and sure as hell insist on a percentage of the gross.' Sage advice, but in this particular instance they were already on to a winner.

The Rock's script sparkled with brilliant lines and good, believable plots. Connery, Cage and Harris presented the audience with three convincing characters and, in an era of Hollywood action movies where little changed from one to the next other than more explosions, *The Rock* provided issues and people that you actually begin to care about.

John Patrick Mason (Connery) is a British spy who 30 years ago stole J Edgar Hoover's secret files, including a dossier containing the true facts about the assassination of John F Kennedy. He was secretly jailed for life without trial and has remained in custodial isolation ever since. Meanwhile, American war hero Gen Francis X Hummel (Harris) claims that the US military establishment has denied the existence of 83 men under his command who were killed on secret operations during the first Gulf War and other conflicts. Gathering a band of renegade Marines he captures the former prison island of Alcatraz and threatens to launch rockets loaded with deadly biological agents across the bay into the heart of San Francisco unless $100 million is distributed among his former comrades' next of kin. Mason, the only man ever to escape from Alcatraz, is recruited to join forces with FBI scientist Dr Stanley Goodspeed (Cage) and outmanoeuvre Hummel. His task is to break back into Alcatraz unnoticed and guide Goodspeed through a maze of underground passages and sewers so he can defuse the weapons.

The movie is punctuated by spectacular action and, as much of the location work is shot in the place where the most famous car chase of all time was filmed with Steve McQueen in *Bullitt*, there just had to be homage to it. It came in heart-stopping style with Connery in a Humvee being pursued by Cage driving a yellow Ferrari, and the added dimension of modern technology. The variation on the McQueen chase was breathtakingly extravagant, with cars, trucks, parking meters and shop fronts disposed of by the second before the climatic and fiery dispatching of one of the city's cable cars. As critic Roger Ebert concluded, 'The film could almost end right there – the sequence comes fairly early – and viewers would feel they got their money's worth.'

But there was much, much more that was noteworthy as the chemistry between Connery and Cage went beyond the demands of the movie. Connery was also making the point that he could still cut it when others of his age and ilk had already hung up their action boots. He proved it by performing stunts that others might have passed to a double, to the admiration of all around him. The audiences, spurred by excellent reviews, turned out in droves and *The Rock* grossed $325 million worldwide against a budget of $75 million.

The Rock also concluded the quintet of back-to-back movies Connery made in the mid-1990s. His 'second wind' had produced some outstanding and memorable work, and it wasn't over yet.

19

KNIGHTED AT LAST

During the making of *The Rock* Connery embarked on one other almost secretive project that harked back to his continuing, if neglected, love of the theatre. He decided to co-finance and co-produce a play by a virtually unknown writer whose work went on to great acclaim and long engagements in theatres around the world thanks largely to his original interest, although initially the credit went to his wife Micheline. She saw the play, *Art* by Yasmina Reza, at a fringe theatre in Paris and implored her husband to come and watch it. It was a three-handed tragi-comedy about three friends who fall out following the purchase of an expensive piece of modern art, although in fact the underlying story was the state of their long-standing friendship.

Reza, who had studied at Paris X University and later at the Jacques Lecoq Drama School, began working as an actress in France and appeared in numerous plays by contemporary authors as well as plays by Molière, Marivaux, and Sacha Guitry. In 1987 she began writing for the theatre and her French translation of Steven Berkoff's adaptation of Franz Kafka's novel *The*

Metamorphosis, for performance by Roman Polanski, was nominated for the 1988 Molière Award for translation. *Art* premiered in Berlin and opened in Paris in 1994, where it won three Molière Awards: Best Author, Best Play and Best Production. Connery was so impressed he decided immediately to bring the play to London after a translation by British playwright Christopher Hampton. It opened in October 1996 at the Barbican, before transferring quickly to the Wyndham Theatre, with an original cast of three of Britain's finest actors, Tom Courtenay, Ken Stott and Albert Finney. The London *Evening Standard* concluded,

> *At last that rare thing, a true adult comedy, with more than mere laughter on its mind, blooms in the West End wasteland. At first, Yasmina Reza's* Art*, which triumphed in Paris and Berlin, looks eager to make traditional fun of a man so keen to proclaim his love of daring abstract art that he buys a blank, white canvas for a fortune. Miss Reza's interest lies not in the picture, but the dangerous antagonisms it sparks.* Art *is a French female's deliciously sharp imagining of how middle-class men relate to each other – or rather how they spectacularly fail to. This is no low shot aimed below the waist. Miss Reza views the male of the species more in amused resignation than feminist anger ... An appealing comedy, whose surface charms conceal a dark and interesting interior.*

The play went on to win an Olivier Award, an *Evening Standard* Award and in 1998, on tour in America, a Tony. The international stage showered Reza with tributes as *Art* was translated into 35 languages and fought over by theatres around the world, including such diverse cities as Tokyo, Bombay, Johannesburg and Buenos Aires. In London, the play ran at the Wyndham until October 2001 and thereafter transferred to the Whitehall Theatre until January 2003. The cast changed numerous times during its UK run, with many of the country's most popular male actors and a number of comedians appearing, as well as a number of

American actors who travelled to London especially to take part. *Art* also went on tour across Britain, America and Europe, becoming one of the most performed plays of modern times, while Yasmina Reza was installed as one of her generation's most discussed, famous and sought-after authors. All in all, it was a hugely successful outcome that resulted from the Connerys' original interest.

Sean Connery himself was also being honoured again for his own work and in January 1996, he collected the Cecil B DeMille lifetime achievement award at the Golden Globe ceremonies in Hollywood. Connery was clearly moved at the presentation, especially as few such honours were coming his way from his home country – other than a bus pass from a local transport company on his 65th birthday. It was also noticeable that the man who has so often bemoaned the fact that he was for ever associated with James Bond chose to make his own reference to the character in his acceptance speech: 'It is the words in between the shooting and the punches and the car crashes that really counts. The scenes between the men and the women that try to say something about how we really behave, what we really feel, that's ultimately what moves people and sends them into the movie houses. In other words, I prefer my audiences stirred, not shaken.' The paraphrasing of the most famous of his Bond quotations came just before Cubby Broccoli died in Los Angeles, at the age of 87, after a long illness with heart trouble. Connery was asked to comment, but issued only a brief, curt statement: 'My previous differences with Cubby Broccoli were well known, but I recently took the opportunity to make my peace with him. I'm extremely sorry to hear of the loss. He will be missed.'

His passing was also marked by an outstanding achievement: that the Bond movies Broccoli created with Saltzman (and, initially, Connery who to this day feels he was badly done down) were just about to go into the cinema record books as the highest grossing series of movies, having topped the $1 billion mark with the international returns for *Goldeneye*. It was the early stages of the enterprise, launched entirely on the Connery image as 007, that formed the profit-sharing dispute between him, the producers and the film company. By the 1990s, of course, the image of any celebrity, film, sports or otherwise, was a most valuable commodity owned entirely by the celebrity and on which substantial royalties had to be paid as of right. By then the management of Broccoli's Bond legacy had passed to his daughter and stepson and, on a grey November day, they helped stage a tribute to their father – 'one of the best-loved producers in Hollywood' – at the Odeon Leicester Square, the home of many Bond premieres. The scene was glittering, with a high celebrity count among the 2,500 guests, including the Bond actors Roger Moore, Timothy Dalton and Pierce Brosnan. Connery's absence was duly noted.

In America, where Cubby himself had been honoured with a place on Hollywood's Walk of Fame, Connery found himself as the nominee for a gala tribute by the Film Society of Lincoln Center, an annual award that had previously featured only four British-born actors, Charlie Chaplin, Laurence Olivier, Alex Guinness and Bob Hope (Michael Caine received the honour in 2004). The gala featured guest appearances by Steven Speilberg, Harrison Ford, Tippi Hedren, Diana Ross, Blair Underwood, Sidney Lumet and Ursula Andress. Film clips shown ranged from the actor's early career to the James Bond series, from Hitchcock's *Marnie* to *Indiana Jones And The Last Crusade*, from *The Untouchables* to *The Man Who Would Be King*, from *Just Cause* to *Robin And Marian*.

By then, Connery had received many such honours, awards and tributes from his peers around the world, but there remained a glaring omission in his home nation, that of recognition by the Queen, on the advice of Her Majesty's Government, of his achievements in the form of a knighthood. In fact, ministers in the outgoing Conservative government had already put his name forward for the award, but he was persistently ignored, and then specifically blocked when New Labour came to power in 1997.

The reasons were entirely political, arising from the feuding north of the border when it became clear that the devolution of government to Scotland, Wales and Northern Ireland was to be set in motion. Connery had often publicly reinforced his long-held and well-known support for Scottish Nationalism, which he compounded with substantial donations.

However, in the summer of 1997 when the campaign for devolution was underway, New Labour's Donald Dewar, Secretary of State for Scotland, had asked to meet Connery to enlist his help in promoting what became known as the cross-party Yes-Yes campaign ahead of a referendum on self-government for Scotland. Dewar, in line to head the first Scottish Parliament if the outcome was successful, had approached the leader of the Scottish Nationalist Party, Alex Salmond, to arrange a meeting with the star. Salmond later revealed that it was Prime Minister Tony Blair's close Cabinet ally Peter Mandelson who persuaded Dewar to bring Connery on board for the campaign because, whatever the media or politicians said about him, he carried influence.

Somewhat grudgingly, Dewar agreed and arranged to meet in London, and over a meal Connery agreed to participate in the final ten days of the campaign prior to the referendum vote on 11 September. Dewar himself was still not fully convinced because of Connery's stout views on Scottish independence, but Labour Party strategists were convinced that one of Scotland's most famous sons would have a major impact on achieving their ambitions for a devolved government with Dewar at the helm, thus becoming what the spin doctors called 'father of the nation'.

What Connery and Salmond did not know then was that only a month previously Dewar had vetoed a proposal for Connery to be given his long-overdue knighthood, originally mooted during the latter stages of John Major's Conservative administration. When the Tories lost the general election this proposal was still on the books but set aside by incoming New Labour on Dewar's say-so. Nor did Connery's agreement to go on to the public platform in support of the Yes-Yes campaign change that view. The antipathy towards him merely heightened among the ranks of New Labour, and Dewar in particular, because of an unanticipated side effect of Connery's contribution to the campaign, eventually won in the September referendum: his supportive words were spoken with such passion that he inspired a new spurt of nationalism among the people of Scotland.

Dewar now saw Connery as a political threat, his continued support for the Scottish Nationalist Party possibly weakening New Labour's position. He maintained the veto on Connery's knighthood and, when this became known, off-the-record briefings – or smears, according to the ScotNats – were made against Connery indicating that his tax-exile status was the cause of his exclusion from the Honour's List.

That consideration clearly did not apply to numerous other recipients. Knighthoods and other high honours abounded among the ranks of those whose main domicile was overseas but who had generously supported the major political parties. Others in the country were given honours for their services to a particular profession or calling, including many in the performing arts who were far less deserving than Connery. This penalisation, as Connery described it, was also eventually extended to prevent him from making an annual donation to the Scottish Nationalist Party. Amendments to the Political Parties, Elections and Referendums Bill meant that he was disallowed from making donations of £50,000 annually, to which Connery responded in *Scotland On Sunday* newspaper, 'We waited 300 years for our own Parliament but still Scots politics are being stitched up from London.'

Mutterings about his decision to live abroad were nothing new, but now they began to appear with an undercurrent of determined malice. Accusations were rife about the tactics he had used to avoid making any substantial contribution to the British exchequer, especially during the 1960s and 1970s, when top-rate income tax was in excess of 80 per cent. He was not alone, of course. Michael Caine, Tom Jones, Engelbert Humperdink were but three of the many high-profile celebrities who simply felt it necessary to pull out of the country at that time because of the decimation of their income. The pointed references to Connery in particular reappeared with a vengeance in the wake of his continuing support for the ScotNats, with one newspaper alleging that he had saved himself £20 million by staying out of the country. These persistent claims annoyed him intensely, as they also usually overlooked his charitable donations and the fact that his film company Fountainbridge brought work and income to Scotland. He had always been open about the reasons for maintaining his residency abroad, notably at his homes in Marbella or the Bahamas (although he did have a house in London). To silence his critics he subsequently decided to open his books and reveal that between 1990 and 2003 he had paid £7.1 million in British taxes. 'Everything I've got is tax paid,' he insisted. 'I don't have any blind trusts and I hope this finally erases some of the cynicism about my financial affairs.'

He made these comments in 2003, fed up with continued briefings against him for his political views and support for the Scottish Nationalists. By then, of course, the politicians in London had relented and he finally became Sir Sean Connery in the Queen's New Year's Honours List on 1 January 2000.

In the intervening period, Connery was back making movies seemingly determined to set aside the fact that he was fighting another battle against an adversary that ultimately he could not beat: advancing years. His period of intense activity in the 1990s ended with a relatively short break from movies, although even as he finished work on *The Rock* other projects were in development, including two that would again involve Fountainbridge.

Fortunately, there was no such personal connection with the next in line – his appearance in the widely panned big-screen version of *The Avengers*. The cult series, which had won huge acclaim on both sides of the Atlantic, was a product of the times in which it was born. The series grasped an unexplored area of British television with a quirky blend of espionage, fantasy and science fiction. Plots were somewhat dated, and in time had no qualms about spoofing the Bond movies. The series began in the UK in 1961 and ran for 161 episodes over 8 years, becoming one of the most popular television series of all time and eventually finding an audience in 120 countries. The pairing of Patrick Macnee and Diana Rigg as intrepid agents John Steed and Emma Peel was a masterstroke. They went about their business with tongue firmly in cheek and each time rode off into the sunset in a different mode of transport.

The series was equally popular in America where it ran until the late-1970s. The revival version, *The New Avengers*, did not enjoy the same level of success and it eventually folded, bequeathing *The Avengers* to its many fanclubs, websites and archives, still going strong almost 45 years after the series ended. The question of whether it should be revived as a movie had been around for some time. Many of the diehards believed it should be left to revel in the quirkiness of its time, available on video and DVD. But Warner Bros did not listen and went ahead anyway with a big-budget production, lashing out $60 million to recast the story into modern times with Ralph Fiennes and Uma Thurman in the leading roles, with Connery providing the villain of the piece, the pompous kilted Sir August De Wynter who is trying to blackmail the world using Prospero, his weather-controlling machine.

The movie was largely filmed at Shepperton Studios, giving Connery and Micheline the chance to use their Belgravia home and the novel experience of driving himself to work each day in his Range Rover. The production did not run smoothly, and the weather was appalling, leaving Connery fed up and bad tempered. He clearly had severe misgivings as filming progressed and his worst fears were confirmed when he saw the final cut. He was furious, and later let it be known that he considered the movie to be 'amateur night stuff'.

Those reviewers, especially in America, hoping to see

something on a par with the original television version were seriously disappointed. Mick LaSalle of the San Francisco Chronicle (in whose city the 1960s *Avengers* was especially popular) wrote of the film, 'The Avengers is a crime: bad casting and poor direction rob the remake of 1960s panache. After a slow opening, the 90-minute movie jolts into climax mode. What happened to the middle? Clearly, this wasn't just edited but gutted. No doubt they did us all a favour, but it doesn't help. Instead of just being a bad picture, the missing middle makes *The Avengers* a bad and weird and strangely off picture. Connery's presence is sprinkled throughout, and he has the best scenes – solely because Sean Connery is in them. He walks into a meeting of various world powers, wearing a kilt, and announces, "From now on you will buy your weather from me." It makes sense: if you're going to walk through a role, walk through it wearing a kilt.' No doubt Connery himself agreed with the sentiments expressed in that review. Only £23 million was taken in the ten weeks the film appeared on the US circuit, topped up by another $25 million worldwide, but the film fell short of production costs.

Thereafter, Connery took one of his familiar turns into a movie that was never likely to enter the blockbuster lists. *Playing By Heart* from the Miramax stable was strictly one for the pleasure of doing it, a small-budget picture that raised itself into creation largely through Connery's own participation. He was so taken with the script for the romantic comedy that he agreed to appear in it for a fee of just $60,000. No one was more surprised than writer- director Willard Carroll: 'He called and said he loved the idea of portraying an intimate, passionate relationship between people in their twilight years.'

Connery also reportedly persuaded other members of the cast, which included Gena Rowlands, Dennis Quaid, Ellen Burstin and Gillian Anderson, to form an ensemble whereby they were all paid the same minimum fee. The arrangements were nailed down hard. Connery would be available for one month, and he would be required on set for no more than eight days. He also insisted that work each day should start precisely on time.

His part, mostly with Rowlands, would be filmed like a running stage play, with minimal retakes. Carroll reported that they rehearsed their scenes in playlike fashion and then the cameras rolled and it went very smoothly. What impressed Carroll most was that Connery had no entourage and didn't play the star. He drove himself to the set where he met an assistant, did the business and went away, leaving a message on the director's answer phone at the end of the job saying it was a pleasure working with him.

His fellow actors were equally impressed. Gillian Anderson said, 'In person, Sean projects the same energy as he does on screen. It's not just sexual. It's radiant, intriguing and powerful and you can sense it the moment he walks in a room.' Dennis Quaid noted that Connery 'doesn't like to hang out on a set. He's there to work. He retires to his trailer when he's not needed. He doesn't invade other peoples' space in case they're trying to concentrate or work.'

Willard Carroll concluded, 'He was a most generous actor, even though he's a larger-than-life star.' It was indeed a curious link-up between an international star and a director whom few in mainstream Hollywood had even heard of: up to that point Carroll's work had consisted almost entirely of producing animated videos for children, the last entitled *Brave Little Toaster Goes To Mars*. Consequently, with the star line-up Connery had helped to assemble, the movie received far greater attention than it otherwise would have, although it was given a slow roll-out by the distributors, limited in the first week to 308 screens across the US compared to the normal average of around 2,600. The screenplay, written by Carroll, was sharp and punctuated by some witty dialogue which is probably what appealed to Connery in the first place.

He could doubtless visualise his own deliverance of such lines, but naturally enough it did not please everyone, quite often because some viewers simply cannot get used to seeing Connery in relatively low-profile roles. As Andy Seiler, in *USA Today*, commented, 'At times, the film resembles an endless audition in which a series of actors do monologues.' On the other hand, Rod Dreher in the *New York Post* called it an 'observant and brilliantly acted film … the calm, constant rhythm of the film mesmerises.' Connery was pleased with the result and director Willard Carroll who had brought it to the screen was simply overwhelmed by the co-operation he received, although immediately thereafter reverted to his previous genre with his production of *Brave Little Toaster To The Rescue*.

Connery, meanwhile, was heading back to the big time and the big action with a project that had been in development for more than a year through Fountainbridge Films under the overall command of Rupert Murdoch's Fox Films, although he was personally listed as the producer. The film was *Entrapment* and, even as it was announced, there was considerable media furore that Connery, 68 years old, was to star opposite Catherine Zeta-Jones, 40 years his junior, who would also be his lover. Although well known to British television audiences for her role in *Darling Buds Of May*, her only major film up to that point had been *Mask Of Zorro* with Antonio Banderas and Anthony Hopkins, and it had not been released at the time she was contracted to partner Connery. She had, however, just become more famous through her recent entry into the House of Douglas, as the future wife of Kirk's son Michael. Even so, the fact remained that she was currently the only Brit actress with the overtly sexual wherewithal to compete against those of similar build and talent in Hollywood.

The pairing was immaculate, and threw Connery straight back into high-octane stunts and situations dangerous, hardly befitting a man of his years and more in keeping with Pierce Brosnan's current Bond movie – 19th in the series – *The World Is Not Enough*. Was it any coincidence that *Entrapment* contained the elements of any Bond film: an unbelievable plot, impossible action scenes, lavish settings and a beautiful woman, occasionally clad in leather, to entertain the male star and extract from him some suitably witty lines of innuendo in a wholly stylish manner?

Locations took them to New York, Scotland (as part of Connery's Fountainbridge commitment to bring film work to his homeland) and on to Malaysia for scenes which supposedly had them hanging on to wire strung between the two tallest skyscrapers in Kuala Lumpur. The plot line has insurance investigator Gin Baker (Zeta-Jones) on the trail of master criminal Robert 'Mac' MacDougal (Connery). She supposedly sets up a scam to trap him by introducing MacDougal to a robbery he can't resist, the theft of a $40 million Chinese mask. But what is her game? And who's playing who?

The whole was an enjoyable, undemanding romp that kept the action going from the start. Some reviewers were a bit sniffy about the unbelievability of some of the stunts and scenarios, and Roger Ebert suggested Connery was lacklustre. There was one other postscript that indicated that Connery's role in the sex symbol department was at last beginning to wane: the American magazine *Film* ran a poll asking readers to vote on the worst movie love scene of all time. The result was, in descending order: Sharon Stone's encounter with Joe Pesci in *Casino*; Sean Connery and Catherine Zeta-Jones in *Entrapment*; and Marlon Brando and Maria Schneider in *Last Tango In Paris*. At least he was in good company.

Regardless of what the critics wrote, Connery, as both producer and star, went on the road to sell the movie and completed more than 60 media interviews in North America and Europe. The result was an outstanding financial success: the movie was produced on a budget of $66 million, and took $22 million in its first weekend in the US on 2,800 screens, and grossed close on $300 million worldwide. This was secured against some very strong competition and as Greg Bulmash of IMDb observed, *Entrapment* was the number four film for that year. Another interesting statistic showed that all the top five films had at least one British actor in a starring role. Apart from Connery and Zeta-

Jones in *Entrapment*, Liam Neeson and Ewan McGregor arrived in *Star Wars*, Hugh Grant (and others) in *Notting Hill*, Anthony Hopkins in *Instinct* and Rachel Weisz in *The Mummy*.

At the time of these further successes, the British government had yet to recommend that Sean Connery should receive an honour for his achievements. As recorded earlier, it was not until the New Year's Honours List, officially announced on 1 January 2000, that he had been awarded his knighthood. By then the US had beaten Britain to the punch with an outstanding honour – he became the recipient of the 22nd Annual Kennedy Centre Honour for lifetime contribution to arts and culture. The award, presented to Connery at a ceremony in Washington by President Bill Clinton, is among the most important in the American performing arts.

Seldom sitting still, Connery was by then already engaged in another Fountainbridge project, once more as producer and star, and again a total change of pace from the previous one. He had been working on it for almost three years with writer Michael Rich who had sent him a screenplay of what became *Finding Forrester*, an appealing, quiet drama of an old man who befriends a talented black teenager. He also recruited director Gus Van Sant who had recently brought the hugely successful *Good Will Hunting* to the screen with Matt Damon, Robin Williams, Ben Afleck and Minnie Driver.

On the surface, this quiet drama about an aging recluse who tutors a young African-American student in life and literature had no great handle but Connery had so much faith in the story that he persevered with Rich and Van Sant to develop it into a project that would interest a major studio and eventually received backing from Columbia Pictures. His character was William Forrester, a Pulitzer Prize-wining author who, shortly after publishing his one and only novel, had retreated to seclusion in a tiny Bronx apartment where he lived anonymously for the next 40 years, sustained by royalties from his book as it was discovered by each new generation of readers, and spending his time keeping watch on his neighbourhood with binoculars from his window.

He befriends a black teenager, Jamal, who is intrigued by 'the man at the window', and as he is tutored in literature by the author, so Forrester is gradually drawn out of his shell. Connery explained in a media interview,

'It's difficult not to think of JD Salinger when you're creating a character like Forrester. His *Catcher In The Rye* has worked for every generation since it was written (in 1951). I'm not playing Salinger but his ghost was always near at hand. Forrester closets himself in his apartment with his books and his royalty cheques. He hated celebrity. He shunned fame. I myself have avoided many of the pitfalls of fame by choosing not to live in Los Angeles. The story took hold of me from the first reading and I knew I had to avoid being sentimental. I wanted people to believe the relationship between Forrester and the young boy could actually develop. It was only when I felt we'd achieved that goal, I agreed it was time to film it, but we still had another big problem. We had to find a black kid who could do all the things the script required and still be just 16 and exactly right for the part – and until we found Rob Brown, I was prepared to scrap the whole film.'

Rob Brown was born in Harlem and raised in Brooklyn. He attended Poly Prep High School in Brooklyn and played on their basketball team, but had never studied drama and had no previous acting experience. In fact, he only went to the audition for *Finding Forrester* when it was advertised locally to get money to pay his cell phone bill. Connery said he was a natural, smart with good instincts and they struck up a rapport that continued off screen as the movie was being filmed. Brown said, 'I spent a lot of time at his apartment while we were shooting and we just talked for hours. I'd be asking him questions and he answered all of them. We went to dinner together a lot.'

That rapport was evident in the film as the depth of the story unfolded, and Brown's basketball connection was also paralleled in the movie when he is torn between the ambitions of his school to pursue the sport, while at the same time expanding his writing talent through Forrester. When the boy, Jamal, wins a scholarship to a private academy he is confronted by an old enemy of Forrester's who refuses to accept that an African-American basketball player from the Bronx could possibly write to such a level. It was a heart-warming tale with current social implications that was well received by the critics and attracted strong business at the box office after a slow start. The distributors, unsure of public reaction, put it on to just 200 screens for the opening week in America at Christmas but within two weeks it had been extended to 2,002 screens across the nation, eventually grossing more than $60 million in the US alone. At the time, there was talk that Connery was in line for a second Oscar, but it didn't happen. 'I'm not in the club,' he commented to an interviewer in Toronto. 'I don't go to Los Angeles unless I have to.' As for young Rob Brown, his future looked positively bright. He was quickly signed for two more movies and television work.

The conclusion of *Finding Forrester* marked a distinct slow-down in Connery's workload and over the next three years he made only one film, this time reverting to the big box-office ambitions of the much-heralded *The League Of Extraordinary Gentlemen*, again as both star and executive producer. Given the film's reception it is quite possible he regretted becoming either. This was a wacky 19th-century adventure that actually had the potential for brilliance but ended up, to steal a phrase from the *Hollywood Reporter*, 'disintegrating before your eyes'. The screenplay was based on a graphic comic-book novel co-written by Alan Moore, who brought us *From Hell* and which had established something of a cult following. The authors filched characters from famous novels and League's line-up consisted of Allan Quatermain from Rider Haggard's *King Solomon's Mines*, Mina Harker from Bram Stoker's *Dracula*, Jules Verne's Captain Nemo fresh from *20,000 Leagues Under the Sea*, RL Stevenson's Dr Jekyll, an American secret service agent named Tom Sawyer who bore no resemblance to Mark Twain's creation, Oscar Wilde's Dorian Gray and Rodney Skinner, drawn around HG Wells's *The Invisible Man*, presumably because the original was the only one in the group not yet out of copyright. To get the point of all this, of course, you had to have at least a minimal knowledge of the books from which these characters stepped, otherwise it was a meaningless romp from the start, and doubtless quite a number of under-25s didn't get lines like, 'You're missing a picture, Mr Gray.'

So why are they brought together in the first place? British adventurer Quatermain (Connery) is summoned from his alcoholic sojourn in Kenya by Her Majesty's Government to defend the realm from a mysterious character, known as Fantom, who wears a mask to hide his facial scaring. Fantom is threatening to instigate a world war with unheard of weapons of mass destruction. Quatermain assembles the fictional personalities to fight this evil character, and the initial battleground is Venice, to which they are despatched in Captain Nemo's massive *Nautilus* submarine. Unfortunately they fail and Venice is blown to smithereens, even thought most of the audiences would know that San Marco's is still there, and has been for some considerable time. The movie was, as they say, action packed, but disjointed and ultimately ran out of steam. It was critically slammed but still did remarkably good business. Made for $78 million, *League* grossed more than $200 million, with good worldwide support, and few could argue that Connery's presence in any movie gave it a headstart.

Although he might not be 'in the club' in Hollywood, there is no doubt that he remained a box-office draw as he moved into his 8th decade and almost 50 years in the business. Connery works for no one but himself, although he can be tempted to loan out his services for what he considers the right price. For years he fought exploitation with undying vigour. He began the movement in Hollywood, which others followed, to halt what he believed to be a corrupt misuse of actors in general, and to encourage actors to fight back.

In his own corner he has, as we have seen, steadfastly hit out at any whom he believed had been less than honest in their dealings with him. He has often displayed a tough, uncompromising exterior and has, on occasions, been accused of using his power and financial strength with quite ruthless determination. His battles were sometimes judged excessive, especially by those who considered that recognition of his incredible good fortune in his chosen field should have made him more circumspect in his fight against exploitation – and that the commercial dogfight of which he has accused others is the same one that allows him and a mere handful of other international movie stars to charge anything from five to ten million dollars, and more, for their services in a picture.

Connery has worked hard in a career in which he has matured into a man capable of unrivalled characterisations and superb performances, pushing himself towards challenging roles that have often been surprisingly subtle and off-beat.

His own analogy – likening his films to a painter's collection of canvases – probably cannot be bettered, and it demonstrates that he himself views his work as an art form much of the time, rather than simply as a commercial venture. Money, though, has always been a major part of the equation.

Fellow actors and friends with whom Connery has worked over the last few decades are at one in their admiration of the man. One commented that in his view the test of working with a good actor was to be doing a scene with him and to believe everything he is saying, and Connery mastered the art so convincingly that he made it look easy, the touchstone of greatness.

Oddly enough, it was some time before Connery was accepted as a *very good* actor, partly because his acting was curiously overshadowed by his charisma – a word vastly over-used in Hollywood but one which describes a quality that was immediately apparent in Connery in his first appearance as James Bond. In post-Bond years his sheer dominating presence on the set or stage enabled him to take supporting roles as frequently as star parts without affecting his standing.

Meanwhile, off screen he always remained unmoved by the glamour and the glitz. Unlike many of his Hollywood contemporaries who are ruled by the prerequisites of being a star

– the parties, the award ceremonies, the constant attention to personal detail – he has shunned the lot. He lives a relatively quiet life with a partner who not only shares his passion for privacy but who has joined him in maintaining it. Friends report an immensely relaxed household, free of tension except when he is close to starting a new film with which he is not yet satisfied. Otherwise, his family takes precedence over all other matters, followed by his work and his artistry. Connery still reads a lot, often revisiting the classics he studied in his early days as an actor. By his meticulous selection of roles he has managed what many others have not – to cross the age barrier while staying fresh, virile and even sexy – precisely the attributes that first made him a superstar.

19

FILMOGRAPHY

No Road Back (GB 1956). Director: Montgomery Tully. Cast: Skip Homeier, Paul Carpenter, Patricia Dainton, Norman Woodland, Margaret Rawlings, Eleanor Summerfield, Alfie Bass, Sean Connery.

Hell Drivers (GB 1957). Director: Cy Endfield. Cast: Stanley Baker, Herbert Lom, Peggy Cummins, Patrick McGoohan, William Hartnell, Wilfred Lawson, Sidney James, Jill Ireland, Alfic Bass, Gordon Jackson, David McCallum, Sean Connery.

Time Lock (GB 1957). Director: Gerald Thomas. Cast: Robert Beatty, Betty McDowall, Vincent Winter, Lee Patterson, Sandra Francis, Alan Gifford, Robert Ayres, Victor Wood, Sean Connery.

Action Of The Tiger (GB 1957). Director: Terence Young. Cast: Van Johnson, Martine Carol, Herbert Lom, Gustavo Rocco, Jose Nieto, Helen Haye, Anna Gerber, Anthony Dawson, Sean Connery, Yvonne Warren.

Another Time, Another Place (GB 1958). Director: Lewis Allen. Cast: Lana Turner, Barry Sullivan, Glynis Johns, Sean Connery, Sidney James, Terence Longdon, Doris Hare.

Darby O'Gill And The Little People (US 1959). Director: Robert Stevenson. Cast: Albert Sharpe, Janet Munro, Sean Connery, Jimmy O'Dea, Kieron Moore, Estelle Winwood, Walter Fitzgerald, Dennis O'Dea, Jack McGowran.

Tarzan's Greatest Adventure (GB 1959). Director: John Guillermin. Cast: Gordon Scott, Anthony Quayle, Sara Shane, Scilla Gabel, Sean Connery, Niall MacGimis.

The Frightened City (GB 1961). Director: John Lemont. Cast: Herbert Lom, John Gregson, Sean Connery, Alfred Marks, Yvonne Romain, Olive McFarland, Frederick Piper, George Pastell, Kenneth Griffiths.

On The Fiddle (GB 1961); USA title: *Operation Snafu.* Director: Cyril Frankel. Cast: Alfred Lynch, Sean Connery, Cecil Parker, Wilfrid Hyde White, Stanley Holloway, Alan King, John Le Mesurier, Barbara Windsor.

The Longest Day (US 1962). Directors: Ken Annakin, Andrew Marton, Bernard Wicki, Darryl F Zanuck. Cast: John Wayne, Robert Mitchum, Henry Fonda, Richard Burton, Richard Todd, Kenneth More, Rod Steiger, Robert Ryan, Robert Wagner, Roddy McDowall, George Segal, Curt Jurgens, Mel Ferrer, Sean Connery.

Dr No (GB 1962). Director: Terence Young. Cast: Sean Connery, Ursula Andress, Joseph Wiseman, Jack Lord, Bernard Lee, Anthony Dawson, John Kitzmiller, Zena Marshall, Eunice Gayson.

From Russia With Love (GB 1963). Director: Terence Young. Cast: Sean Connery, Daniela Bianchi, Pedro Armendariz, Lotte Lenya, Robert Shaw, Bernard Lee, Lois Maxwell, Desmond Llewelyn, Eunice Gayson, Walter Gotell, Martine Beswick, Vladek Sheybal, Nadja Regin.

Woman Of Straw (GB 1964). Director: Basil Dearden. Cast: Gina Lollobrigida, Sean Connery, Ralph Richardson, Johnny Sekka, Alexander Knox, Andre Morell.

Mamie (US 1964). Director/Producer: Alfred Hitchcock. Screenplay: Jay Presson Allen, from the novel by Winston Graham. Cast: Sean Connery, Tippi Hedren, Diane Baker, Martin Gabel, Alan Napier, Bruce Dern.

Goldfinger (GB 1964). Director: Guy Hamilton. Cast: Sean Connery, Honor Blackman, Gert Frobe, Shirley Eaton, Tania Mallet, Harold Sakata, Martin Benson, Cec Linder, Nadja Regin, Burt Kwouk, Richard Vernon.

The Hill (GB 1965). Director: Sidney Lumet. Cast: Scan Connery, Harry Andrews, Ian Hendry, Michael Redgrave, Ian Bannen, Alfred Lynch, Ossie Davis, Roy Kinnear, Jack Watson.

Thunderball (GB 1965). Director: Terence Young. Cast: Scan Connery, Claudine Auger, Adolfo Celi, Luciana Paluzzi, Rik Van Nutter, Marline Beswick, Guy Doleman, Molly Peters.

A Fine Madness (US 1966). Director: Irvin Kershner. Cast: Scan Connery, Joanne Woodward, Jean Seberg, Patrick O'Neal, Colleen Dewhurst, Clive Revill.

You Only Live Twice (GB 1967). Director: Lewis Gilbert. Cast: Scan Connery, Donald Pleasence, Akiko Wakabayashi, Tetsuro Tamba, Mie Hama, Karin Door, Teri Shimada, Charles Gray, Burt Kwouk, Alexander Knox, Tsai Chin.

Shalako (GB 1968). Director: Edward Dmytryk. Cast: Brigitte Bardot, Sean Connery, Stephen Boyd, Jack Hawkins, Peter Van Eyck, Honor Blackmail, Woody Strode, Eric Sykes, Alexander Knox, Valerie French.

The Molly Maguires (US 1969). Director: Martin Ritt. Cast: Sean Connery, Richard Harris, Samantha Eggar, Frank Finlay, Anthony Zerbe.

The Red Tent (Italy/USSR 1969). Director: Mikhail K Kalatozov. Cast: Peter Finch, Sean Connery, Claudia Cardinale, Hardy Kruger, Mario Adorf, Massimo Girotti, Luigi Vannucchi, Edward Marzevic, Boris Kmelnizki.

The Anderson Tapes (US 1971). Director: Sidney Lumet. Cast: Sean Connery, Dyan Cannon, Martin Balsam, Ralph Meeker, Alan King, Christopher Walken, Val Avery, Dick Williams, Garrett Morris, Stan Gottlieb.

Diamonds Are Forever (GB 1971). Director: Guy Hamilton. Cast: Sean Connery, Jill St John, Charles Gray, Lana Wood, Jimmy Dean, Bruce Cabot, Putter Smith, Bruce Glover, Norman Burton, Lawrence Naismith, Joe Robinson.

The Offence (GB 1972). Director: Sidney Lumet. Cast: Sean Connery, Ian Bannen, Trevor Howard, Vivien Merchant, Peter Bowles, Derek Newman, John Hallam, Ronald Radd, Anthony Saghar, Howard Gorney.

Zardoz (GB 1974). Director/producer/screenplay: John Boorman. Cast: Sean Connery, Charlotte Rampling, Sara Krestleman, Sally Anne Newton, John Alderton.

Ransom (GB 1974); USA title: *The Terrorists.* Director: Casper Wrede. Cast: Sean Connery, Ian McShane, Norman Bristow, Isabel Dean, John Cording, William Fox.

Murder on the Orient Express (GB 1974). Director: Sidney Lumet. Cast: Albert Finney, Lauren Bacall, Martin Balsam, Ingrid Bergman, Jacqueline Bisset, Jean-Pierre Cassel, Sean Connery, John Gielgud, Wendy Hiller, Anthony Perkins, Vanessa Redgrave, Rachel Roberts, Richard Widmark, Michael York, Colin Blakely, Denis Quilley, Jeremy Lloyd.

The Wind and the Lion (US 1975). Director: John Milius. Cast: Sean Connery, Candice Bergen, Brian Keith, John Huston, Geoffrey Lewis, Vladek Sheybal.

The Man Who Would Be King (US 1975). Director: John Huston. Cast: Sean Connery, Michael Caine, Christopher Plummer, Saeed Jaffrey, Shakira Caine.

Robin And Marian (US 1976). Director: Richard Lester. Cast: Sean Connery, Audrey Hepburn, Robert Shaw, Richard Harris, Nicol Williamson, Denholm Elliott, Kenneth Haigh, Ronnie Barker, Ian Holm, Bill Maynard, Peter Butterworth.

The Next Man (US 1976). Director: Richard C Sarafian. Cast: Sean Connery, Cornelia Sharpe, Albert Paulsen, Adolfo Celi, Marco St John, Bob Simmons.

A Bridge Too Far (US 1977). Director: Richard Attenborough. Cast: Dirk Bogarde, James Caan, Michael Caine, Sean Connery, Edward Fox, Elliott Gould, Gene Hackman, Anthony Hopkins, Hardy Kruger, Laurence Olivier, Ryan O'Neal, Robert Redford, Maximilian Schell, Liv Ullmann, Denholm Elliott, Jeremy Kemp, Donald Pickering, Ben Cross.

The First Great Train Robbery (GB 1978). Director: Michael Crichton. Cast: Sean Connery, Donald Sutherland, Lesley-Anne Down, Alan Webb, Wayne Sleep, Michael Elphick, Pamela Salem.

Meteor (US 1979). Director: Ronald Neame. Cast: Sean Connery, Natalie Wood, Karl Malden, Henry Fonda, Trevor Howard, Brian Keith, Martin Landau, Richard Dysart.

Cuba (US 1979). Director: Richard Lester. Cast: Sean Connery, Brooke Adams, Jack Weston, Martin Balsam, Denholm Elliott, Hector Elizondo, Chris Sarandon, Walter Gotell, David Rappaport.

Time Bandits (GB 1981). Director/Producer: Terry Gilliam. Cast: John Cleese, Sean Connery, Shelley Duvall, Katherine Helmond, Ian Holm, Michael Palin, Ralph Richardson, David Warner, Peter Vaughan, Craig Warnock, Jim Broadbent.

Outland (US 1981). Director: Peter Hyams. Cast: Sean Connery, Peter Boyle, Frances Sternhagen, James B. Sikking, Kika Markham, Steven Berkoff, Clarke Peters, John Ratzenberger, Nicholas Barnes.

The Man With The Deadly Lens (US 1982); USA title: *Wrong is Right*. Director/Producer: Richard Brooks. Cast: Sean Connery, George Grizzard, Robert Conrad, Katharine Ross, Leslie Nielsen, Hardy Kruger, Dean Stockwell, Ron Moody.

Five Days One Summer (US 1982). Director/Producer: Fred Zinnemann. Cast: Sean Connery, Betsy Brantley, Lambert Wilson, Anna Massey, Isabel Dean, Sheila Reid.

The Sword of the Valiant (GB 1982). Director: Stephen Weeks. Cast: Miles O'Keeffe, Sean Connery, Cyrielle Claire, Leigh Lawson, Trevor Howard, Peter Gushing, Ronald Lacey, John Rhys-Davies.

Never Say Never Again (US 1983). Director: Irvin Kershner. Cast: Sean Connery, Klaus Maria Brandauer, Max Von Sydow, Barbara Carrera, Kim Basinger, Bernie Casey, Alec McCowan, Edward Fox, Pamela Salem, Rowan Atkinson, Valerie Leon, Pat Roach, Ronald Pickup.

Highlander (US 1986). Director: Russell Mulcahy. Cast: Christopher Lambert, Roxanne Hart, Clancy Brown, Sean Connery, Alan North.

The Name Of The Rose (Italy/Germany/France, 1986). Director: Jean-Jacques Annaud. Cast: Sean Connery, F Murray Abraham, Christian Slater, William Hickey, Michael Lonsdale, Ron Perlman.

The Untouchables (US 1987). Director: Brian De Palma. Cast: Kevin Costner, Robert De Niro, Sean Connery, Charles Martin Smith, Andy Garcia, Richard Bradford, Jack Kehoe, Brad Sullivan, Billy Drago, Patricia Clarkson.

The Presidio (US 1988). Director: Peter Hyams. Cast: Sean Connery, Mark Harmon, Meg Ryan, Jack Warden, Mark Blum, Dana Gladstone, Don Calfa.

Indiana Jones And The Last Crusade (US 1989). Director: Steven Spielberg. Cast: Harrison Ford, Sean Connery, Denholm Elliott, Alison Doody, John Rhys-Davies, Julian Glover, River Phoenix, Michael Byme, Alex Hyde-White, Alexie Sayle.

Family Business (US 1989). Director: Sidney Lumet. Cast: Sean Connery, Dustin Hoffman, Matthew Broderick.

The Hunt for Red October (US 1990). Director: John McTiernan. Cast: Sean Connery, Alec Baldwin, Scott Glenn, Sam Neill, James Earl Jones, Tim Curry, Richard Jordan, Peter Firth, Joss Ackland.

The Russia House (US 1990). Director: Fred Schepisi. Cast: Sean Connery, Michelle Pfeiffer, Roy Scheider, John Mahoney, Klaus Maria Brandauer, James Fox, Ken Russell.

Highlander II: The Quickening (US 1990). Director: Russell Mulcahy. Cast: Christopher Lambert, Sean Connery, Virginia Madsen, Michael Ironside.

Robin Hood: Prince Of Thieves (US 1991). Director: Kevin Reynolds. Cast: Kevin Costner, Morgan Freeman, and Sean Connery appearing as King Richard.

Medicine Man (US 1992). Director: John McTiernan. Cast: Sean Connery, Lorraine Bracco, José Wilker, Rodolfo De Alexandre.

Rising Sun (US 1993). Direct Philip Kaufman. Cast: Sean Connery, Wesley Snipes, Harvey Keitel, Cary-Hiroyuki Tagawa, Kevin Anderson, Ray Wise.

A Good Man In Africa (US 1994). Director Bruce Beresford. Cast: Colin Friels, Sean Connery, John Lithgow, Diana Rigg, Louis Gossett jnr, Joanne Whalley, Sarah Jane Fenton, Maynard Eziashi, Jeremy Crutchley.

Just Cause (US 1995). Director Arne Glimcher. Cast: Sea Connery, Laurence Fishhburne, Kate Capshaw, Blair Underwood, Ed Harris, Christopher Murray, Ruby Dee, Ned Beatty, Lynne Thigpen, Taral Hicks.

First Knight (US 1995). Director: Jerry Zucker. Cast: Sean Connery, Richard Gere, Julia Ormond, Ben Cross, Liam Cunningham, Christopher Villiers, Valentine Pelka, Colin McCormack, Ralph Ineson, John Geilgud.

Dragonheart (US 1996). Director Rob Cohen. Cast: 9voice of) Sean Connery, Dennis Quaid, David Thewlis, Pete Postlethwaite, Dina Meyer, Jason Issaacs, Brian Thompson, Lee Oakes, Wolf, Christian, Terry O'Neill.

The Rock (US 1996). Direct Machael Bay. Cast: Sean Connery, Nicolas Cage, Ed Harris, John Spencer, David Morse, William Forsythe, Michael Biehn, Vanessa Marcil, John C McGinley, Gregory Sporleder.

The Avengers (US 1998). Director: Jeremiah S Chechik. Cast: Ralph Fiennes, Uma Thurman, Sean Connery, Patrick Macnee, Jim Broadbent, Fiona Shaw, Eddie Izzard, Eileen Atkins, John Wood, Carmen Ejogo, Keeley Hawes, Shaun Ryder.

Playing By Heart (US 1999). Director: Williard Carroll. Cast: Gillian Anderson, Ellen Burstyn, Sean Connery, Anthony Edwards, Angelina Jolie, Jay Mohr, Ryan Phillippe, Dennis Quaid, Gena Rowlands, Jon Stewart, Madeleine Stowe, Matt Malloy, Christian Mills.

Entrapment (UK/US/Germany 1999). Director: Jon Amiel. Cast: Sean Connery, Catherine Zeta-Jones, Ving Rhames, Will Patton, Maury Chaykin, Kevin McNally, Terry O'Neill, Madhay Sharma, David Yip, Tim Potter.

Finding Forrester (US 2000). Director Gus Van Sant. Cast: Sean Connery, Rob Brown, F Murray Abraham, Anna Paquin, Busta Rhymes, April Grace, Michael Pitt, Richard Easton.

The League Of Extraordinary Gentlemen (UK/US/Germany/Czech Republic 2003). Director Stephen Norrington. Cast: Sean Connery, Naseeruddin Shah, Peta Wilson, Tony Curran, Stuart Townsend, Shane West, Jason Flemyng, Richard Royburgh, Max Ryan, Tom Goodman-Hill, David Hemmings, Terry O'Neill.